Chicken Soup for the Soul.

Laughter Is the Best Medicine

101 Feel Good Stories

Amy Newmark

Chicken Soup for the Soul, LLC

Cos Cob, CT

Changing the world one story at a time®
www.chickensoup.com

Chicken Soup for the Soul

Laughter Is the Best Medicine

Chicken Soup for the Soul: Laughter Is the Best Medicine
101 Feel Good Stories
Amy Newmark

Published by Chicken Soup for the Soul, LLC www.chickensoup.com
Copyright ©2020 by Chicken Soup for the Soul, LLC. All Rights Reserved.

The publisher gratefully acknowledges the many publishers and individuals who granted Chicken Soup for the Soul permission to reprint the cited material.

Front cover photo courtesy of iStockphoto.com/coolendelkid (©coolendelkid)
Back cover and interior photo of raccoon courtesy of iStockphoto.com/Sonsedska (©Sonsedska), back cover photo of giraffe courtesy of iStockphoto.com/prapassong (©prapassong)
Photo of Amy Newmark courtesy of Susan Morrow at SwickPix

Cover and Interior by Daniel Zaccari

Distributed to the booktrade by Simon & Schuster. SAN: 200-2442

Publisher's Cataloging-In-Publication Data
(Prepared by The Donohue Group, Inc.)

Names: Newmark, Amy, compiler.
Title: Chicken soup for the soul : laughter is the best medicine : 101
    feel good stories / [compiled by] Amy Newmark.
Other Titles: Laughter is the best medicine : 101 feel good stories
Description: [Cos Cob, Connecticut] : Chicken Soup for the Soul, LLC,
    [2020]
Identifiers: ISBN 9781611599992 | ISBN 9781611592993 (ebook)
Subjects: LCSH: Laughter--Literary collections. | Laughter--Anecdotes. |
    Wit and humor--Literary collections. | Wit and humor--Anecdotes. |
    Embarrassment--Literary collections. | Embarrassment--Anecdotes. |
    LCGFT: Anecdotes.
Classification: LCC BF575.L3 C45 2020 (print) | LCC BF575.L3 (ebook) | DDC
    152.43--dc23

Library of Congress Control Number: 2020931436

PRINTED IN THE UNITED STATES OF AMERICA
on acid∞free paper

25 24 23 22   09 10 11

Table of Contents

❸

~Parenthood~

❹

~Happiness Ever Laughter~

❺

~Pets and Other Creatures~

❻

~Mistaken Identity~

❼

~Work Whoops~

❽

~Laughing at Ourselves~

9

~Child's Play~

10

~Not What I Meant!~

11

~Innocently Inappropriate~

⑫

~Family Fun~

Introduction

Welcome to Chicken Soup for the Soul's first-ever collection of humorous stories! Of course we've published thousands of funny stories over our twenty-seven-year history, but never before have we had a volume 100% devoted to them.

We had a great time putting this book together. I must have sounded like a crazy person cackling away in my office while I was selecting and then editing these stories. Even on the third pass through them I was laughing.

If laughter is the best medicine, then this book is your prescription. Turn off the news and spend a few days *not* following current events. Instead, return to the basics — humanity's ability to laugh at itself.

Maybe you should even do a news cleanse for a few days! Hide under the covers and read these stories instead. Or read a chapter a day, or one story a day for 101 days. Whatever works for you. All I can promise is that these pages contain the antidote to whatever is troubling you. They will definitely put you in a good mood.

I don't want to ruin the surprise endings or the punch lines in these stories so I'll forego my usual in-depth review of what's inside. But rest assured that you'll find stories about embarrassing things that you and yours have probably done, too, and you'll also find stories that are so "out there" that you can't even imagine living through what our writers did.

No one is safe from our writers, from spouses to parents to children to friends to other relatives. And of course, the funniest of all are the stories they tell about their own mishaps. No one is holding anything back, and quite a few of our writers are telling their stories publicly for the first time ever… and then running for the hills!

Chicken Soup for the Soul is often the place you turn to for advice — on positive thinking, forgiveness, gratitude, self-esteem, raising kids, caring for the elderly, etc. This time, we're not providing any of that — this is just plain fun.

So enjoy your "medicine." And let me know what you think, by shooting me an e-mail at amy@chickensoupforthesoul.com. I'm hoping this humor book is a big bestseller and we can make another one for you, because this is the most fun I've ever had editing a manuscript. It's been a blast for our whole team.

With hopes that these feel-good stories make you feel as good as we do…

Amy Newmark
Editor-in-Chief and Publisher
Chicken Soup for the Soul
January 23, 2020

Domestic Disasters

Home Alone

As soap is to the body, so laughter is to the soul.
~Yiddish Saying

After my husband left for work, I put our dogs outside and began my morning chores. I stopped mid-chores to use the bathroom. Although I was alone in our home, I closed the bathroom door out of habit. I switched on the ventilation fan, and made a mental note to have it looked at because it was making such a loud rattling sound.

Despite the old fan's noise, I suddenly heard a loud thud against the bathroom door. It startled me to attention. Then it thudded against the door again.

I knew I had put the dogs out, and I was almost positive I had locked the front door. We live in the woods so I thought it could be an animal. Could a bear have gotten in through the sliding door in the back? Or worse, could it be a two-footed intruder?

Before I could logically consider my own questions, the door was hit for a third time. I was truly frightened. I watched a distinct shadow slowly pass by, visible through the little bit of space at the bottom of the door. There definitely was something out there, banging on my unlocked bathroom door, trying to get in.

I moved to the door and quietly depressed the button on the flimsy lock. It wasn't much protection, but maybe it could buy me some time. I strained to hear any clue as to the intruder's whereabouts, but the noisy ventilation fan made that impossible. I thought about shutting off the fan to hear better, but I ruled that out because it might signal to the intruder that someone was in the bathroom.

I felt raw fear. I had no exit but through that bathroom door. I had to think clearly, but I was panicking. I told myself to slow down and think this through. Our dogs hadn't barked and normally they would alert us to an intruder. But maybe the rattling fan kept me from hearing their warning. After all, I had clearly seen that shadow.

I rested my ear against the door, but heard nothing. I needed a plan of action. I looked about the bathroom for something I could use as a weapon, but was frustrated immediately by my limited choices. I remembered a metal, alligator-type hair clip in the top drawer. It was strong, long, and tapered almost to a point at its end. Grasping it like a dagger, I raised it high in the air, testing its feel. I caught my reflection in the bathroom mirror. I looked like a desperate woman arming herself as best she could, but a woman who knew she was no match for a bigger intruder. I wanted to cry, but there was no time.

I was tempted to make a mad dash for my cell phone left in its charger in an adjacent room, but I had no idea what waited for me beyond that door. Did I dare risk a confrontation I probably couldn't win? Maybe the intruder was just waiting for me to make a break for it. Besides, even if I reached the phone first, I live in the country. It would take time for any help to reach me. I decided I should stay put and not force an immediate encounter.

Finally, I couldn't stand it. I needed to know where the intruder was. I let five more silent minutes pass and then I quietly unlocked the door. With my makeshift hair-clip dagger held high, I opened the bathroom door a crack and peered out. I saw nothing unusual.

But I hadn't imagined that moving shadow. It was real.

Then I looked down and saw the intruder who had banged on the door — my trusty robot vacuum cleaner, now silenced and still, having turned itself off after it got stuck under a chair.

— Jennifer Clark Vihel —

In the Kitchen, With the Knife, No Clue

A recipe has no soul, you as the cook
must bring soul to the recipe.
~Thomas Keller

Several years ago, my wife and I were enjoying one of our favorite dishes: Beef Burgundy (or Boeuf Bourguignon, if we really want to sound fancy). As I reached for a second helping, my wife looked across the table and said, "You know, you could make this. It's really easy. The recipe is in my notebook."

It sounded like a dare to me. A month or two later, I got home from work early and decided to give it a try. Sure enough, I found her handwritten Beef Burgundy recipe right where she said it would be. I started gathering the ingredients she had listed: two pounds of stew meat, some mushroom soup, two cups of sliced carrots, eight ounces of mushrooms, a can of red wine... Wait a minute, a *can* of wine? I'll be the first to admit that I have had trouble in the past searching for items in the grocery store, not knowing whether I was looking for a jar or a box or a bottle or a carton. (Where do they teach that kind of stuff anyway?) I knew one could buy wine in a box, but I had never heard of wine available in cans. And was there something special about canned wine over bottled wine? Baffled, I decided to get on with my task and postpone that ingredient until later.

When my wife finished her workday, she called to say she was on her way home. I told her about my quest to cook dinner, but that I had a question. "What size can of wine do you use for the Beef Burgundy?"

There was a pause on the other end. Then, in a puzzled voice, she asked, "What are you talking about?"

"You specify a can of wine in your recipe," I pointed out.

"Oh, right," she said matter-of-factly. "After you scoop the mushroom soup out of its can, pour some red wine into the can, and that's how much you'll need."

Perhaps I'm too literal, and I'm sure "a can of wine" made sense to her when she wrote down the recipe long ago, but I'm convinced that something got lost in the translation.

In fact, a lot gets lost in translation when it comes to this husband's talent in the kitchen. An example is this real-life conversation:

"Nick, would you grab a thirteen-by-nine pan from under the counter?" my wife asks. Immediately, I open up a drawer. "What are you doing?" she demands. "I said it's under the counter."

"I'm getting the tape measure," I reply.

"I don't need the tape measure."

"But I need it to see which pan is thirteen inches by nine," I say.

"No, you don't," she says. "You just tell by looking at it."

So I open the cabinet and pull out a pan. "Is this it?"

My wife looks at me as if I was born on Mars. "Never mind, I'll get it," she sighs.

After other failures such as this, I wanted to prove that I could be creative in the kitchen. So I decided to prepare something new for dinner one evening. I was home all day while my wife was at work, and I looked through a cookbook and found what appeared to be a tasty recipe for Shrimp Linguini. I jotted down the ingredients and took the list to the supermarket. I had no trouble finding the shrimp and the pasta, but some of the other ingredients proved more elusive. Finally, I found a store clerk and asked him, "Are you out of roasted red peppers? I've been all over the produce section and can't find them."

"Roasted red peppers aren't in the produce section," he told me. "Try aisle eight."

On aisle eight, I found cans of green chili peppers, cans of chipotle peppers, cans of sweet corn with peppers, but no cans of roasted red peppers.

"They usually don't come in a can," the clerk told me after I found him again. "They come in a jar." (Seriously, does anybody know where I can sign up for that "What Comes in a Jar, What Comes in a Box, What Comes in a Bottle and What Comes in a Carton" class?)

After I discovered that, yes, roasted red peppers do come in a jar, I looked at my list again and read, "Three cloves of garlic." I had seen the garlic in the produce section, so I returned and found an abundance of lovely white garlic heads. I chose three of the best and put them in a bag.

Once home, I followed the recipe carefully. It told me to finely chop the three cloves of garlic and sauté them in butter. I chopped up one of the heads and tossed it into the pan. As it sizzled, the kitchen filled with the definitive and pungent aroma.

That's a lot of garlic, I thought. *Three of these might be more than we really need.* So I put away the other two heads of garlic and moved on.

By the time my wife got home, I had set the dining room table with our best china and lit the candles. The Shrimp Linguini was ready. We sat down and dug in.

As she readied to take her second bite, my wife paused and asked, "Where did you get this recipe? It's pretty heavy on the garlic!"

"And get this," I told her, "I put in only a third of what the recipe called for. It actually specified three cloves, but I think that would be way too much." (I couldn't hide the pride I felt in my ability to modify a recipe on the fly.)

She looked at me suspiciously. "Did you save the cloves you didn't use?" she asked.

"Yes."

"Can I see them?"

I went to the kitchen, fetched the other two heads of garlic, and presented them to her.

"These are the other two cloves of garlic?" she giggled.

"Yes," I said, though I didn't see what was so funny. "What's the big deal?"

"Nothing that can't wait," she said softly. "Sit down and let's finish this wonderful meal."

— Nick Walker —

H Is for Humor

If you would not be laughed at,
be the first to laugh at yourself.
~Benjamin Franklin

It was almost midnight and my husband was sound asleep, tired to the bone. With the weekend's back-to-back thunderstorms, Jeff had already worked thirty hours of overtime to help restore power and might be called out again. So, I tiptoed past him to the bathroom, just five feet from his side of the bed.

I was exhausted too. And sad. We had moved recently and missed being a part of our military community. As I squeezed the toothpaste onto my brush, I thought about our friends back in Texas.

About two seconds into brushing my teeth, I realized something was fishy. I mean, it *smelled* fishy. The natural toothpaste I use does have a weird smell and a unique taste, but this was weirder than usual. Looking at the lack of foam on my brush, I sniffed it, shrugged, added water, and continued brushing. There were still no bubbles, so I leaned toward the mirror to look at my teeth.

The white stuff I saw was a little too pasty and a tad too white. I looked into my toiletry basket sitting on the sink. There, right next to my toothpaste, sat a long-forgotten tube of Preparation H. At first, I felt foolish and thought it was a stupid thing to do. But as I took a closer look at the ointment snuggled nice and tight between my teeth, I thought, *Oh dear, this can't be good. Will my gums shrink and make my teeth fall out?*

I felt the giggles coming and managed to stop them. I rinsed out my mouth over and over, and wiped my gums with a washcloth. Then I re-brushed my still-intact teeth. With toothpaste.

As I crawled into bed next to Jeff, those giggles bubbled up again. Trying to hold them in only made the bed jiggle, and I snorted, which jolted him awake.

"What in the world... What's so funny?"

Now, with permission to let loose, it took a minute to contain myself. "I brushed... my teeth..." Jeff was already laughing... "with Preparation H."

"With what?"

"Do you think my teeth will fall out?"

We laughed until we were wrung out. Like kids at a slumber party, we breathed deeply to calm ourselves, "Okay. For real, we gotta get some sleep." And then one of us would snicker and start it all over again — good, cleansing belly laughs with the works: snot, tears, and tissues. Eventually, we fell asleep and woke up feeling lighter.

I tried to remember the last time we had laughed like that. Somewhere in the stress of missing our friends, and adjusting to new jobs and a new home, we let too much seriousness sneak into our days. Everyday irritants and busyness pressed in and squeezed out life's funny side. That laughter was just the medicine we needed.

— Robin K. Melvin —

Stuck in the Ceiling

A well-balanced person is one who finds
both sides of an issue laughable.
~Herbert Procknow

The annoying, intermittent chirps began at 4:00 a.m. I woke on the second shrill beep and saw the blinking red light of the smoke detector on the ceiling over my head. Half asleep, my husband and I shuffled to the guest room to catch a few more hours of shut-eye.

Over breakfast, my husband George announced he was going to change the battery himself. "I'm cheap. I'm not going to pay someone to do a job that I can do. It'll be easy peasy."

"Easy peasy my foot, George. That smoke detector is eighteen feet above our bedroom floor. You'll break your neck if you fall."

"I got this," he said smugly.

At 10:00 a.m., against my better judgment, I steadied a twelve-foot ladder as George stood on the top rung. He threw his left leg over the ornate crown molding of the tray ceiling and crawled onto the narrow deck. Standing up, he stretched as far as possible to reach the still chirping smoke detector. This certainly was not a place I wanted my seventy-five-year-old husband. But in no time at all, George had removed the dead battery and installed the new one. I sighed in relief. Now he could come down.

Kneeling on the fuzzy bathroom rug I'd tossed up to him, George attempted to get one leg over the bulky trim to reach the first step.

He missed. I directed him to move left and then right, but nothing worked. After several attempts, George lay prone on the deck of the tray ceiling with one arm dramatically draped over the crown molding.

I couldn't hide my concern. "Now what?"

"Go get the guys working on the neighbor's gutters and have them bring their extension ladder."

"George, they're being paid to clean out his gutters." I walked out of the room with a feeling of panic rising in my chest.

At that point, I had no choice but to call our local fire department. I explained our "emergency."

As soon as I hung up the phone, our daughter Margie called to check on us. When I explained that her dad was stuck in the tray ceiling, she said, "I'll be right there."

I returned to the bedroom to inform George that I'd called the fire department and was going outside to wait for them.

"Really?" he said plaintively, lifting his sweaty head from his forearm. "You really called the fire department?"

"Yes, I did," I said on my way out of the room. "I'll be in the garage waiting for them to get here."

Ten minutes later, Margie pulled into the driveway and hopped out of her car. She ran toward me. "Where's Dad?"

"In the bedroom right where I left him, stuck in the tray ceiling. Why don't you go keep him company until the firefighters get here?"

Five minutes later, a white pickup truck turned into our driveway. I thought, *Oh good, a firefighter is here.*

The truck door opened, and Margie's pastor jumped out.

"Pastor Nate, what are you doing here?"

"Margie called me. She said something about George being stuck somewhere."

"Yes, he is. Follow me. We could use a prayer right now."

I returned to watch for the firemen and was rewarded with the sight of a massive red fire-rescue vehicle parking in front of my home.

"I understand you have a situation," said one of three firemen.

"You could say that." I looked at their nametags. "Brandon, Jonathan, and Marty, my husband is stuck in the tray ceiling." They tried not to grin.

"Follow me," I instructed.

The bedroom was officially crowded as six pairs of eyes looked up at my red-faced husband peering over the edge of the crown molding.

Marty addressed George. "Hello, sir. Do you think if I guide your left foot to the top rung that you can swing your other leg over to stand on the ladder?"

"Yes, I can," George responded. "You guys didn't really need to come."

"We were in the neighborhood," Jonathan lied.

Marty said, "Sir, put your leg over the edge. I'm going to grab your ankle and guide your foot to the ladder. Are you okay with that?"

"Yes," George confirmed. A shaky leg appeared over the top of the molding as George scooted closer to the edge. The rescue began.

When both his feet were firmly on the floor, George shook hands with each of the firemen.

Jonathan turned to him and said, "You don't need to change batteries anymore."

George said, "Why is that?"

"We do it free of charge," said Brandon.

George nodded. "Free is good."

— Nancy Emmick Panko —

Amish Friendship Bread

Bread for myself is a material question.
Bread for my neighbor is a spiritual one.
~Nikoli Berdyaev

It all started when a friend paid me a surprise visit. She knocked frantically on the door. I found her standing on the porch, teary-eyed and holding a Tupperware bowl in one hand and a wooden spoon in the other. Her bottom lip trembled as she spoke. "No matter how many times I give it away, it just keeps coming back. Take it." Cautiously, I lifted the container from her hands.

I whispered, "What is it?"

"It's Amish Friendship Bread. Like, a special cake mix."

This stuff didn't look like any cake mix I'd ever seen. It didn't even come in a box.

"Listen," she continued, "this stuff has a mind of its own. You have to follow the rules."

Cake rules? My friend was babbling like she'd had one too many Chardonnays.

"Keep it comfortable. Room temperature is best. And don't put the lid on too tight or it will blow its top. Now, for the first five days, you have to stir it. But never with a metal spoon — it hates that." She thrust the wooden spoon at me.

"Never forget to stir it, or it gets angry and tries to escape. On Day 5, add one cup each of milk, flour and sugar. Then, continue the stirrings for another four days."

I grabbed a pen and scribbled her instructions. I couldn't remember the passcode to my Wi-Fi. How could I be trusted with a bowlful of neurotic cake batter?

"On Day 10, feed it again. Scoop out one cup of batter for yourself. Here's a recipe for bread. Then divide the rest equally into three containers and give it to your friends. But don't bring me any. I won't be home." As she ran to her car, she hollered over her shoulder, "Don't forget to stir it every day."

I lifted the lid and sniffed the batter. Ick! My son's wet gym socks didn't smell this bad. Gagging, I snapped it shut and sat it behind the toaster.

How hard could this be? I thought. I Googled "Amish Friendship Bread" and found entire websites dedicated to the stuff—which I find ironic as I assume that Amish bakers likely do not spend much time on the Internet. The online recipes and instructions were just as my friend had advised.

On Day 2, as I dropped bread into the toaster, I was reminded of my friend's parting words.

The lid had ruptured, and the mass, triple in size, flowed from the confines of its Tupperware prison. Smelly globs bubbled on the countertop. Using the designated wooden spoon, I scooped it back into the bowl and gave it a vigorous stir.

For days, I approached my brew with caution and spoke softly, hoping it didn't sense my apprehension. On Day 5, I "fed it," gently stirring in the milk, flour and sugar.

That night, I woke with a start, sensing something wasn't right. I tiptoed down the hall to find that my smelly countertop companion had grown to enormous proportions and was attempting its escape. It crept wildly over the sides of the container and appeared to be moving toward the front door. I spent the rest of the night scooping and wiping. By morning, I had it contained in an ice-cream bucket.

Over the next seventy-two hours, I didn't leave the house, suspecting the creature would be oozing from the windows upon my return. I found myself running to the kitchen hourly to stir it. I didn't dare let in the cat for fear he would be consumed.

I was up at daybreak on Day 10, eager to feed the monster and give it away. I added the necessary ingredients, scooped out just enough to bake the bread, and then divided the rest into three containers. Within minutes, I was on the road, in search a few unsuspecting friends. I made three deliveries and then raced home to reclaim my kitchen.

As I pulled into the driveway, I spotted a dish sitting outside my front door. I approached it cautiously. When I saw the wooden spoon, my fears were confirmed. It was accompanied by a note, "I offer you this starter batch of Amish Friendship Bread. Enjoy." It was signed simply, "Your friend." I didn't know who the culprit was, but I was pretty sure she wasn't Amish. And, sure as sourdough, she was not my friend!

— Ann Morrow —

Tuna Delight

But some secrets are too delicious not to share.
~Suzanne Collins, Mockingjay

Early in our marriage, we had what we call our "poor years." First, we were paying off our college debts and the mortgage on the little farm we bought. Then came the kids, and we were always saving up for new shoes, a station wagon, school supplies, and winter coats.

We had a lot of spaghetti and mystery stews during those years. Our four kids were hearty, active, outdoorsy and busy kids with appetites to match. Luckily, I had taught our oldest child the fine art of making sandwiches, so he could make an afternoon snack for himself and the other kids when he got home from school.

Our son was proud of his new skill at preparing lunch. One Saturday afternoon, when all of us were coming in from working in our massive garden, he volunteered to start "fixin" while I helped the younger ones wash up. Most of us were content with PB&J sandwiches, but Dad wanted his favorite tuna salad.

I wasn't sure we had any canned tuna in our cupboard, but our son said he had found two cans on the bottom, plenty enough for sandwiches for his dad. I offered to help him, but he wanted to make them all himself.

While we readied for the meal, cleared away ongoing homework and set the table, our son put together a meal worthy of a mass of farm hands: a mountain of PB&J sandwiches for me and the kids and a plate of tuna-salad sandwiches for Dad. He had even found a bag of chips to accompany the meal, as well as a gallon of sun tea.

We ate like the starving farmhands we were. Dad complimented our son on the perfection of the tuna sandwiches and finished every one. Later, while we cleared away the mess and prepared for our afternoon — naptime for the baby, laundry for me, and a garage project for Dad — he stopped to compliment our son again.

"Best ever," he added, bending low. "Even better than Mom makes." He also bragged about the amazing sandwiches to his brother later that day.

During a rare quiet moment that afternoon, I went to the kitchen for a glass of sun tea and a handful of the few remaining potato chips. The bag was down to broken fragments, so when I finished them off, I stuffed the empty bag into the trash bin.

That's when I found two empty cans of 9 Lives tuna-flavored cat food in the trash. I nearly choked on my tea as I sat and laughed out loud.

I've never told a soul that delicious secret until this very moment.

— NancyLee Davis —

7

Holly and Mistletoe

*I love being married. It's so great to find one special
person you want to annoy for the rest of your life.*
~Rita Runder

I sang at the top of my voice as I danced into our lovely, pastel bedroom to pick out a chic, flattering outfit for the night's festivities. "I'm gonna shake, rattle and roll! Yes, shake, rattle and roll."

Every Saturday night, ten of us would go out for a sumptuous dinner followed by dancing. We had a marvelous time de-stressing from the obligations of being parents. We exercised our bodies, bared our souls and had the time of our lives.

As I fumbled through my clothes, prying the hangers from one another and de-squashing one dress from another, I swore under my breath. "I really need my own closet—a place where my dresses can breathe, my slacks can stay creased, and my blouses won't have to share hangers with my skirts."

Rob didn't have that many clothes, but his were bigger and took up half of the closet. With four children in the house, there was no way I could use the closets in the other rooms, either.

"I hate wrinkles. Why do I even bother ironing when I'm just going to cram them into a crowded cubbyhole?" I ranted. "There has to be a better way."

And then it hit me.

We had a perfectly good linen closet just outside our bedroom door. Those sheets and pillowcases could easily be stored in my mom's cedar chest. It was near empty with only the kids' christening gown wrapped up in blue tissue paper. *What a brilliant mind I have,* I told myself.

I raced to our barn to find two steel rods that would house Rob's shirts on the upper level and his pants on the lower level. I came in with several lengths until I found two that would work. With hammer in hand, I busted out the shelves. With this funny shaped tool, I carved a hole in each piece of board that I nailed to the wall. I smashed the steel rods into those holes. It was a little primitive, I must admit, but it did the trick. I was extremely proud of myself as I color-coordinated all Rob's pants and shirts and lined them up with the hangers all facing the same direction. He was going to be so surprised!

My clothes were so happy. My flared skirts flared again, my dresses spread out, my blouses had elbowroom, and my slacks stayed creased. Tears burned my eyes as I gazed at my spacious, organized closet. No more wrinkles for *moi*!

Rob came in from work, late as usual.

"Hurry, honey. They'll be here any minute. Now jump in the shower."

Rob took his five-minute shower and sprinted to the bedroom as I answered the door.

"Come in, Gail and Larry, and have a seat. How are you doing, Roy and Joyce? What would you like to drink, Romeo and Patricia? Rob's running late, as usual. He should be ready any minute."

"Barb, where are my clothes?" came Rob's plea from the bedroom.

"Oh, yeah, honey, they're in the hall closet. I was planning to surprise you."

"The what?"

"The old linen closet. It is now all yours to enjoy," I chuckled.

I should mention that the back wall of our living room is totally mirrored. It reflects the upstairs and really makes the whole house look larger.

Rob opened the bedroom door with his towel around his waist. He reached up to get down a shirt, and all six people sitting in the living room got a bird's-eye view of holly and mistletoe. And it wasn't

Christmas, if you know what I mean. Their laughter shook the house.

"Barb!" Rob bellowed. It took him a few minutes to compose himself enough to make his blushing entrance.

Bright and early on Monday morning, Todd, our local cabinetmaker, was busy rebuilding our linen closet.

Rob's clothes are back in our closet where he thinks they belong. And I've made my peace with wrinkles!

— Barbara Bondy-Pare —

8

Dieting Disasters

*It is bad to suppress laughter. It goes back down
and spreads to your hips.*
~Fred Allen

I decided to diet — again. Like an addict flushing pills or dumping alcohol, I purged my kitchen cabinets and refrigerator of all temptations. I couldn't be trusted around cookies and candy.

An unopened bag of chocolate-covered graham crackers made me pause. How could I trash all those delicious cookies? But they had to be banished. My willpower — or lack of — was no match for chocolate-covered anything.

Julie, a friend and fellow teacher, loved those cookies, too. Ahh, that was the answer. I'd surprise her with a treat for lunch at school.

Early the next morning before I got ready for work, I put the cookies into a brown paper bag, folded the top and left it on the kitchen counter. Later, I threw my tote bag over my shoulder, grabbed the bag and kissed my husband Ed goodbye.

Julie and I didn't share the same lunch period, so I sent one of my students to give her a note: "Please stop by my room before your lunch." I couldn't wait to see the expression on her face.

During the class change, Julie popped through the door. "Hey, what's up?"

"Come on in." I reached behind my back into my tote and produced the paper bag with a grand flourish. "Ta-da!"

Julie took the bag, tilted her head and furrowed her brows. "What's this?"

"A surprise. Open it. You'll see."

She opened it, pulled out a paper towel and a Ziploc full of potato chips.

My jaw dropped.

Next, she took out a sandwich and an apple. She placed the food along the edge of my desk. Wrinkling her forehead, Julie looked at it.

That didn't make sense. I shook my head. "Where did that come from?"

"What do you mean?" She lifted her hands and shrugged. "You brought it."

"No, I didn't. I brought you a bag of chocolate cookies."

She held up the apple. "Well, what's this? And where are my cookies?"

"Oh, no!" I plopped into my chair.

"What?"

"That's Ed's. He packs his lunch every day. I must've picked up the wrong bag."

"Uh-oh." She laughed and stuffed everything back into the bag except the potato chips. "Well, gotta go. Thanks for lunch." Munching on a chip, she breezed out the door.

I rarely called Ed at work, but I phoned his office on my lunch break.

"What's wrong?" he asked.

"Oh, nothing really. Have you had lunch yet?"

"Yeah, but I had to go out to get some fast food. Some moron played a trick on me and swapped my lunch with a stupid bag of cookies. What a jerk."

"You didn't wanna eat the cookies?"

"What… cookies for lunch? No way."

I took a breath and closed my eyes. Confession time. "It's my fault. I… I took the wrong bag. I wanted to give those cookies to Julie. I'm so sorry."

"You've got to be kidding. I asked everyone in this office which wise guy switched the bags."

"You really thought one of them ate your lunch?"

"What else could I think?"

"I'm sorry. Just tell them your crazy wife was the culprit."

"Yeah, right."

The next day, I took Julie the contraband cookies—minus a couple.

Several days of dieting later, I was dressing for work. My slacks were so loose around the waist that they wouldn't stay up. I'd never worn a belt. I hadn't needed one. But that day I had to search for one to hold up my corduroy pants.

How wonderful, I thought. *I must've lost a lot of weight. So fast, too. Good thing I got rid of those cookies.*

During the first class change, I headed to the bathroom. I unhooked the belt and pulled down my pants. Something about them seemed strange. I noticed the label: Waist thirty-six, length thirty-two.

"What on earth?"

They weren't my pants. They were Ed's. We both wore khaki-colored corduroys. After doing laundry, I must've hung his in my closet. Good grief, I'd done it again.

That night, I told Ed about my latest misadventure. He just shook his head and rolled his eyes. "I don't know about you. First, my lunch, now my pants."

"If I hadn't been on that dumb diet, I would never have thought those slacks were mine." I paused. "Hey, if you start missing your underwear, we're really in trouble."

I laughed. Ed didn't.

No more ridiculous diets for me.

—Linda Carol Cobb—

Chapter 2

That Was Embarrassing

9

Breakdown on the Batchellerville

There is nothing more deceptive than an obvious fact.
~Arthur Conan Doyle

As dusk descended, my uneasiness grew. My husband, Chuck, should have been home long before this. He'd spent the day driving all over the county, locating supplies he needed to build our new house. His last stop of the day was at our middle son's house, where he was picking up a snowmobile trailer to use to transport larger loads.

Even allowing for talk-time at each stop, Chuck should have been home by now. I'd tried his cellphone several times without luck. My mind was eased, though, by the knowledge that he no longer drove the rusted, fourteen-year-old truck that had left him stranded multiple times the previous year. Despite the late hour, I knew Chuck was safe and sound in his brand-new Nissan.

Finally, the phone rang.

"You'll never believe what happened," Chuck began in a stunned voice. "My truck died!"

"What? Where?" I cried, every bit as shocked as Chuck.

"One-quarter of the way across the Batchellerville Bridge," he explained, referring to the 3,000-foot-long bridge that spanned Great Sacandaga Lake. "No sooner had I started across when the entire dashboard lit up — every imaginable light! — and the truck stopped dead.

I can't even get it out of gear now, and the engine won't turn over."

"But it's brand-new," I sputtered. "That truck wasn't supposed to break down for years!"

"I know," my husband sighed. "Worse yet, I'm hauling the snow-mobile trailer—and blocking one lane of the bridge!"

When I asked what I could do to help, Chuck said there was nothing at the moment. He'd just called our insurance company, which provides free towing, only to be told that their regular truck would only tow our vehicle—not the trailer. But they promised to check other sources and call him back.

On the bright side, Chuck told me that several cars had already stopped to see if he needed help. He thanked everyone but explained that his new truck was under warranty, so he just needed to get it towed back to the dealer.

Shortly after hanging up, Chuck called back, excited. "The insurance company found a guy who will tow both the truck and the trailer. But it'll cost $80 for the trailer."

We lived just five miles away, but the expense seemed well worth it to get my husband off the bridge and home safely. Ninety minutes later, a fully loaded tow truck pulled into our driveway.

"Man, this is a first for me," the driver remarked to Chuck as he unhitched the trailer. "Nissans never break down, especially new ones!"

But, moments later, I was stunned to see the man leave—with an empty flatbed!

"Why didn't he take our lemon-of-a-truck?" I snapped in frustration.

Chuck explained that, since his valuable tools and building equipment were stored in the back of his truck, he needed to unload everything first and put them in the shed before getting the vehicle towed. "But don't worry," he added. "The truck's warranty includes free towing within a fifty-mile radius. I'll call them tomorrow."

"Do you have any idea what the problem is?" I asked.

"Not a clue," he replied wearily.

Later that night, as we crawled into bed, Chuck told me that no fewer than fifteen to twenty people had stopped to offer assistance during his long, lonely wait on the bridge. That was the night's silver lining, for sure. It warmed our hearts to know there were still so many kind and caring people in the world.

Bright and early the next morning, Chuck called the dealership, explained the situation, and requested a tow. In no time, we watched as our vehicle was loaded on a flatbed and taken away for what we feared might be a lengthy repair.

Hours later, worried, Chuck called the dealership for an update.

Standing nearby, I watched my husband's body language morph from alarm to relief.

"Oh, no. You're kidding me! Really? Okay, then, we'll be right over to pick it up."

I was thrilled to hear this last part! But when Chuck hung up the phone and turned toward me, he looked oddly uncomfortable.

"What did he say?" I asked, eager for details.

"Well," Chuck hedged, "the guy said our truck worked just fine... uh... once they put some gas in it."

For a split second, his words didn't compute.

"No way!" I gasped suddenly. "You mean, you ran it out of gas?"

When Chuck nodded painfully, I burst out laughing, tickled to think that in all his running around the previous day, my incredibly smart, savvy, engineer-of-a-husband had failed to check one tiny detail.

At length, Chuck was laughing too, albeit sheepishly. And we laughed even harder when it hit us that — during the entire time Chuck was camped out on that bridge, declining offers left and right — there was a gas station just up the hill on the far end of the bridge! During his long wait, Chuck could have walked there and back many times.

As we headed to the dealership, my husband sheepishly shared one last piece of news.

"The mechanic who worked on our truck even gave it a free diagnostic testing, hoping to find something, anything, the matter with it."

"Why would they want to find a problem?" I asked, puzzled.

"Well, the service manager was really sorry to have to tell me this, but because there was nothing technically wrong with the truck, they'll have to charge us for the tow."

For the second time that morning, a strange mix of incredulity and delight bubbled up inside me. "How much?"

"$120," Chuck sighed.

Somehow, that got us laughing again — not that spending $200 on an "Operator Error" was funny, exactly. Still, the entire episode had all the markings of a topnotch, primetime sitcom.

"Would you go inside and pay them, please?" Chuck asked as we pulled up to the dealership.

"No way," I grinned. "This one's all yours."

As Chuck trudged slowly toward the entrance, I headed home, happy to know that my husband was safe, our new truck wasn't a lemon after all, and we had a terrific tale to tell our family and friends. It had been an expensive twenty-four hours with a hard-learned lesson.

But laughter had lightened the load.

— Wendy Hobday Haugh —

Beginners Welcomed

Laugh at yourself first, before anyone else can.
~Elsa Maxwell

The sign was pinned on the post office bulletin board: *Wanted. Quilters. Beginners welcomed.*

I'd always wanted to quilt, but I didn't know how. So the very next Monday morning, I showed up in the Powassan United Church basement, where I found seven women seated around a queen-sized quilt. One woman waved at me to sit beside her. She was in her eighties and had been quilting her whole life, with the calluses on her fingers to prove it.

She learned how much of a beginner I was when she had to show me how to thread my needle, which was about as long as my arm. She demonstrated how one should have six stitches to the inch — if one is an average quilter. It's ten stitches if one is accomplished.

The ladies chatted about everything. The weather. Apron patterns. The price of strawberries at the market. The upcoming music festival. No gossip. Not a word. Then they talked about a coffee break and the homemade butter tarts waiting for us in the kitchen.

"Did you know that the stitches on the underside of the quilt should be as lovely as the ones on the top?" one lady told me.

"No," I said. "Thanks for telling me."

When I realized that everyone had left the room ahead of me, I

decided to go under the quilting rack and see how my stitches looked. Only one thing was wrong: I'd sewn myself to the quilt.

— Mary Lee Moynan —

11

A "Short" Misunderstanding

*Things aren't often what they appear
to be at first blush. But embarrassment is.*
~Jarod Kintz

I t never changed throughout thirteen years of school. I was always the most vertically challenged person in my class. By the time I was in fifth grade, I no longer had to wait for the music teacher to tell me where to stand for the annual Christmas concert. I marched straight to my position — left lower row, outside corner.

As an adult, it takes some intuition and creativity to make my life easier. I keep stepstools handy on each floor of my house. If my husband borrows one and forgets to put it back, well… it's not pretty. When we put in new kitchen cabinets last year, I insisted on one of the best inventions ever — a spice cabinet that sits between my stove and the dishwasher. I actually get to bend over to retrieve the thyme and turmeric. (T through Z resides on the bottom shelf.)

I haven't resorted to those gripper tools yet, but a long-handled wooden spoon has come in handy multiple times when in pursuit of something on a top shelf. Attempt this at your own risk — an uncaught five-pound bag of sugar can make an awful mess when it splits open on the counter.

Needless to say, I've heard my share of "short jokes" throughout these last sixty years. There have also been a lot of subtle — or maybe not

so subtle — insinuations related to my stature. Grade-school classmates affectionately called me "Shrimp." High-school classmates razzed me about the stack of pillows I needed while driving. As a thirty-year-old, candy was passed through the bank's drive-up window to me (unless, of course, I was driving).

For the most part, I've been able to handle these things with grace, but occasionally something hits me wrong. Years ago, I was working as a clinic nurse in Laramie, Wyoming. We had several satellite clinics across Wyoming and Colorado where we would fly to provide orthopedic care. The surgeons employed their own full-time pilot, and Randy was a personable young fellow. It was his duty to keep us safe in the skies. Randy took his job seriously; if he didn't think it was safe to fly, we didn't.

One particular day, we were heading to Fort Morgan, Colorado. I was on one of the phones in the hallway, talking with one of the Fort Morgan medical personnel, when Randy came up the corridor. He realized by listening to my side of the conversation that I was on with the Fort Morgan folks. He leaned against the wall as I finished talking. Then we took off down the hall together, chitchatting for a minute or two. Suddenly, Randy peered down over his mustache and muttered the five words I have heard time and time again: "How's the weather down there?"

I threw out my arm with the strength of Wonder Woman, landing it squarely into Randy's abdomen. He gave out a surprised "umpf," grabbing his middle and bending forward. His facial expressions led me to believe he was astounded at what I had just done. After regaining his balance, Randy stared at me like I owed him an explanation. No worries. I had already planned to give him one.

"Randy," I said with lips pinched, "I get short jokes all the time, and this morning I'm in no mood."

Randy shook his head as if clearing the cobwebs from the crevices. "Oh, I get it," he said finally, starting to laugh. This did nothing to soothe my irritation. I glared at this pompous man who dared to laugh at my expense. Amid continued chuckles, Randy dropped the bomb. "I just hoped to find out what the weather was doing in Fort Morgan."

Oh, crap. If the only hiding place available had been a thorn bush, I would still have dived under it. Of course, it all made sense *now*. With less than half an hour to be in the air, Randy's mind was focused on weather, not petite co-workers. Only then did I remember the severe weather warnings I had heard on the way to work that morning.

—DeLila R. Lumbardy—

12

Restaurant Rules

I turn over a new leaf every day.
But the blots show through.
~Keith Waterhouse

The December chill in Vancouver had us bundled in bulky sweaters as my husband Gord and I buckled our two little girls into their car seats. We were off to experience a wonderful dinner in a restaurant highly recommended by friends. Eating out was a luxury for us, so we were excited about our evening.

But there was a bothersome issue. I was eight months pregnant, and constantly tired and bloated. It was hard to get comfortable these days, and my family waited patiently as I adjusted the seat a few times.

As we made our way up the North Shore Highway, snow-capped mountains rose majestically before us, and whitecaps on the water lapped against the boats in the marinas. The massive city of Vancouver looked like a miniature village in the distance. It was spellbinding. Even our little ones seemed to appreciate it.

Although the girls were only two and four years old, we spent a few moments during the drive reviewing restaurant rules. Two little heads bobbed in agreement that nothing but good manners and quiet voices would be displayed throughout dinner.

I was quite happy when the one-hour drive was over. It turned out the baby boy I carried would enter this world at twelve pounds, so it was no wonder that every joint and muscle was stiff and sore. With great difficulty, I struggled out of the car and waddled into the restaurant, leaving Gord to manage the girls. Thankfully, there was no wait, and we were quickly directed to a table tucked into a comfortable corner.

Before the waiter had time to take our orders, I had to rush off to use the facilities, and that was when it happened.

I was washing my hands in the restroom and I noticed a statue beside the sinks. It was a naked man. And even more shocking was the strategically placed fig leaf… on a hinge. Now I was pretty sure I knew what was under that leaf, but having always been an inquisitive type, I couldn't curb my curiosity.

I watched as several women chatted while touching up lipstick and washing their hands. Not one of them even glanced at the statue. I found that quite unbelievable! What was wrong with these people? A tiny niggling of warning prickled at the back of my mind, but I ignored it and plotted my course.

I decided to wash my hands very slowly until the women had finished up and exited.

Before long, the women were gone, and it was just the statue and me. Pressing my huge belly up to the counter, I reached over to quickly lift that leaf before anyone else came in. I didn't need to dally. Just a quick peek would do.

As my hand firmly grasped and lifted the leaf, a loud, long, piercing alarm sounded suddenly — strong enough to shake a building! I dropped the leaf like it was on fire.

With paralyzing horror, I knew immediately that the leaf was connected to that alarm. This was obviously someone's twisted sense of humor.

Now what was I to do? Being the only one in the restroom, leaving now would alert everyone that I had lifted the leaf… and in my obvious condition! Lord, have mercy! I needed a plan.

This was not the first time I had found myself in a predicament, so I drew on all my faculties to find a solution. As the wheels turned, an idea formed.

I decided to wait for a diversion and keep washing my hands until some unsuspecting soul came in. I hoped it would be soon as the recent adrenaline rush caused me to think I might need to use the facilities again, and that could mean missing the opportune moment when it arrived.

Before long, two ladies came in. I continued to wash my hands with purpose as they did what they needed to do and then made their way to the sink. Ignoring their smiling glances my way, I put more effort into my performance… and added soap. I knew this must end soon. My fingers were turning into prunes.

When they finished up and left, I grabbed the opportunity and hurried to slip in behind them.

To my horror, smirking busboys and waiters had lined up along the walls by the washrooms to honor the return of the bell ringer and celebrate the "lifting of the leaf." Their grins in my direction said it all. They knew it was me. Waddling by like a walrus on a mission, my face burned with embarrassment. Then it got worse… They started to clap and cheer. There was no place to hide!

Entering the eating area, I became aware of several smirks directed at me. I searched frantically for my little family. Finding them again, I kept my face down and slid awkwardly into my chair.

Apparently, the little girls were remembering their restaurant manners, which only made me feel worse. I turned to Gord and whispered, "Did you hear a loud, ringing bell out here a few minutes ago?"

"Yeah," he garbled with a mouth full of bread. "It was weird. I wonder what that was about?" He swallowed. "Hey, what took you so long anyway?"

I murmured quietly, "It's a long story. I'll fill you in on the way home."

We continued our meal, and as we enjoyed our dinner, my embarrassment subsided, and the humor of it all began to hit me. My giggles started, and at Gord's questioning look, I choked out my series of unfortunate events. His hearty laugh joined mine, and the little girls picked up on the hilarity of the moment, chuckling along with us.

Over time, we've had some great laughs over that incident. Through the years, I have realized it is not just an embarrassing story; it's a human one. Sometimes, we take ourselves too seriously and miss out on the funny side of life. Humor heals and helps us through the tougher times.

It wasn't the last time I embarrassed myself, but it certainly stands out as one of the most memorable. But one tragic disappointment haunts me to this day: I'm still not sure what was under that leaf!

—Heather Rae Rodin—

13

Fishin' and Sinkin'

The rate at which a person can mature is directly
proportional to the embarrassment he can tolerate.
~Douglas Engelbart

take fishing seriously. Not fishin', which I do when I want to relax
and have a beer with my guy friends and do rude man stuff best
left at the lake.

Fishing is to fishin' like wrestling is to wrasslin'. The upper
echelon is angling, which only Brits and rich tourists pursue.

But fishing, my favorite, involves pursuing trophy-sized fish with
expensive equipment, which works out to about $27.50 per pound
per fish. While this might not be a bad investment if the fish were kept
and eaten after being prepared by a noted French (i.e., Cajun) chef, the
fish is usually released after a photo op. Still, it is a great investment
for those who own stock with the equipment manufacturers.

Being a purist, I do save some money by catching my own baitfish:
shad. None of that glittery, fake, plastic, namby-pamby bait for me.
This requires predawn excursions; shad are sometimes hard to locate.
Shad are the favorite food of striped bass, i.e. stripers, a word that, if
an extra "p" is added, can lead to heartache, despair, and even divorce,
especially at 4:00 a.m. when this story started.

My fishing partner, Belle, was a Golden Retriever who loved fishin',
with or without the "g." Although she couldn't hold a fishing pole or
bait a hook, she would amuse herself by standing in the bow of the
boat, barking at the water and, every so often, jumping in to retrieve

a bobber someone had thrown nearby.

On one of our mornings out, a fog settled as I began the launch of my boat, something I'd done solo many times. Belle took her place in the bow, and I removed the straps holding the boat on the trailer, tied the anchor rope around a rock, and backed the car and trailer down the steep ramp using the side mirror as a guide. Watching the boat as it floated onto the water, I stopped just as my back tires touched water.

This one-man launch was an art, a dance I'd perfected. I knew just how to make a sudden stop to gently float the boat off the trailer. Then it would be held by the anchor rope until I pulled it ashore and boarded. I'd done this successfully a thousand times.

This was the 1,001st time.

I watched as the rope pulled taut as it should, then tauter, and then slack again as it slipped off the rock and into the water, following the boat as it drifted away. Throwing open the door, my plan was to chase the rope. However, in turn, I was suddenly being chased by my open door — and it was faster, knocking me to the pavement.

In hindsight, I should have put the car in "Park" first.

Lying there, I had a great view of the front tire rolling over both of my ankles. I groaned and rolled into the water, my only hope being that maybe the pain of my crushed ankles would make drowning less traumatic.

But then a miracle happened. I found that I could stand up, which gave me a better view of my empty boat trailer as it disappeared into deeper water. The still-running car dutifully followed on the surface, the windows rolled up and the door having shut itself after attacking me. The motor was purring smoother than it ever had.

The car floated impressively until mid-channel. There, the back was pulled down by the weight of the trailer, and the automobile's front rose from the water in the fog, giving a dramatic visual of what the *Titanic* might have looked like if it had wheels and was made in Detroit. The motor ran until the last second, making a "glush" sound as water replaced gasoline in the cylinders. Then, all was quiet.

By luck, the boat drifted to shore. Belle, who'd been watching from the bow, leapt to my aid as soon as it touched land — her idea of aid being to grab a nearby stick and look at me to throw it. Instead, I tied the boat to a nearby dock, and we headed toward the main road. I was soaked and muddy, limping pitifully, and Belle ran in circles around me with a wet stick. Crossing the bridge over the boat launch, I looked down and saw the eerie glow of headlights—my own; the taillights dim red globs a few feet behind. Shad leaped like little trained porpoises in the lights' glow, begging to be eaten by large stripers, "p" singular.

A combination bar and live-bait store was nearby. Although closed, a neon beer sign still flickered. A few early travelers were now on the road. I yelled and waved frantically at the passing cars as Belle barked for them to throw the stick. The first three cars sped up, probably assuming I was the reason the beer sign was still lit. Finally, a car stopped.

"I sunk my car," I told the driver, who rolled the window down only an inch in case I was dangerously unsober.

"I'll pull you out," he said.

"No," I insisted, "I *sunk* my car." I pointed to the lights underwater, which could be seen from where we were.

"That's your car?" he asked.

"Yup."

"I'll call a wrecker."

The sun was coming up, and the early morning boating crowd began to arrive. Numerous authorities were also present, including two wreckers, an agent from the Department of Natural Resources, three deputies and, in case anyone might miss the spectacle, two police cars with flashing blue lights. The car was deemed a navigational hazard by someone of authority, so it was necessary to close the ramp. I was given the task of notifying those waiting to launch their boats.

"I can't launch because some idiot sunk his car?" one man exclaimed angrily.

"Yes, sir," I replied. "Some idiot did."

Another said, "My cousin, Thad, did that once." This made me feel a little better—until he added, "Thad was a real idiot."

By midmorning, a vehicle retrieval plan was hatched. By now, my son and wife had arrived (nobody wanted to miss this spectacle, not even family), and my son volunteered to swim the wrecker hook out to the car. Soon, we discovered one doesn't just swim with a forty-pound iron hook and chain. Instead, he grabbed the hook and began walking along the lakebed until he reached the car. Blindly hooking onto something, he surfaced and signaled the wrecker.

There was a collective "ooooh" from the now-numerous spectators as the car rose from the depths. Where my son had blindly impaled the hook, a fluorescent green liquid poured from a fresh hole in the radiator, the newest equipment on the car.

I'd been limping along all morning, but once I removed my shoes, my ankles swelled immediately, and I could not walk.

"Tell me again what happened," the emergency-room doctor said, as the nurses and several other patients strained to hear. Repeated several times among staff, the hospital was soon abuzz with the tale about a man who'd been run over and almost drowned, saved by his faithful dog. At least nothing was broken, except my pride and a car with a new radiator.

—Butch Holcombe—

14

The Naked Truth

I learned that there's a certain character that can be
built from embarrassing yourself endlessly.
~Christian Bale

I was so excited to vacation in Florida for the first time, thanks to my sister. She had invited my daughters and me to go with her family and she even lent me her brand-new, very expensive bathing suit. It was made of soft natural fibers and was so comfortable.

The first morning we were there I donned that bathing suit and we headed to the crowded beach. We hit the water running, taking in the sights and sounds of the ocean: the waves, the breeze, fish that nibbled on our toes, white sand, squawking seagulls, flying pelicans, seashells, and whatever else captured our attention. I was mesmerized by it all while I bobbed in the cool ocean water.

Suddenly, a deep pain pierced my right arm, stiffening it instantly. My sister saw my face and rushed to my side. I lifted my arm to find huge blisters that circled the entire length of my arm like that of a coiled snake. I had been stung by a jellyfish.

My sister was a diver and trained EMT, so she quickly led me out of the water to head back to our room. She wanted to put a special ointment on the blisters, give me Benadryl to counteract any ill effects from the sting, and keep me under her watchful eye in hopes I wouldn't have to be rushed to the hospital.

I didn't want to alarm anyone, so I emerged from the water quietly with my arm now hanging completely stiff at my side. We had forgotten our towels that morning in our eagerness to get to the ocean, so I shivered as we walked in silence.

I began to notice people staring at me and pointing me out. It seemed as if the entire beach was fixated on me.

Then I looked down and saw why. I was naked! That beautiful, expensive bathing suit was completely transparent now that it was wet! Not only was I shining in all my glory on a crowded beach, I also had no towel for the long trek back to the room!

Then, to add more salt to the wound, I had to walk past all the people at the swimming pool, too. Like everyone else, they could not believe their eyes and stared at this either very brave or extremely stupid woman who paraded naked past them! All I could do was keep my head down and hope I didn't hear any catcalls. I have great peripheral vision and could see their shocked faces and gaping mouths. I could only imagine the pool attendant cussing me for having to clean up all the mess from the dropped beverage cups!

Finally, we made it up to the twelfth floor where my sister lovingly gave me an antihistamine and rubbed salve on my blisters. When she saw I was going to be okay, she began laughing uncontrollably. Who in their right mind could refrain from laughing at such an obvious opportunity? I'd heard of pranks, but this was the mother of them all. I accused her of doing it deliberately! She swore up and down that she had never worn the suit and didn't know it would totally vanish when wet.

Well, good and bad came from my situation. The good news was I didn't have to go to the hospital. I learned that the suit I wore was for lying out in the sun, not for swimming. Believe me, the difference was "transparent"! I also saved my sister from crippling embarrassment had she worn it. Plus, the cell phones at that time did not have the capability to take pictures so at least I wasn't plastered all over social media. My incident did, however, become a "classic" family event to laugh about again and again.

The bad news was that I had to walk past all those people again later that day to get back to the beach. I'm sure those beach lovers will never forget the day I gave their kids a quick education on the human anatomy.

— Kathy Dickson —

Detained by the CIA

Because the greatest part of a road trip isn't arriving
at your destination. It's all the wild stuff
that happens along the way.
~Emma Chase, Tamed

My cousin, Colonel Sharon Mack, was retiring from the U.S. Army and asked me to sing the national anthem at her retirement party. I agreed, of course, and my husband John made arrangements to get off work. To attend this soirée, we needed national security clearance, so our applications were submitted months in advance. No problem. Our records were squeaky clean.

We decided to fly out a week early and make a vacation of it. Instead of renting a car, we purchased bus and train passes to simplify our transportation. We stayed at a no-frills hotel in Alexandria and spent a week taking in all the historic sites, plus a few plays, shows, and concerts.

Our second Saturday in the D.C. area was dedicated to my cousin's Army retirement activities. Public transportation got us safely to Fort Myer Army Base that morning for the Army's group retirement ceremony. It was a moving, solemn event with lots of pomp and circumstance.

Afterward, Sharon paired us with friends of hers from Pennsylvania who agreed to let us ride with them. First, we went to a restaurant where friends and relatives were grabbing some lunch before heading to Sharon's private retirement bash later that afternoon at the Liberty

Crossing National Counterterrorism Center.

About ninety minutes before the next party was slated to begin, we and the couple left the restaurant. The Liberty Center was just thirty minutes away, but we wanted to allow some extra time just in case. That was a good call. Right out of the parking lot, the husband drove us fifteen minutes in the wrong direction before realizing it. Not to worry. We still had an hour left to travel forty-five minutes.

John rode shotgun, and I was in the back seat with the wife and their GPS. We learned quickly that the husband was not only directionally challenged, but also hard of hearing. Invariably when his wife said something like, "At the next corner, turn right," he would turn left. Then we would have to circle around to get back on track. This wrong-turn/circle-around scenario was repeated over and over until we were hopelessly lost.

We tried to call my cousin Sharon to tell her what was going on, but the terrain was hilly and cell phone reception unreliable, so we never got through. Sharon's husband left several frantic voicemails wondering where we were. Time was running out, and civility was wearing thin in the car.

Frustrated, my husband began repeating the wife's driving instructions to her husband. Miraculously, things improved. Apparently, John's low-pitched voice was literally on the right wavelength for the husband to hear. In a flash, we were on the correct highway, just minutes from Liberty Center.

Sadly, that's when their GPS froze. We would have to stop for directions.

Just then, I saw a large green highway sign announcing that the George Bush Center for Intelligence — the CIA — was just ahead. Surely, someone at the CIA would know where the Liberty Center was.

When we pulled into the driveway of the CIA headquarters, an official-looking fellow waved us over to the curb. In seconds, our car was surrounded by men in black — no guns drawn, but clearly packing heat.

Their spokesman approached and asked, "May I help you?"

The husband mumbled something unintelligible.

"What is your business, sir?" the spokesman demanded.

The husband giggled.

That's when I piped up from the back seat, "Sir, we just need directions to the Liberty Center."

"Why are you going there?" the fellow wanted to know.

"My cousin's retirement party is being held there."

"Who is your cousin?"

"Army Colonel Sharon Mack." He looked skeptical, so I added, "We were at Fort Myer this morning for the public retirement ceremony. I can show you the program, but it's in the trunk."

He signaled for me to retrieve said artifact, which I did — walking slowly and not making any sudden moves. With the program in hand, I pointed out my cousin's name listed with the other retirees.

With the veracity of our story becoming more likely, the spokesman inquired, "Do you understand, ma'am, that you can't enter the Liberty Center without national security clearance?"

I assured him we had taken care of that months earlier, but the agent he sent inside to check out our story came back with bad news: Our names were not in their system.

On the verge of tears, I looked at my watch and told the man, "Look, I'm supposed to sing the national anthem at the gathering in three minutes."

Another agent spoke up. "You know, I think the Liberty Center may have their own separate security database. Let me go check." Minutes later, the agent reported that our names were indeed in the appropriate database and added sheepishly, "They are expecting you."

The security team flanking our vehicle backed away, and the spokesman's demeanor changed from "national-security-threat-mode" to "kindly-nephew-helping-his-crazy-aunt-mode." And armed with the directions he gave us, we were at the Liberty Center in less than five minutes.

The personnel at the gatehouse ran us through their security check in record time. The man in charge said, "It's just a short drive from here to the building where the retirement party is."

"Can't we just leave the car parked here and walk?" I asked, fearful of getting lost again.

Sensing my angst, he replied, "Sure. Follow me."

When we arrived, much of the program honoring my cousin was already over. Fortunately, we did get to see her mom and husband honored and heard Sharon's beautiful farewell speech.

Later, I learned that Sharon's pastor had led everyone in singing the national anthem in my absence. What a relief! I would have been devastated had our unfortunate incident in any way marred the occasion.

During the reception that followed, I tracked down the gentleman who had escorted us from the gatehouse and thanked him for his kindness. "It was my pleasure," he responded. And then, making small talk, he asked, "So, where are you and your husband staying?"

"At a hotel in Alexandria."

"How are you getting back there?"

"With the people who brought us, I suppose," I sighed, "unless there's a train or bus station nearby."

"There's a train station about a mile from here."

"Is it easy to find on foot?" I asked hopefully.

"You know what? I pass that train station every day on my way home," he said with a twinkle in his eye. "I'm about ready to leave for the day. I'd be happy to drop you off. Would you like to hitch a ride?"

Trust me, he didn't have to ask twice.

— Carol Senn Ruffin —

Treasure Hunting

Yet the best determining factor of how comfortable
we are with ourselves, is our ability
to laugh at ourselves.
~Wes Adamson

My husband and I love treasure hunting at local garage sales, thrift stores, and estate sales. We like to rise early on Saturdays, grab a cup of coffee, and head out for a day of bargain shopping. These days we use the Internet to find sales, but back in the day we had to find our treasure hunts in the classified section of the local newspaper.

A number of years back, while we were still in manual mode, we stopped at a local convenience store for our weekend newspaper. When we pulled into the parking lot, we could tell it was busier than normal because of the number of cars already parked there. I decided to wait in the car in case I needed to move it while my husband went inside to purchase the paper.

As I waited, I noticed a few people leaving the store, but it seemed as soon as one car pulled out two more would pull in, so the parking lot was a constantly shifting mass of cars.

After several minutes passed, I was relieved when I saw my husband finally exit the store. It was obvious he had become impatient because of the long wait; he already had the newspaper flipped back to the classified section, and his nose was buried in the want ads. Oblivious to the world around him he slowly made his way down the sidewalk.

I was certain he would trip over his own two feet and fall flat on his face, but he managed to stay upright as he stepped off the sidewalk, and headed straight toward the car. The one parked next to ours, that is.

A tickle of laughter began to build in the back of my throat. Surely he would look up. The bubble grew into a hiccup of laughter when he reached out to grab the door handle, and then my hiccup burst into a roar of laughter when he yanked the door open and climbed inside. I watched in horror as he pulled the door shut, rested his newspaper on the steering wheel, and continued to peruse the want ads. I waved my hands in the air in the hopes of catching his eye. No luck. Oblivious to the world around him, he continued to read.

Not wanting to draw attention to him, I was hesitant to blow the horn. After several failed attempts to get his attention, I knew I had no other choice, so I reached over and gave the horn a quick toot. Nothing, still content in his new ride my husband continued to read his paper. I gave the horn another quick toot but still got no reaction, and to my surprise he wiggled in the seat to make himself more comfortable.

I was laughing so hard by this point I couldn't think straight. Then the horrified thought that the owner of the car might be watching from the long line inside the store registered in my brain. Did they think he was trying to steal their car? Had they called the police on him?

I reached over and gave the horn a long blast, then tapped it again when I got no response. Finally, my husband stirred in his seat. I watched his mouth move and could only assume he was speaking to me, thinking I was sitting next to him. I watched his mouth move as he said something else. The silence must have tipped him off that something was not quite right, because seconds later he slowly turned toward me, and when our eyes met through the glass of the car door, I gave him a small wave with my fingers.

The look of surprise on his face caused me to burst out laughing at that point. His adrenaline must have then kicked in because he swung open the car door, vaulted to his feet, slammed the door shut, and raced over to our car as if he were being chased by some unseen monster. Not wasting any time, he wrenched open our car door, climbed inside, cranked the engine, shifted into drive, and zoomed out of the parking lot.

I tried to speak, but every time I opened my mouth nothing but loud laughter bellowed out. I waited a few seconds and tried to speak again, but once again, nothing but laughter. Finally after several minutes of silence I began to gain control, I reached up and wiped the tears from my eyes and even managed to swallow back a few wayward giggles. With great effort I managed to get control of my laughter, then my husband glanced over at me, and I lost control again, and within seconds he and I were both bellowing loud chuckles.

I'm not sure how long it took for us to be able to talk about it, but at some point we finally managed to gain control, but dared not try to discuss it, because when either of us tried to bring it up our words would turn into laughter within seconds.

— Sharon Rosenbaum Earls —

The Handcuffs' Tale

But with your life you make a few bad decisions,
get unlucky a few times, whatever,
but you have to keep going, right?
~Cecelia Ahern

've done some pretty dumb things in my life. Many were, in fact, downright idiotic. But among my uncountable brain cramps and stupendous errors of judgment, few compete with what I did on a Sunday morning in the early '90s.

A week earlier, I had found a pair of what appeared to be bona fide, police-issue handcuffs. Someone had either lost or dumped them at curbside in front of the Santa Monica apartment building where I had lived for years.

There they were, relaxing in the gutter, waiting for an innocent like me to notice them. When I came along, the cuffs gazed up at me and issued a dare: "C'mon. You know you want to…"

I'd never seen genuine, functional handcuffs before, except maybe on a police officer's belt. The only ones I had ever handled were those cheesy pretend-cuffs sold in toy stores or placed in gift bags doled out at kids' birthday parties. But these cuffs certainly had to be real. They looked legit, had heft and, well, they just oozed authenticity.

And the keys? None in sight. But what did I care? It's not like I rode with a posse or cruised the city looking to bust perps. Still, I figured, why not keep them? If only for the sheer novelty.

Flash forward to Sunday morning. My then-girlfriend, Kathie, had stayed over. When we woke, she noticed the cuffs where I'd left them: draped over the outstretched, palms-up hand of Sid, the six-foot wooden statue of a man I'd inherited from my dad.

"What," she asked while examining the cuffs, "are these?"

"Oh, I think you know what they are."

As the words left my mouth, Kathie spotted a floating, glowing light bulb that appeared above my head. *What,* she wondered, *was I up to?*

Now, understand, I haven't a kinky bone in my body. But just the novelty of a romantic interlude with these items seemed like benign but irresistible Sunday morning fun.

But when I explained all this, a visibly nervous Kathie remained unconvinced. I reassured her everything would be all right because I had tested the cuffs the day I found them. I did so by rotating the shackle bracelet on its hinge in a full circle, completing the 360-degree route unimpeded. By design, the ratchets on the rotating shackle, which lock the cuffs when in use, never meshed at all.

Wahoo! I spun the shackle over and over that day in the gutter. Piece of cake, so who needs a key?

This, of course, was where all my presumed logic, reason and assumed intelligence simply evaporated. A verifiable Bachelor of Arts degree-holder, I had fallen victim to a world-class brain cramp. I had forgotten that when a human wrist becomes, uh, involved with handcuffs, the manacles' rotating shackle cannot complete a harmless 360-degree pirouette because something blocks its path: the presence of a human wrist.

Unfortunately, this realization occurred while the cuffs were on Kathie's wrists instead of my own. The normally good-natured Kathie, wrists bound together in front of her, exploded. "Get me out of these things. Get the key!"

Incredibly, I managed to make things worse: I laughed, first at the sight of my hapless handcuffed honey, and then at my own off-the-charts forgetfulness of the laws of science. Standing there, I envisioned someday sharing this hilarious mishap with our grandchildren. Certainly, they'd squeal with delight over the day that Grandpa forgot to mention he never had the key, right? I also believed that Kathie would join in the mirth at any moment.

I was wrong.

The devastated Kathie alternately raged, cried and swore. Instantly, I was recast in the urban melodrama as the ridiculous "Jerk Boyfriend." (When they make the movie, get Seth Rogen to play me.)

What to do? We couldn't possibly call friends or family to ask for help; we'd never live down the humiliation. Who could save us?

Another epiphany: This was a job for the police.

Somehow, we managed to pull a sweatshirt over Kathie's nightshirt, which, believe me, is not a good look. Our drive to the police station was a study in stony silence — except when I tried to convince the mortified Kathie that we'd laugh over this slapstick morning years later.

Kathie made it clear she'd never find the humor in this. Ever.

When we walked into the West Los Angeles station at 7:00 a.m., a few uniformed cops were hanging around the front desk. The sight of us produced a loud chorus of laughter, which fulfilled Kathie's worst fear: public mortification.

The coup de grâce came when the desk sergeant sized us up and deadpanned, "I don't even wanna know."

The cops, it turned out, didn't have heavy-duty bolt cutters. They sent us to a nearby fire station where, in seconds, a grinning firefighter used large, industrial-strength cutters to quickly liberate my wary, not-laughing girlfriend.

We broke up about a year later. I've now been happily, and sometimes even laughingly, married for twenty-two years. We have a daughter in college. All's well that ends well. And Kathie? We've been out of touch for nearly thirty years.

But I'll bet she's still not laughing about this.

— Barry M. Grey —

Chapter
3

Parenthood

Shower Shock

It's important to learn to laugh at ourselves,
don't take life too seriously.
~Geri Halliwell

peeked in on my two-year-old. He had picked up my husband's iPad and was watching *Baby Shark* for the eightieth time in a row. I was about to walk over and take it away when a thought struck me. I could take a shower in peace while he was zoned out. It would be a midweek miracle. Quietly, I backed out and hurried toward the shower.

I was basking in five whole minutes of uninterrupted, independent bathing when I heard a man's deep voice right outside the shower door inside my bathroom! "Steve?" it boomed. "Steve, is that you?"

I froze. Why was there a strange man in my bathroom at 10 in the morning asking for my husband? Frantically, I searched the shower for some kind of weapon. The best I could find was an economy-sized bottle of Pantene.

Heart pounding, I tried to get the nerve to take the offensive and attack first. Just as my hand touched the handle, the door burst open. I was staring not at a beefy guy named Marco with a Louisville Slugger but at a sleek metal square held by two chubby hands.

It took me 1.2 horrifying seconds to realize that Cody had decided to abandon *Baby Shark* and access my husband's contact list. There I now stood, in fact, on a live FaceTime call with "Randy from accounting" wearing nothing but shock and my birthday suit.

"Steve?"

I've never stopped, dropped, and rolled so fast in all my life, slamming the glass door closed as I tumbled. The bottom of the shower was fogged with steam, so I crouched in the fetal position to be well hidden. I needed to end the call fast. I inched over to the door as Cody started cracking up at his mother's soapy crawl of shame. Before he could raise the iPad higher and reveal me through the steam, I gripped the shampoo bottle and shot my hand out the door, hitting the screen hard enough to knock it from his hands and smack it to the ground. I scrambled out, careful to keep a wide berth from the camera. I stretched out my arm as far as I could while my face pressed into the linoleum and slammed "End" on the screen.

A few hours later, Steve got home. "How was your day, Cass?"

"You need to quit your job. We're moving to Wyoming."

"What?"

"I'll explain after I put the house on the market. Please pack a bag."

— Cassidy Doolittle —

Are You There?

Back of every mistaken venture and defeat is the
laughter of wisdom, if you listen.
~Carl Sandburg

'm the kind of guy who likes to have all his ducks in a row. I'm fairly disciplined and expect the members of our family to do things in the most efficient way, like I do.

I especially like us to get to places on time. To help my family, I tell them the precise time we're going to leave to go somewhere. That means they have to be seated in the car, with all their shopping bags, lunch bags, and assorted gear. I calculate how long it takes to drive somewhere and, if we're visiting someone, the time we'll arrive.

I even tell our hosts when to expect us. If I'm a few minutes early, we'll drive around the block or engage in other stalling behavior in order to arrive at the precise time. I have quite a reputation to maintain. "They'll be here at exactly one o'clock, just as they said," people would say.

When we were raising our children we lived in the country, so there were many opportunities to drive places and train everyone to leave at the proper time. One such "distance drive" was to hockey practice. The ice surface in the arena in the small village in which we lived was not big enough for Bantam hockey, the minor hockey division for thirteen- to fourteen-year-olds. That meant we had to drive to the next town, thirty miles away on a winding mountain road. Naturally, I had to have my commute timed just right to get there on time.

To save time, I had my son put on his hockey gear before we left on one of those drives. I could work those last few minutes after school where I taught and then walk home in five minutes, in time to drive him to his practice. Meanwhile, said son was supposed to be getting ready and putting on his gear. This did not always work exactly the way it should have. Alex would get distracted by something, not having the same sense of discipline I had developed over the years. Or if his brothers happened to be in the same room, there would be some kind of teasing, or even an argument going on.

"Alex! Get going and get dressed!" my wife would call out. "Dad will be here in a few minutes!" Usually, I left it to her to organize him while I headed straight for the car, which was parked in the carport. But on this particular day, I first went into the house to grab a snack. Minutes ticked by, however, and I didn't see Alex. *Where is that boy? I wondered. He should be here by now. We have to leave!* I was seeing red by then.

Impatiently, I got into the car, slammed the door, and started backing out of the driveway, tires spinning and spitting gravel. Out of the corner of my eye, I caught a glimpse of Alex sitting in the back seat, but was too angry to say anything. It was a quiet ride. Inside, I was fuming. I didn't feel like talking. I was used to this drive to the next town, and I focused on the curves and twists of the road instead. This day, I drove a bit faster than usual, fearing we would be late. Alex needed to make the most of every minute of his time on the ice.

Meanwhile, back at the house, another scenario was being played out. I heard about it later. Apparently, Alex had come around the corner to meet me in the driveway. He had come out of the house through the basement door on the other side. He didn't see the car anywhere. My wife was in the house, and he ran back inside.

"Mom! Dad left without me!"

"Just wait a few more minutes; he must be coming back to get you," said my wife.

Alex waited in the driveway, not knowing what to make of this turn of events.

After a while, as I drove along, I imagined my blood pressure going down a bit. We were already three quarters of the way there. I glanced back in the rear-view mirror to finally say something.

"What?" I yelled out loud. Where was he? I was sure he was in the car. Looking back again, I saw that what I had thought was Alex's head with his helmet on was really a basketball on the ledge under the rear window.

Looking back, I don't remember how the events of the day sorted themselves out, or if they ever did. Shortly after the incident my wife urged me to relate the details to some visiting friends. They roared with appreciative laughter, but I felt terribly sheepish as I relived my incredibly embarrassing moment.

— Terry Burnett —

20

Getting Gobsmacked

You can learn many things from children.
How much patience you have, for instance.
~Franklin P. Adams

J W (not his real name because he threatened to sue if I use his given name) has always been overdramatic. He was only four months old when he affected a rapid distaste of pureed spinach by using his spoon to shoot the spinach as a liquid projectile at the dog. When he was three, he shoved a screw up his nose to protest napping.

At six, his melodrama reached its zenith when the school nurse came into my classroom to announce that JW entered her office eating a biscuit and claiming he had anorexia. Two days later, the nurse stated that JW limped in to her office and alleged he had shrapnel in his shoulder. The next visit had the nurse in hysterical laughter. JW professed to having undescended testicles, which required immediate care away from school.

To say I was gobsmacked would be an understatement! As far as I was aware, my son's appetite was good, he had never been in a war, and after countless diaper changes, I was sure JW had normal equipment.

Not surprisingly, JW was mute about how he had acquired his medical knowledge. This was way before we allowed him on the computer. My husband, Dave, was equally puzzled about JW's new enterprise in self-diagnosis.

But the answer became clear when Dave resumed his recorded

House episode after putting JW down to bed. The plot line concerned a patient with undescended testicles, and I spied a sneaky JW crawling down the hall to watch this banned-for-kids TV show surreptitiously. The previous *M*A*S*H** had been about—wait for it—a soldier with shrapnel in his shoulder. To this day, we can't figure out how a six-year-old knew about eating disorders.

JW's now eighteen years old. His melodramatic antics have slowed down, but we've blocked WebMD and hospital sites on our home computer to be proactive.

— Christy Breedlove —

21

Nightlight

People who say, they sleep like a baby
usually don't have one.
~Leo J. Burke

Dustin and I were both exhausted, living through the first few weeks of caring for our new baby. We were sleep deprived and trying to grow accustomed to our life as parents. It was proving to be more taxing than anyone could have prepared us for.

We had finally closed our eyes and were snoozing away when Randy woke up for one of his nighttime feedings. I whined to Dustin that I was much more tired than he was, and he needed to fix the bottle. Little did I know how tired Dustin actually was that night.

Dustin seemed to be taking a very long time in the kitchen so I called out to him to see if he was okay. He yelled back that he was, but he couldn't get the bottle "fixed" and was trying to find another one. Finally, he made it back to the room and fed the baby.

The next morning, as I was washing the dishes, I noticed a flashlight and batteries (separate from each other) amongst the dirty dishes. I called Dustin to ask if he knew why the flashlight and its batteries were in the sink.

He began to laugh, realizing that the "broken" bottle he was making the night before must not have been a bottle after all. He said he would put in the formula, put on the top, and then turn it over to check the temperature, but each time he did it would dump all the formula out. He made up the baby's formula in this "bottle" several times, thinking each time that the top was just not on tight enough.

Dustin had grabbed the flashlight we kept by the kitchen sink. New-parent fatigue is in a category all its own.

— Shannon Cribbs —

22

Hair Raising

*Everything is funny as long as it is happening
to someone else.*
~Will Rogers

It was time to start a vegetable garden. My kids were twelve and nine years old, and I wanted them to have the experience of growing their own food.

I like to think that I'm pretty handy. I love putting a good power drill to work, so I knew that buying a DIY raised vegetable garden wouldn't be too much for me to handle.

After reading online reviews and perusing a few gardening catalogs, I picked a kit and watched two YouTube videos about how to put it together. It looked straightforward, so I ordered it.

Our new raised garden arrived a few days later. I pulled out a wrench and my power drill, which also worked as a screwdriver, and set to work.

After about half an hour, I almost had the whole thing done. I was just leaning over to align the tip of the screwdriver into the X in the top of one last screw when I felt a pull on my scalp and smelled something burning.

I tried to move the drill as the blood drained from my face. My long hair was wrapped around the drill bit and being sucked into the drill.

Not needing to look, my hand felt its way around the drill and pushed the "reverse" button. But the drill only took in more hair, and the smell of burning was even stronger.

Terror flooded my mind. Quickly, I moved to unplug the drill's cord from the electrical outlet. I knew that with another touch of a button, I could possibly scalp myself.

Cord unplugged, I tugged at the drill. It pulled on a large clump of the hair attached to my scalp. I felt around with my other hand. There seemed to be only about an inch of hair between the drill and my scalp. I tugged harder. There was no movement — and the pulling really hurt.

I now had a power tool attached to the side of my head — possibly forever.

My first instinct was to call 911. This was certainly an emergency. But what would the EMTs think when they zoomed up the driveway to find a blond lady with a drill attached to the side of her head? Plus, rewind, what would I say to the 911 operator? No, that wouldn't work.

My twelve-year-old daughter, Gigi, was inside, doing homework upstairs, but I couldn't let her see me in such an idiotic position, not to mention my frantic mental state. I was the mom. I was supposed to know what I was doing.

Suddenly, it dawned on me that the pool guy was here. Maybe he could help. But that could be worse. I'd be famous all over town — but not in a good way.

I decided to call my husband. There wasn't much he could do from his workplace an hour's drive away, but at least he could guide me with a clear head.

Using the one hand that wasn't holding the heavy drill, it took a few times to dial the cordless phone since its rounded back kept sliding across the kitchen counter. Finally, it rang and rang, and the call went to voicemail.

As I listened to the familiar recording, I wondered what message I could possibly leave. None. I hung up. I waited for approximately three seconds, with my drill-holding arm aching more and more, and tried again. Voicemail.

With the drill-arm aching, I walked to look at the situation in a mirror. How bad was it really?

Really bad. I took one look at my distressed face, above which I saw a large, heavy, orange-and-black power drill snared in my locks.

I pulled again, hard. Searing pain, but no movement. Guided by looking in the mirror, I tried to untangle the hair with my opposite hand, but any jarring physical movement made my scalp scream.

Finally, I realized that I couldn't handle this on my own. Gigi was my only hope. I was going to have to humiliate myself to become free. I would get down on my knees in front of my daughter and beg for help.

"Gigi!" I screamed.

"Mom, are you okay?" I heard her yell from upstairs as she ran quickly from her room down to the kitchen. I guess she could tell from my voice that something was really wrong.

She took one look at me and laughed — hard. But she stopped when she saw me crying. Twelve-year-old girls know how important hair is.

The drill and I walked to the dining room table, and she followed. I desperately needed to sit down and rest my aching arm, and I explained how I had gotten myself into this horrible position.

Trying not to let me see her smile, Gigi got straight to work.

"Ouch!" I screamed. I heard my hair ripping, and it hurt. "Be gentle!" I shrieked.

Within a few minutes, Gigi had freed me from the drill. I stood up and hugged my baby girl, relief flooding my core. I pulled away from her, looked her deep in the eyes, and said, "You know you can't tell anybody about this, ever, right?"

"I promise," Gigi said.

If only her mom had any of her good sense.

— Jennifer Quasha Deinard —

23

Chicken Soup for the Soul

Milestone

I thought I used to "worry" a lot when my kids
were little. Then I had teenagers. You know what
I would give right now to worry about
sippy cups and naptime?
~4BoysMother.com

'd been a single dad for just over two years, and I thought I had things well in hand. But that was before my eleven-year-old daughter, Mary, sat down calmly on the coffee table opposite me one Saturday evening and announced, "Dad, I need a bra!"

The words reverberated in the room like a ping-pong ball in a shaken jar.

Five words were all it took for my perfect, pure little girl to burst my safe Daddy Bubble and take our relationship to a whole other level of danger. A bra meant she was growing up... and that meant boys... and I knew what boys meant, being a large one myself.

Breathe deeply, I said to myself as I looked at my innocent baby in her cut-off shorts and size-zero T-shirt. I was without words. I mean, what can a father say to an opening line like that?

"Dad, I need a bra," she repeated.

My skin turned a clammy shade of pale as I blurted out unthinkingly, "For what?"

In retrospect, I can say with complete and total assuredness that that was not the perfect response.

As I tried to regroup, my size-zero daughter pointed calmly to two completely flat areas on her shirt, one on each side of the bright yellow smiley face design, and said simply, "See."

As a father, I knew that behind that innocuous yellow, silk-screened smiley face, there were parts that, in time, would develop. I was fully prepared for this eventuality. My preparation for the inevitable had begun shortly after her birth with my purchase of a samurai sword.

Her mother, I knew for a fact, had purchased bras in the past. But for whatever reason, my daughter came to me instead of her mom. It is still a mystery. Gratifying, yes, but a mystery nonetheless.

I needed a plan.

You can imagine how little sleep I had that night, but I had a perfect plan by morning. After a breakfast of age-appropriate Mickey Mouse–shaped pancakes, we saddled up and headed out into the great unknown: the bra section at our local Target.

I reasoned that any decent Target would have a few bras for sale. I also figured that Sunday morning was a quiet time of late family breakfasts, collegiate hangovers, and the faithful attending church. I was betting on an empty store, a fast fitting and an unseen getaway.

Good plan, right?

As planned, we were the first two customers to enter the store, and we headed straight for the ladies' section. Making our way past the make-up aisles, I thought a little conversation was in order just to break the tension — *my* tension, that is. I asked, "So, sweetie, exactly what kind of bra are we looking for today?"

She didn't hesitate as she responded casually, "One of those push-up ones, Daddy, the ones with the underwire." Now, I may not be the brightest bulb in the pack, but I knew that this was one of those moments when laughter and humor were definitely not the way to go.

"Ya know," I said off-handedly, "I think we should look at a nice cotton sports bra, don't ya' think?" She said nothing as we continued on, passing the lace undies.

We made it through undies and into the bra section unseen, but we were now confronted by a staggering assemblage, an eye-popping potpourri, of female breast-support apparatus. This took choice to a whole other level.

We pressed on, passing the pointy Viking-like contraptions, the scary lace offerings, and some others that were horrifyingly grown-up looking. It took some looking, but we finally found the cotton sports bras… the starter section.

Compared to the bras we had just passed, these were so small that they actually looked more like apparel for an American Girl doll.

"So, what size do you need, sweetie?" She gave me her best "I don't know" shoulder shrug.

"Okay," I said, "so here's what we're gonna do."

Kneeling down behind the display and using my softest voice, so as to go unseen and undetected, I picked out a likely little white cotton sports thing and commenced putting it on over her smiley-face T-shirt. I figured that if it fit, we'd buy one size smaller and be on our way with no one the wiser.

Good plan, right?

Crouching down behind the display, we struggled to get the thing on over her shirt. She began giggling. I began sweating.

As providence would have it, someone up there must have been watching and sent in the cavalry in the form of a friendly face I recognized from our neighborhood.

"What in heaven's name are you two doing down there?" came the decidedly female voice looking around the end of the display at us.

Still in my crouching position and now sweating profusely, I tried to explain the plan. I was cut short by, "I need a bra," coming from my little girl.

"Come with me, child," the kind, smirking woman said as they walked off, leaving me sweaty and alone on the cold linoleum floor.

They exited the ladies' dressing room several minutes later with a selection of little cotton thingies, which I joyously paid for without looking at them. Many times after that morning in Target, the neighbor lady smiled when we passed on the street. I truly believe she thought more kindly of me because of my pathetic efforts that day on the floor in the bra section.

Mary is now thirty-three and, thankfully, buys her bras without my help. I know that somewhere in Target's security department, there are men, other fathers, who have seen my bra-buying efforts on some video recording. They have played and replayed it over and over again, laughing themselves silly, all the while giving thanks that it wasn't them down there on the floor that morning with their little girls.

As for me, I wouldn't have missed the milestone moment for anything.

— Daniel Ginsberg —

24

Four-Letter Words

*Children have never been very good at listening to
their elders, but they have never failed to imitate them.*
~James Baldwin

One day, I was over at my brother and sister-in-law's place, visiting my niece and nephews. They were twelve, ten, and four years old. My sister-in-law was a chatty, shopaholic, gossipy sort who was usually so preoccupied with the conversation that she didn't always look around when sharing verbally.

So it wasn't a surprise to anyone but her when her children would repeat certain words or phrases she commonly used, as kids do. It was always followed by an entertaining lashing-out at them to "watch your mouth!" That would be immediately followed by a spirited reply from the offending child: "You said it first!"

On this particular day, my sister-in-law said they were planning to go to the mall and asked if I wanted to come along. We piled in the van, with my niece in the front passenger seat and my older nephew in the back. I sat beside the youngest, Chris, who was in his car seat.

My sister-in-law began telling me about some of the stores she wanted to visit and some of the deals she had found over the years, especially for the kids' school years and Christmas. The West Edmonton Mall has always been a destination hot spot for serious shopping, and that's where we were heading.

Around this time, precocious little Chris piped up and declared, "I know what Mom's favorite four-letter word is!" Thinking he was going to shout out one of his mother's favorite "colorful" words, we all stopped talking and chanted, "No! No! No! No! No!"

But he didn't disappoint when he yelled out, "Sale!"

That was the greatest laugh of the day. Not only was it a great jab at his mom's obsessive shopping, but a jab at all of us for assuming the worst.

—J. E. Erickson—

Chapter
4

Happiness Ever Laughter

My Wife Tried to Kill Me

I did a push-up today. Well actually I fell down, but I
had to use my arms to get back up, so close enough.
~Author Unknown

Anyone who has been married or in a relationship for a long time knows what "support" means. When your spouse is trying something new, it's your duty to help in any way possible. You may not agree with the decision or even believe it will work, but if his or her mind is made up, you need to support the effort one hundred percent.

In my marriage, these little plans usually come and go, like the time my wife decided we were going to use scent-free laundry soap or start a cardboard recycling program to help save the world. No harm, no foul. But imagine my trepidation when she included me in "our" New Year's resolution to improve our physical fitness.

It sounded simple enough at first. We were already eating fairly well, so all I had to do was join her in doing something called "planking." Since it seemed to involve staying still I was all in.

For those who don't know, a plank is basically a pushup without moving. After my wife explained it to me, I figured this had to be the easiest exercise known to mankind. "You mean, I get in a pushup position and then don't actually do any pushups?" I was incredulous. The world record for holding a plank is five hours; she suggested we start with thirty seconds. I scoffed.

While she set the timer, I confidently dropped to the floor with dreams of my new rock-hard abs dancing through my head. She said, "Okay, go!" I lifted myself up, making sure my back was straight, and waited, wondering why the world record was only five hours for this. After some time passed, I noticed that my stomach muscles were complaining a bit. Surprisingly, my arm shook a little. I refocused. Then it shook again, but more pronounced. My arms started to shake a lot. "How much time?" I asked, starting to doubt my original estimate of an hour's duration for my first-ever plank.

"Twenty seconds to go," she said.

Twenty seconds to go? Meaning only ten seconds of our easy thirty had elapsed?

My stomach muscles started to complain. I started to regret how easy I had made their life. I'd been nicer to them than I was to our kids.

My wife called out, "Ten seconds!" My discomfort turned to pain, and I noticed that my arms were no longer the only things shaking. My shoulders and legs also shook like the paint mixer at a hardware store, while my stomach started a full revolt, threatening to collapse and leave me in a heap on the floor.

"Keep your back straight. You're slouching. Five more seconds!" she barked.

She was no longer the sunshine of my life. At this point, I was convinced that she was pure evil, the root of everything that is pain in this world. I'm also pretty sure she was laughing at me.

As my wife and personal trainer counted down from five, I glanced down, half expecting to see a pool of blood on the floor. Actually, I would not have been surprised if I found myself face to face with a small alien head as it ripped itself out of my stomach like in the movie *Alien*.

"Four!" she called out as I envisioned the alien climbing free of my innards.

"As seen on TV!" crossed through my mind, and I started to giggle.

"Three!" The countdown continued, and the giggles increased. Apparently, the pain was making me delusional.

"Hi, little guy," I imagined I'd say to my new friend as he peered out of my intestines. I started laughing harder. This chuckling did not match up well with the shaking the rest of my body was doing.

It occurred to me that this whole fitness thing was a terrible idea. I decided I would rather walk an actual plank at knifepoint than do these planks any longer.

"Two!"

She had to be lying about the time. She was evil incarnate.

I realized that I wasn't breathing. That was probably part of her plan.

"One!"

My face hit the ground first. As I lay in a sobbing, laughing, sweating, heaving pool on the floor, I did an assessment to see if I had a bloody nose. Apparently, the human nose is not designed to stop the body from a free fall, which is pretty poor engineering. I didn't dare look to see if any fluids were leaking onto the carpet. It was her idea. She could do the cleanup after I expired.

An hour later, after the stomach pains had subsided and I regained the use of my arms, I stood in front of the mirror, saw absolutely zero improvement, and considered moving to Tibet until my wife's fitness craze passed. But I am not a quitter! (Or I am not allowed to quit, which is kinda the same thing, isn't it?) With the same resolve that allows a woman to have another child after enduring the pain of childbirth, I decided I could press on. I mean, I'm only four hours, fifty-nine minutes and thirty seconds away from the record, right?

— Marty Anderson —

The Headlight

To be fully seen by somebody, then, and
be loved anyhow — this is a human offering
that can border on miraculous.
~Elizabeth Gilbert, Committed:
A Skeptic Makes Peace with Marriage

"Honey, the headlight on my car is burned out," I told my husband Eric.

"If you can pick up the new bulb, I'll change it out this weekend," he answered.

The next day, I headed to the auto-parts store and purchased the replacement headlight. I put it in the center console, so I'd know exactly where it was when Eric needed it.

But he got busy that weekend and didn't have time to change the headlight. The same thing happened the following weekend and the weekend after that.

I'd been driving around with the replacement bulb in the center console for about a month when a policeman pulled me over.

"Ma'am, I stopped you today because you've got a headlight out," he said. "I'm going to have to write you a ticket."

I yanked the bulb from the center console — still in the package — and put it in the officer's face. "With all due respect, sir, I did my part," I told him. "I went and bought the bulb a month ago. That was my role in this repair. My husband hasn't made time to actually install the light I purchased, so if you're going to write someone a ticket, it will have to go to him."

"But, ma'am, you're the one driving the car. I can't write him a ticket because the violation is called 'driving with faulty equipment.' You're the one who is doing that."

"I am only driving with faulty equipment because my husband did not do his part." I held up the aforementioned bulb. "I did my part. The ticket goes to him."

The officer's lips twitched, and then he grinned. "You win. What's your husband's name?"

I told him, spelling it for him and everything. He went back to his squad car and returned minutes later. He handed me a written warning, made out in Eric's name. At the bottom, he'd written, "Change your wife's headlight! You don't want that woman mad at you!"

When I got home, I handed Eric his warning ticket. "I got this on my way home. I told the officer that it was your fault, so he made the ticket out to you."

Eric laughed. "There's no fine to pay, but if there was, I'd pay it out of our joint checking account, honey. You'd be out the same amount, regardless of whose name was on the ticket."

I folded my arms across my chest. "I know, but it's the principle of the thing. I did my part. I should not be ticketed because you didn't do your part."

The next day, Eric came home from work early to fix the headlight. He changed clothes and headed to the garage. An hour later, he came back in the house.

"All done?" I said.

He scowled. "No, I can't figure out how to get to it. And the directions in the owner's manual say to take it to the dealership. I'm not paying the dealer hundreds of dollars to change a stupid light bulb. That's ridiculous."

I nodded sympathetically. "I'll be upstairs if you need anything."

Fifteen minutes later, I came back downstairs with a basket of laundry to be washed. I heard a string of expletives coming from the living room.

I was beyond shocked. My husband did not speak that way. I

looked around frantically for our children, hoping they could not hear the tirade.

I headed in the direction of the voice, convinced Eric really needed my help. But when I found him, he was sitting in a chair in the living room with his laptop. He seemed calm for someone who'd been screaming profanities seconds before.

"What is wrong with you?" I asked.

"Nothing. I'm just watching a YouTube video that shows how to change the headlight on our SUV, but the guy in the video has a really foul mouth."

I burst out laughing.

"Yeah, the guy was like, 'The bleeping car manufacturer makes it so bleeping hard to change the bleeping headlight, all so they can get more of our bleeping money,'" Eric chuckled. "He was really upset about it. I only watched the video long enough to figure out what to do, and then I turned it off before the kids heard it."

"Thank goodness for that," I said. "So the guy with the foul mouth was helpful?"

"Yeah, you have to go through the wheel well to get to the headlight."

Eric headed back out to the garage and, within thirty minutes, he was back inside, wearing a smile. "Once again, you have two working headlights," he said. "No more traffic tickets for you."

I kissed his cheek. "Thank you. But, actually, it's no more tickets for *you*."

— Diane Stark —

King Solomon's Sheets

A problem well stated is a problem half solved.
~John Dewey

Inside our little farmhouse wedged in a cold creek valley in Floyd County, Virginia, it will soon be time for the battle between Venus and Mars. The gods of love and war will wax wrath at one another over the indoor temperature in our house until June.

The wife and I don't seem to be able to find a happy medium when it comes to winter comfort zones — except in bed. And even this has not always been an island of peaceful thermoregulation.

In winter, there is the matter of the sheets. In the summer, this is no problem. Cool sheets are deliciously pleasing to us both on a June night when the windows stay open to the balmy country air. And I was — but she was not — perfectly happy in winter with these same cotton sheets. I knew that, upon crawling between layers of chilled cotton in January, there was that catatonic instant when the body went rigid and breath came in short shivering gasps. In my Martian opinion, though, this bracing chill served as an anticipatory counterpoint to the soothing warmth that would come eventually. It was painfully pleasant, like the transition from an ice-water swim to the blissful relaxation that will follow in the sauna.

"A pox on your cotton Polar Bear Club preliminaries," said the wife, insisting on the instantaneous gratification of the sauna. That woman between cold sheets was a horror to witness. On cotton sheets in winter, she immediately turned blue, stuttering and convulsing. She cursed through chattering teeth that I should have blankety-blank put a half-dozen more logs on the fire before I came to bed. Worse than that, when the lights went out, she became a shape-shifting, heat-seeking parasite whose bony appendages conformed to every nook and cranny of my agitated, unsleeping form. If she was cold, we could forget the demilitarized zone in mid-bed. In the pursuit of nocturnal warmth, the woman would slink and slither where angels fear to tread, leaving me pinned on the very brink of my twenty percent of the bed, sweating from uninvited physical contact.

Then, after a dozen or more years of uneasy winter bickering, she discovered her nirvana: flannel sheets. On that first night of flannel, Her Skinniness slipped between powder-blue cloth and commenced to making embarrassingly sensual sounds of contentment. I tell ya, it sort of made me feel inadequate that a woman could derive such pleasure from her bedclothes. She was so happy with our new linens that I tried to love flannel, too. But after a week, I decided I'd rather spend eight dark hours naked in an electric wool sock than sleep under flannel. She pulled 'em up; I threw 'em off. She purred contentedly; I fanned the covers all night, with nightmares of slow death by Crock-Pot.

Marriages have ended over controversies less trivial than this. The solution came to both of us simultaneously: In the wisdom of King Solomon, we divided the "baby," and our marriage-maintenance sheets were invented. We cut one cotton and one flannel sheet down the exact middle and sewed them together. We created a full sheet that is his and hers — half electric wool sock and half Polar Bear cool cotton! We now sleep where the covers suit our alien thermostats and temperaments.

Hybrid sheets are our small contribution to Galactic Harmony. My next mission will be to find a win-win solution to the dreaded Toilet Seat Conundrum. Wish me luck.

— Fred First —

Man Shall Not Live on Bread Alone

The only time to eat diet food is while you're waiting
for the steak to cook.
~Chef Julia Child

Last night, as I put the finishing touches on a batch of roasted pumpkin meatballs, I got a text from my husband. "Hey, are you cooking tonight?"

I wiped my hands on a kitchen towel and replied, "Yep. Found a new recipe online today. It's almost ready."

He responded, "Running late. Won't make it home for dinner. Sorry."

That's when I realized my husband was cheating. Rather than having dinner with his wife, I knew he was headed across town, where he couldn't wait to get his hands on that old hen he'd been sneaking around with. And I knew when he came home I'd be able to smell the perfume on him — eau de fried chicken from the grocery-store deli.

I should've seen it coming. He showed signs of food infidelity the first time I served a Pinterest meal and told him it was time for us to incorporate clean eating into our lives. He poked at the zucchini noodles on his plate and frowned at me. "But I like it dirty," he said. And by dirty, he meant battered, deep-fried and extra crispy.

My husband doesn't like change, especially when it comes to food. He's a Midwestern boy who's spent a lifetime gobbling dinners comprised of his three favorite food groups: meat, potatoes, and bread. So, when I started making changes to the way I shop and prepare meals, he was convinced that I was trying to starve him to death.

For the past two years, I've been trying to prove to him that removing gluten, sugar and processed foods from our diet is a part of living healthy, not a form of punishment. But he's still trying to figure out what he did wrong. He used to finish a meal by patting his belly and telling me it was delicious. Now he leaves the table and asks, "Are you mad at me for something?"

My kitchen cabinets were once filled with food magazines and cookbooks. These days, my smartphone is my cookbook; I find all my recipes on websites and social media. Oh, I know, just because some Paleo expert posts it on Facebook doesn't mean it'll taste good, but I like to think of my kitchen as a healthy test lab.

However, just as in the laboratory, there are a few dangerous concoctions that should be avoided. I realized this when I made cauliflower soup for dinner and served black-bean brownies for dessert. That night, as he slept, my husband serenaded me with gassy honks so noxious and loud that the dog got up and left the room. Those two food items, along with cabbage steak and herbed Brussels sprouts, have been taken off the menu. Forever.

Don't tell my husband this, but some of the dishes I've tried have been hard for even me to handle. A few weeks ago, I cooked up a pot of chickpea pasta. The texture and smell were reminiscent of something we once used to patch our driveway. And recently, I attempted roasted eggplant. Minutes into slicing the ingredients, I discovered I was allergic to the purple produce. Just the process of handling it prompted an itchy rash that quickly spread across the backs of my hands and up my arms. The eggplant took a trip down the garbage disposal, and dear hubby still believes we have poison ivy growing amidst the herbs in our back yard.

All those relationship books that encourage couples to experiment probably aren't referring to gluten-free, low-sodium meal prep. But healthy adventure cooking is about as exciting as things get around here. I just hope there'll come a day when my husband no longer feels the need to cheat on his diet. Until then, I'll remind him that quinoa isn't birdseed, and kale isn't a conspiracy against the potato industry. Until then, he'll probably continue to sneak around with the greasy broad he met downtown. After all, she does come complete with a side of biscuits.

—Ann Morrow—

29

The "Invisible Chair"

You can't deny laughter; when it comes, it plops down
in your favorite chair and stays as long as it wants.
~Stephen King

Every week after our writing group I stop at the Habitat for Humanity ReStore. It's on my way home, and I enjoy browsing their eclectic collection. I usually find something I like, whether it's for me, my kids, or a friend. The prices are reasonable, so whatever I purchase is a good buy.

On one visit, I spotted an attractive, old oak chair with a high, curved back. I didn't need another chair, but it looked so inviting that I had to try it out. It was the most comfortable chair I'd ever sat in. I was hoping it would have one short leg, a broken spindle, a nail sticking out through the seat, or something to deter me. It didn't. It was flawless and in topnotch condition.

I was already rearranging furniture in my mind, trying to find a suitable place for this chair. If I moved my bulky, stuffed chair to the sunroom, I could put this more compact piece in its place. Or, if nothing worked, I would give the chair to my daughter. In any event, the price was right, and I took it home.

I carried the chair into the house and brought out the furniture polish. After a vigorous workout, the chair looked shiny and brand-new. I shifted furniture, set down my bargain and enjoyed my new acquisition. It took up less space than the bulky chair and made the room look larger.

I knew my significant other would flip out when he saw another chair in the house. I decided not to tell him and wait to see if he was observant enough to notice it on his own.

Art walked past the chair many times and didn't say a word. *Is the chair invisible?* I wondered. *Is Art waiting for me to admit that I bought yet another piece of furniture, or is he waiting for my next move as I am his? If I can notice a crumb on the floor or a candy bowl that has been moved just one inch within seconds, why can't Art notice a brand-new chair? It's not the size of an ant.* Trying to make it more conspicuous, I placed a brightly colored pillow on the "invisible chair." He still didn't notice it.

A week later, I decided to sit on the chair wearing a bikini. When Art walked past, he remarked, "Nice bikini."

If Art hasn't seen the "invisible chair," I hope he doesn't see the "invisible player piano" I'm having delivered in two weeks!

— Irene Maran —

30

First Anniversary

*Marriage is a bond between a person
who never remembers anniversaries and another
who never forgets them.*
~Ogden Nash

t is easy to put my finger on the most embarrassing moment in my adult life. It came on the first anniversary of my marriage to Kyra. I had one failed marriage and was determined to make my second one work. The only disagreement we had in our time together came before we were married. Kyra wanted to be a June bride when the trees and flowers were in full bloom and foliage. I was superstitious about June because that was when my first marriage took place.

Kyra was adamant and said a silly superstition should not keep her from the wedding that she wanted. I continued to push and urged her to either elope or move the date up. Kyra won that argument, and we married in early June.

I wanted our first anniversary to be special, so I made special arrangements for dinner at a place known for gourmet eating and had the local flower shop deliver a dozen long-stemmed red roses.

All day, I thought of how happy I must have made my wife. I had visions of her jumping into my arms for a big hug. I couldn't wait to get home from the office. I escorted my last client to the door and handed him his hat. I had my hand on his back so there was no doubt that the meeting was over. I left five minutes early and told the secretary to lock up.

The weather was warm, so I walked the several blocks to my house, getting more eager with every step. I almost broke into a sweat as I bounded up the steps, threw open the door and announced, "Honey, I'm home!"

Kyra was standing at the sink, washing something, and she didn't even turn around. I saw the long-stemmed roses still in the open box, so I knew she had received them. That was strange behavior for Kyra. She is usually glad to see me, even if I am not bearing gifts.

I put my hands on her shoulder, but she didn't turn around. I asked her what was wrong. "Nothing," she said. I don't know much about women, but I know that when they say "It's nothing," then it's something.

I couldn't figure out what I had done. I wracked my brain — and then it hit me. At the same moment, Kyra blurted out in her best Ricky Ricardo voice: "Doug, you got some 'splaining to do!"

Wrong day, wrong wife! Or maybe wrong day, right wife. All I know is that I sent a dozen roses to my wife on the day that I married my *first* wife. I had gotten the days mixed up — just like I had imagined in my "silly superstition."

Needless to say, I wasn't eating gourmet food that night; I was eating crow. I spent my first anniversary apologizing and 'splaining.

—Doug Sletten—

31

A Soft Whisper in the Ear

With mirth and laughter let old wrinkles come.
~William Shakespeare, The Merchant of Venice

Premature gray hair runs in my family. My dad was completely white by the time he was in his thirties. I found my first gray when I was eighteen. I spent most of my twenties and thirties in heavy combat, attacking the dreaded skunk-stripe that seemed to arrive only a few weeks after my monthly attempt to cover up what my DNA decided was my natural hair color.

In my late forties, I gave up the chemicals and let my white hair shine. My husband James was a big supporter of my natural look. Other women stopped me in shopping malls and at the grocery store to tell me how much they liked my long, frosty-white hairstyle. All in all, I was exceedingly pleased with my decision to go au naturel.

I must admit, though, that I'm asked far too often for my liking if I'm over sixty-five when I'm at a checkout that offers senior discounts. Usually, the clerk is under thirty and can be forgiven for not being able to distinguish between the sagging skin of an eighty-five-year-old versus the droopy flesh of someone barely fifty. I get it. I didn't pay much attention to the over-thirty crowd when I was her age, either.

However, my husband finds this particularly hilarious because he knows it annoys me. I've even been known to stifle the question before it escapes the dewy-skinned clerk's mouth when I happen to be in a store on a seniors' day.

"Don't ask," I say preemptively. And, thankfully, they usually oblige.

However, there have been occasions when my white hair has been the source of a good laugh. My husband and I like to frequent thrift shops and antique stores. I'm a genealogist and collector of old photographs. I often find old carte de visite photographs or cabinet card images in these shops. One of my hobbies is reuniting old family photos with genealogists.

On one of our visits to a local thrift shop, my husband was in an exceedingly goofy mood. We had watched an old *Saturday Night Live* episode the evening before, and James was doing a poor imitation of Steve Martin's "wild and crazy guy" character, Georg Festrunk, as we entered the store. I went off to look at the knickknacks, hoping to find old photos, while he went into the housewares section of the store.

I didn't find any interesting pictures or tchotchkes, so I headed over to join my husband in the hunt for some nice kitchen gadgets. I noticed he had walked up behind an older woman. She was wearing the same color and style of coat as mine and had beautiful, flowing white hair. I headed over just in time to hear him whisper into her left ear, "See anything you like?" in his most salacious, "wild and crazy guy" voice.

The woman turned around. She was clearly well into her eighties and didn't seem to find his closeness particularly unsettling. She gave him a good look up and down. "Maybe," she said with a smile.

The surprised look on James's face was priceless. I couldn't help it. I laughed out loud. The elderly woman looked at me, and then at James. She figured out the mistake immediately.

"Nice jacket," she said to me.

"Thanks," I replied. "And you have the most gorgeous hair."

We all had a good chuckle. I think the woman was quite pleased to be mistaken for someone thirty years her junior. And you know what? I didn't mind, either.

—Carol L. MacKay—

32

Money Talks

A wedding anniversary is the celebration of love,
trust, partnership, tolerance and tenacity.
The order varies for any given year.
~Paul Sweeney

My husband was always nagging me to discuss our finances. I was always avoiding the topic. And then, one Saturday morning, I skidded into the living room wearing my slipper socks and spied my husband parked on the sofa.

He was surrounded by yellow notepads and papers and there were four pens neatly arranged on the coffee table. He looked open for business. My heart sank.

"Glad you're up," he said, maintaining strong eye contact and a thin smile. "I've saved you a seat."

Uh oh.

"Do you have a few minutes to talk about our finances?"

I needed to find a way out.

"Umm, I have an appointment in five minutes."

I couldn't look him in the eye.

"Come on," he said, patting a spot next to him. "It's the weekend."

For the past few months, he'd been hounding me to review our finances.

"Seriously, this is important," he said. "You need to understand our finances. Do you even remember how to access our banking information? What would you do if I wasn't around?"

"I'd call your best friend, Jeff. He probably knows the passwords to our bank account."

"What?"

"Just kidding. Fine. You have my attention." For the next three minutes was what I meant.

He shoved a pen and pad of paper into my hand. "Might want to take a few notes."

I had to act dumb and make this go away.

He droned on and on about budgets, long-term versus short-term investments, financial portfolios, goals, emergency funds, dividends, blah, blah, blah, and taxes.

I heard nothing.

"Let's begin by discussing the college fund," he said, waving his arms.

I glanced at my watch. Only ten minutes had passed since I sat down, but it felt like an eternity. He pulled out the laptop and balanced it on his knees. Using a pencil as a pointer, he flashed charts bearing all types of data on the screen. My eyes blurred under the strain of bar, pie, and line charts.

He was so well prepared.

"What level of risk are we willing to take with the 529 Plan? Do you think a market risk is best?

"Oh... um... sure. I agree," I said, nodding like a bobble-head dashboard dog. "You are so smart."

I had no idea what he was talking about. And I never wanted to know. Ever.

"Do you think you can start looking into the difference between capital gains and dividend income on an annual basis for some of our investments?"

Was he still talking to me? If he figured out how to work our washer and dryer I would pay attention to his capital gains spreadsheets.

After forty-seven minutes, I slumped over the sofa arm and pretended to hang myself. I wrapped an imaginary rope around my neck and stuck out my tongue for emphasis.

"Seriously?" he said in a whiny voice. "I lost you already? This is important."

"Do you really think I can go from doing nothing to making major decisions about our finances?" I said.

"I believe in you. I know you're capable of helping."

"Won't it all work itself out in the long run anyway?"

"What the heck are you talking about?" he said through gritted teeth.

"Or how about this?" I said, touching his arm. "I'll take baby steps and begin by collecting our yearly expenses."

"That sounds good. Let's follow up on this next month."

Ugh. I thought I had bought myself more time than a month. I did say "yearly."

He left the room, shaking his head and mumbling something like, "God help us."

The low hum of the dryer and the muted thumping of tumbling clothes resounded from the laundry room.

My husband swaggered into the living room with a puffed-up chest and a "Well?" attitude.

"Fine," I said, sighing dejectedly. "You win."

We made a deal. My husband likes a challenge, so now he makes sure my shirts are wrinkle-free, and I'm learning about itemized deductions.

— Stacey Gustafson —

Chapter
5

Pets and Other Creatures

33

Playing It by Ear

Without my dog, my wallet would be full, my house
would be clean, but my heart would be empty.
~Author Unknown

A fter he had twelve ear infections in three years, I decided the time had come to take him to a specialist. Of course, this visit wasn't covered by insurance, and it cost an obscene amount of money to determine there was nothing wrong with his eardrums or his ear canals or anything even remotely ear-related.

The problem, it seemed, was allergies. And the solution was to change his dog food.

"You're telling me the dog is getting ear infections because he's allergic to his food?" my husband asked incredulously.

"Yes."

"And the person who told you this is a Dog Allergist?"

"That's right," I said.

"And I paid actual money for us to find this out?"

"Lots of it," I responded.

He sighed and glared at the dog. The dog wagged his tail and then scratched at his ears.

"There's a special hypoallergenic food we have to feed him, and he can't eat anything except that food," I explained.

The next day, I went out and bought a bag of the new dog food. Apparently, the main ingredient was gold because it was ten times as expensive as his old stuff. For a week, we transitioned him from the old chow to the gold chow, and all was well. But then one night as my husband and I watched TV and the dog lay snoring on the rug, an odor wafted up at us that singed my nose hairs and made my eyes burn and water.

My husband and I looked at each other in horror and then looked down at the dog. He didn't twitch. He didn't utter a sound. Not one piece of fur on his prone body moved. And yet we knew the smell had undeniably come from the dog. It was, without a doubt, the worst thing I'd ever smelled. Coming from someone who routinely has angry skunks in her back yard, that's saying a lot.

There was no doubt it was the new dog food. The special food gave the dog such strong gas that it not only forced us to leave the room, but it probably punched a hole in the ozone layer and contributed to global warming. I decided that the reason they called it flatulence is because it knocked us flat off our feet.

"What's in the new food you're feeding him?" my husband asked through the pillow he held in front of his face.

"Rotten eggs and dead fish, obviously," I said through my own pillow.

"You have to switch his food," said my husband desperately.

"We can't," I replied. "The doctor said the dog can't eat anything but this stuff for twelve weeks to see if it helps his ears."

"It won't help his ears if we suffocate to death and can't feed him," said my husband.

Ultimately, we decided to stick with the plan. The dog ate only the gold chow, and my husband and I invested in some army surplus gas masks.

We suffered for three months. Then it was the dog who revolted. One morning, we came downstairs to find the entire contents of our kitchen garbage strewn across three rooms. There were wrappers, jars, and shreds of paper everywhere, but not a crumb of food in sight. In the middle of the mess lay the dog in a sated heap. The only evidence of anything edible remaining were the telltale coffee grinds on the end of the dog's nose.

"Oh, no! The dog ate the entire bag of garbage," I moaned. "I hope it doesn't make him sick."

My husband sniffed the air. "It could only help."

Eventually, the Great Smelly Dog Experiment came to an end. I took the dog back to the vet to get checked.

"I have some good news and bad news," I told my husband. He had just come in from walking the dog.

"Give me the good news first."

"Okay. The vet doesn't think the dog's ear infections are from a food allergy after all, so we don't have to keep feeding him that hypoallergenic food," I said.

"Hallelujah," shouted my husband. He was understandably jubilant.

"But the bad news is, they did some blood tests and found out the dog has some other allergies." I read from the list the doctor had given me. "He's allergic to trees, grass, pollen, mold, dust mites, fleas, insects in general, and wool."

My husband dropped the leash and leaned wearily against the counter.

"So, the dog is basically allergic to everything inside the house and out, right?" he concluded.

"Yes," I paused. "And he's also allergic to us."

"Come on," he said.

"He's allergic to human dander," I added.

My husband threw up his arms. "I guess the dog is going to have to live in a plastic bubble."

"Actually, they want to give him allergy shots," I told him.

He rolled his eyes. "You know, our actual children aren't even this much work. Can't we just give him an antihistamine or something?"

I looked at the dog splayed out on the wool rug laden with mold and dust mites, and I sighed.

"Good thing you're so cute," I told him. He scratched at his ears.

The next day, I took him back to see the pet specialist. The waiting room was filled to capacity with some pretty miserable-looking creatures… and those were just the pet owners. The dogs did not look much better. There were old dogs and new dogs; huge dogs and tiny dogs. Dogs that itched and dogs that sneezed; dogs that twitched and dogs that wheezed. Dogs with no fur and dogs with no hair. Allergic dogs… everywhere!

I opted not to sit next to the wheezing guy with the matching wheezing Bulldog or the lady with blue hair with the hairless cat. I finally settled on a seat next to a woman with a dog at her feet and a cat in her lap.

"Wow, you have two pets here," I said, stating the obvious. "What are their problems?"

"Allergies," she replied succinctly.

"Oh, really? Mine, too," I said, not unlike everyone else in the waiting room. "What are they allergic to?"

"The cat is allergic to the fish in his food."

I laughed. "That's funny. A cat that's allergic to fish. What about your dog?"

She sighed.

"He's allergic to the cat."

— Tracy Beckerman —

34

No Good Deed

Great deeds are usually wrought at great risks.
~Herodotus

I didn't really know Darlene, but my friend, her daughter, wanted me to meet her. She thought we would like each other. That's how I came to knock on her door at the edge of town one spring afternoon.

She looked a little harried as she answered the door. "Would you help me do something before we sit down?" she asked. "I need to return a chicken to the neighbor." I thought that made a good first impression and agreed to go with her.

The chicken in question was still fuzzy with down underneath the sparsely feathered wings. It was also wet with dog slobber from her Great Pyrenees. Darlene had rescued the little bird from the mouth of their gigantic dog, who had noticed the intruder slip under the fence between the two back yards.

She cupped the chick in her hands and locked the dog inside the yard, and we walked down to the corner and around the block. Unlike many western Washington spring days, the sun was shining and the birds were singing in the tall Douglas firs. *How nice,* I thought. *We'll do a good deed together and then go sit by her koi pond and get to know one another over a glass of iced tea.*

The neighbor lived in a nice trailer, set back off the road, and accessed by a longish driveway. I don't think Darlene noticed the steel-gray Pit Bull that came out of a doghouse by the mailbox. The dog stood silently as we walked by. I nodded to him as we passed and got a slight wag of the tail in reply. Apparently, two gray-haired women — one carrying a resident chicken — didn't require so much as a warning bark. The dog only watched us walk up the steps to the door and then lay down in the shade to keep us under surveillance in case he'd misjudged our intentions.

Darlene knocked and then waited patiently while the neighbor, an older Korean man, looked us over from a front-facing window. When he opened the door, Darlene gave him her biggest smile and held the chick up to him. "I'm returning your chicken," she said. The man did not reply. He didn't smile either.

Thinking that he didn't understand, she gave further explanation. "It got into my back yard, and I'm sorry that my dog got to it first, but I think it will be alright. It's just a little wet." At first, the man didn't respond. Then he took a step backward and put both hands into his front pockets. And I realized long before Darlene did that he was not going to take the chicken. Ever. "It's your chicken," she said. She smiled again and pushed it toward him. He sighed.

"Son buy chickens this year. Not good chickens." He shook his head sadly. Then he perked up as an idea occurred to him, and he did smile just a little. "You want another chicken?"

"What?" I could see that it was starting to dawn on Darlene that this good deed was not going to go as planned. Still hopeful and holding the chick out to him, she tried one more time. "No, this is your chicken that got into my yard, and I want to return it to you. It's *your* chicken."

I admired her persistence and her innocent belief that doing the right thing was the right thing to do no matter how difficult it might be. And really, returning a neighbor's property should be the easiest thing in the world.

Or not. The gentleman pulled the door closed behind him as he stepped off the porch. I noticed that his hands returned to his pockets as if he were afraid that Darlene would force him to take the chick. "Follow me," he said. We did.

I thought I saw the Pit Bull smile.

We followed him around the house to the pen where the rest of his not-good chickens lived. "Which one you want?" he asked as he stepped over the short fence.

Darlene and I looked at each other. She shrugged. "You choose," I said to the man, and he did. The chick he handed me was identical to the one that Darlene still held, except that it wasn't sticky from dog drool. We thanked him and headed back toward the street. The Pit Bull thumped his tail on the ground as a goodbye. He didn't seem to care that two of the resident chickens were being carried off by a pair of gray-haired women. I couldn't help myself. I started to laugh.

By the time we got back to her house, she'd already pulled a cell phone from her pocket and called my friend to request that she stop and get chicken feed on the way home. Listening to her side of that conversation had me nearly in tears as she explained how we had attempted to return one chicken to its rightful owner but came home with two instead.

After the chicks had been safely installed in a large dog crate with water and bedding, we sat by her koi pond to enjoy a bottle of wine.

I asked my new best friend if she had any neighbors who owned ponies. I'd always wanted a pony, and if one slipped into her back yard, I'd be delighted to come by and help her return it.

— Linda Bittle —

35

Bitsy and the Pickup Truck

Being stubborn can be a good thing. Being stubborn can be a bad thing. It just depends on how you use it.
~Willie Aames

Every summer, I volunteer as an assistant dog trainer at the free obedience classes my vet friend Rosa teaches. This always leads to more than its fair share of humorous moments, as one can't get a large group of completely novice dogs and completely novice humans together without at least a few hilarious misadventures. One time, the ballroom dance teacher who used the school gymnasium after us joined, quite cheerfully, in a long discussion about the treats Rosa was planning for "Shane's twelfth birthday party," only to be completely horrified when Rosa said she'd had trouble getting enough raw liver at the store. Shane was Rosa's champion Border Collie, not her son, as the ballroom teacher had surmised.

Then there was the time we were tossing tiny bits of hot dog on the floor so the dogs would leave their owners, who would then lure them back with an even bigger and better treat. One first-time trainer with very bad aim scored a direct hit in the scoop neck of my tank top, and the hot-dog bite went straight down into the front of my bra. That would have been embarrassing enough, but then Romeo the Labradoodle decided to put his paws on my shoulders and go after his treat anyway.

Still, the funniest thing that ever occurred didn't happen until after class, when our training was finished for the day and everyone should have been heading home in their cars. It involved a Great Dane named, I kid you not, Bitsy. Teaching a beginning dog class means that you quickly become immune to incongruent dog names. You only have to make the acquaintance of a few Princesses who drool like it's going out of style or Killers who are frightened of their own shadows before you learn how to shrug and just get on with the task at hand.

But even by free-obedience-class standards, Bitsy stood out as being particularly misnamed. He wasn't just big, he was huge, measuring nearly three feet high at the shoulder and weighing close to two hundred pounds. He considerably outweighed his four-foot-ten-inch owner. He even dwarfed the small, quarter-ton pickup truck she used to transport him, making it look like a toy truck into which some optimistic child had tried to fit a much bigger stuffed animal. In short, Bitsy wasn't "itsy" at all.

Bitsy was never destined to be a star obedience pupil. Teaching him to heel was a particular challenge. After many, many tugs at his collar and waves of treats under his nose, his owner finally induced him to stand up and walk with her... for all of three steps. Then he'd sit down again, progressing in steady stages from resting on his bottom to slumping down onto one hip, his hind legs sliding out across the floor. From there the rest of his body would slowly follow his bottom and legs down to the ground, until all two hundred pounds of Great Dane had gently oozed to the floor like a giant melting marshmallow.

This process took several minutes to complete, and it was really quite fascinating and hypnotic to watch. Many times, the entire class would stop training to simply stand and stare. We'd watch the slow-motion ooze until Bitsy was nothing but a spread-out puddle of dog, utterly boneless and completely at ease. After several classes full of fruitless attempts to get him to move once he'd achieved this state, Rosa eventually nicknamed this puddle "Lake Bitsy." She urged the rest of us to ignore him and just keep working around him.

It was certainly a novel way to learn how to heel around obstacles.

Bitsy may not have been our star pupil, but he definitely enjoyed coming to class — so much that he decided he didn't want to leave one day. Rosa and I were cleaning up after class when Bitsy's owner stuck her head through the door, asking for our aid "with a small problem." The moment we stepped out the door, it was plain to see what the problem was: Bitsy was refusing to get into the back of his owner's truck. She had managed, heaven only knows how, to get his front feet up onto the open tailgate, but that was as far as Bitsy would go; nothing would convince him to jump into the pickup bed. He simply stood there, front feet up and back feet down, panting happily while his weight pushed the truck into a definite slant.

Rosa and I tried everything. After giving him a thorough exam to make sure he hadn't hurt his legs or back, we went through Rosa's entire arsenal of dog treats, trying in vain to find one that was yummy enough to tempt Bitsy the rest of the way. We did the same thing with our entire collection of training toys, all to no avail. Finally, we resorted to brute force. Rosa, Bitsy's owner, and I all gathered at Bitsy's hind end. We each planted our hands squarely on Bitsy's furry bottom and shoved forward and up with all our might.

The truck rocked like a boat in a storm, but Bitsy stayed put.

By this time, the dance class was gathering, so we quickly amassed quite an audience: fifteen couples all liberally bedecked in sequins and body glitter, watching us like we were the most entertaining thing they'd ever seen. I can't deny that we made a hilarious impression: three grown women in blue jeans gathered at the base of a tiny pickup truck, all pushing rhythmically on the bottom of an elephant-sized Great Dane who simply stood there with his tongue lolling out, looking around innocently as if he didn't understand what all the fuss was about. Fortunately, several of the dancers were also dog lovers, and with true small-town spirit, they volunteered to help despite their fancy clothes and shoes. They crowded in around us, and with a "Five! Six! Seven! Eight!" we all pushed on Bitsy's butt in unison.

It took three tries, and quite a few ballroom beads and feathers got detached, but it worked eventually. Bitsy was in the truck!

Bitsy's owner opted to have private lessons after that. She paid

Rosa to come out to her farm, where Bitsy did eventually learn how to heel, though he never quite managed a non-oozing sit. But it doesn't really matter that I never saw Bitsy in class again. All I have to do is close my eyes, and I can still see him: the rocking truck, the pushing people, and most of all, Bitsy's hilarious, utterly serene face. It never fails to make me laugh and raise my spirits when they are low. Long live Bitsy!

—Kerrie R. Barney—

36

Guest Appearance

The great pleasure of a dog is that you may make a
fool of yourself with him and not only will he not scold
you, but he will make a fool of himself too.
~Samuel Butler

O ur neighbor had a wonderful Golden Retriever named Dudley
and we often dog-sat for him. Dudley got along very well
with our Aussie Shepherd, Gus. They were pals.

On one such dog-sitting adventure, my husband Ron and I
were sleeping soundly in the wee hours one Friday morning — 4:30, to
be exact. Suddenly, I realized the bed was jiggling. What in the world?
Ron slept like a log next to me, unmoving. I shook my head, trying
to emerge from my not-awake state of mind. Earthquake? Unlikely
in the foothills of Colorado. Windstorm? What could shake the bed?

I went on the assumption that Gus must be leaning against the
bed scratching his neck, so I whispered, "Stop it!" I did my best not
to wake myself any further from this semi-functioning state, but the
bed continued to jiggle. So I whispered again, as if the dog could
understand what I said, "What are you doing?" I tried not to wake
Ron. How he slept through this jiggling had me baffled.

Then I heard claws scratching the wood floor, causing a spinning,
sliding, clawing-for-dear-life noise. Now fully awake, I realized there
was a dog under the bed. I reached over the side of the bed, snapped
my fingers and whispered firmly, "Come out here whoever you are!"
I looked over the edge.

Suddenly, a large Dudley face stretched its way out from under the frame of the bed. I repeated, "Come on, Dudley! What are you doing?" Again, did I think the dog would answer me?

Now the claws were really scratching, pulling, and slipping, unable to grip anything substantial. He was flattened against the floor with his front paws way out to the side. His paws continued this butterfly swim against hardwood flooring as he tried with all his might to get himself out from under the bed.

I began to mutter to myself about the lack of intelligence of the eighty-pound dog who was stuck under the bed that I was blissfully sleeping in just moments ago.

Thinking I had better get my weight off the bed since that was most likely hindering his progress, I knelt down on my bad knees after grabbing my flashlight and attempted to pull him out. Much like trying to assist a breach calf that refuses to come out, I tried to swing his legs under him to get him on his side, thinking he'd come out easier. That didn't work either.

Dudley just looked up at me in the beam of light with his big, sad Retriever eyes. I pulled and pondered how this was going to end.

Ron woke finally, rolled over and said, "What is going on?"

"Dudley is stuck. Under the bed."

Being the helpful guy that he is, Ron started cracking up.

Meanwhile, I was trying to pull on a huge dog to get him unstuck (Did I mention my bad knees?), and Ron was... laughing. Not helping. Totally cracking up.

I realized I was going to have to lift the side of the bed and hope that Dudley could crawl out. It's a king-sized bed.

Ron was still laughing.

I lifted and said through a strained voice, "Come on, Dudley, come out!"

Ron was still laughing.

The only other sounds besides my grunting and Ron's laughter was mad clawing, dragging, and sliding as Dudley finally pulled his large, furry body out from under the bed.

Ron was still laughing, totally out of control, *on the bed*. He was hysterically enjoying this early morning event of trying to obtain a dog's autonomy.

Finally, Dudley was free! He had a plastic newspaper dog toy in his mouth that he must have found under the bed. I'm so glad he was able to save the daily news. He lay unscathed in the corner with the toy between his teeth, happy as a clam, making his Chewbacca noise.

I got to crawl back under the warm covers, joining Ron, who was still laughing. He was holding his stomach and rolling back and forth on his back, hoping he didn't blow open another hernia.

I explained to him what I found when I felt the bed jiggling, which sent him into a laughing fit all over again. That got me giggling. We kept making jokes about what Dudley must have been thinking as I tried to birth him from under the bed. It took us an hour to settle the laughter and try to fall back to sleep.

At least I could rest knowing there were no more dust bunnies under our bed.

We slept late that morning.

— Sandy Nadeau —

37

The Telltale Meow

If cats could talk, they wouldn't.
~Nan Porter

Recently, while cat sitting for my neighbor's two felines, I had quite the scare. As I doled out kibble, I heard a loud meow that seemed to be coming from behind the stove.

Of course, I was startled. Heart racing, I opened the stove and saw that it was empty. Quickly, I searched the small condominium for the cats. I could only find one. Panic set in. Could Diesel have crawled behind the appliances? Was he trapped or hurt?

I hurried across the hallway to retrieve my cell phone and dialed Mary, the owner. Her voicemail kicked in and announced that her mailbox was full. Shoot! What to do?

It occurred to me to call the fire department. Wouldn't they be willing to help a lady who was looking out for the welfare of a beloved pet? I called the non-emergency phone number and explained my situation.

"Well, I suppose we could send a firefighter out to see if he can help. We haven't any emergencies at the moment."

Diligently, I began to look in every nook and cranny for M.I.A. Diesel. Having a cat, myself, I was aware that they could hide in the oddest of places. "Diesel. Kitty, kitty. Come on, Diesel, I have a treat." As I continued to hunt, I felt lightheaded and nauseous. "Dear Lord, please let him be alright," I prayed.

"Meooow," I heard again. The sound was definitely coming from the kitchen wall. That poor cat had been stuck in there at least fifteen minutes since the last time I heard him. I ran to the spot and, with a closed fist, began to tap the wall. I heard nothing.

My investigation was interrupted by the knocking on the front door. "Come in!" I shouted.

Two extremely fit and handsome firemen entered. *Stay focused,* I chided myself.

Introducing themselves, I realized I was clad in pajamas and slippers that weren't a pair. *Stay focused!*

I explained the situation quickly as my panic returned. "He must be stuck!" I cried.

"Meooow!"

"Goodness, it sounds like he's in the wall!" exclaimed blond Rob.

Stay focused! This is a serious situation!

"I suppose we can open the wall," Rob continued. "This is your condo?"

"No, I'm cat sitting. I live across the hall."

"We'll need to contact the owner before we do any damage."

"She isn't answering her phone, and her voicemail is full."

"Hmm. Does he know his name? I'm a dog person. I must admit I know little about cats."

"Yes, but cats rarely come when called."

Gorgeous Tim piped in, "Maybe we can shake his food bowl. Perhaps he'll try to come for food."

The three of us stood facing the oven as kibble sounds emanated from the bowl. We heard nothing. "Dear Lord," I prayed again aloud. "Please let him be alive!"

The sweet Lord answered with, "Meooow!" but this time it was coming from behind us.

Rob turned and asked, "How many cats does she have?"

I turned, too. Sitting not three feet behind us were Diesel and Mitsi. "What? She has two, these two," I sighed as I pointed. "Who is trapped in the wall?"

We looked at one another. Tim shrugged his shoulders, and Rob said, "Hmm. This is the damnedest thing. Are you sure she only has two?"

"Positive." I turned again. Was the furry pair smirking? Honestly, I am quite sure they were.

Silence.

"Meooow!"

Rob began to laugh as he reached for the clock mounted above the stove. Twelve cats on a round disc were positioned as the décor on this timepiece.

Rob turned the minute hand slowly until it reached the feline at quarter past.

"Meooow!"

— Kathleen Gemmell —

38

Making a Good Impression

Etiquette can be at the same time a means of
approaching people and of staying clear of them.
~David Riesman

fluffed up the sofa pillows and glanced around. No ice cream bowls on the end table. No stinky athletic shoes to trip over. No backpacks tossed in the corner. No dog nose prints decorating the window. Yes, this living room could grace the cover of a magazine.

To top off this perfect scenario, the four kids were playing quietly in the back of the house. Fortunately, Sherlock, our English Bulldog, was with them. I heaved a sigh of relief since Sherlock's manners could not be considered genteel.

The front doorbell rang. I knew it must be my guest since friends popped their heads in the back door, yelled "Hi," and came on in. Mrs. Williams would never do that. She was the poster child for proper etiquette. I ushered her in, got her seated, poured some tea, and handed her the cookie plate. So far, so good.

Just as Mrs. Williams reached the high point about her elite women's club and how she wished to sponsor me, I heard movement in the hall followed by snickering. I tried to ignore the commotion, but it became difficult with the bursts of smothered giggling. Mrs. Williams frowned slightly. I concluded either she was childless or had spawned perfect offspring.

As I looked up, Sherlock waddled into the room wearing an old pink tutu stretched around his large, squat body. Topping off his ensemble was a pair of boy's jockey shorts resembling a crown that he wore proudly on his head. Like a professional model, he paraded around the living room. I must admit by now I was having difficulty stifling my laughter. Sherlock stopped by Mrs. Williams and looked up at her with large marble-like eyes. He leaned against her leg and waited to be petted. I could tell from her expression that she was not a dog lover.

With what looked like a shrug, Sherlock padded into the kitchen. He plopped down with his nose pressed against the side of the refrigerator, enjoying the motor's vibration. The culmination of his high-fashion act was a deep burp followed by an enormous escape of gas from his other end.

Mrs. Williams departed.

The kids dove into the cookie plate.

Sherlock snored.

I figured that elite club probably wasn't for me.

— Sharon Landeen —

39

Impressive

*Of all days, the day on which one has not laughed is
the one most surely wasted.*
~Sebastien Roch

'd just returned to Colorado from Alaska where I'd been working for the Forest Service on a wildlife crew. I had a new boyfriend, and he wanted to go on a backcountry camping trip in
Yellowstone. This was right up my alley; he might be a keeper.

At the backcountry office, we were told that a huge bear had
been seen in the area where we planned to hike. "They have huge
territories," I said with confidence. "He'll move on."

The new boyfriend smiled. That was back when he loved everything I said.

The first snowfall of the season was expected that night. I had
two below-zero sleeping bags, warmer than what he had, so I offered
him one of mine, and he accepted.

We hiked in that afternoon to a clear lake at the base of several
mountains. As we were rounding the lake to the designated campsite,
a huge boulder moved just ahead of us. The new boyfriend and I
backtracked quickly, my scalp tingling the way it did when I thought
I might die. I was without the .375 I hiked with every day in Alaska.
I had bear spray, but that stuff never worked. How ironic, I thought,
to survive five years in the Alaskan backcountry to get shredded in
Yellowstone, five miles from the truck.

The bison exhaled and got to his feet. The new boyfriend breathed out as well. "Close one."

I cleared my throat and rubbed at my hairline. We went around the lake in the other direction, and the bison ignored us, grazing not too far from where he'd been pretending to be a rock.

We set up the tent and talked about the bear. Soon enough, we both had to go to the bathroom. I explained that we should pee in a wide circle around the tent. That way, if the bear stumbled upon us in the night, he'd know for sure what we were and not feel the need to come any closer to investigate. This was what we did in Alaska.

I was dehydrated from the hike, so I drank a bunch of water, which made me have to pee in the night. It was cold and starting to snow, and the new boyfriend was asleep, so I peed pretty close.

I woke up a few hours later to breathing right outside the tent. My eyes caught the new boyfriend's, who had woken up at the same time. He was too big for the women's sleeping bag I had lent him, so I'd helped him get zipped in earlier. Neither of us thought it was a big deal that his arms were stuck at his sides — until now. The zipper would be too loud. No need to move unless the bear decided to attack. He was only breathing at the moment. I inched my hand to the bear spray on my left side. The new boyfriend's eyes tracked my slow-motion movement. The bear moved closer. Black fur pressed up against the side of the tent right over the top of the new boyfriend. There was the tearing of grass and a wet smacking sound. *That's weird,* I thought. *Bears in Alaska don't eat grass.*

The bear took another step and ripped up another mouthful of grass, this time next to the new boyfriend's hip.

This continued. Neither of us breathed or moved once I had a finger on the bear-spray button. My scalp tingled, and my heart beat so hard it felt like I might throw up. The bear moved to my side of the tent. I could feel the warmth of him through the fabric. Eventually, he moved on.

The new boyfriend gave me a look that said something like *I cannot believe you zipped me into this bright purple bag.* Or maybe, *Just unzip me, please.* I don't know. We didn't know each other all that well yet. Once that was done, we lay there listening until dawn.

The next morning, there was no sign of the bear, and we were high on having survived. At the backcountry office that afternoon where we'd gone to sign out, the new boyfriend mentioned that his new backcountry Alaskan girlfriend had likely saved us both because I'd peed a circle around our tent so the bear knew what we were and didn't need to attack to find out. The backcountry ranger cocked an eyebrow at me and explained that, unlike Alaska, salt is in high demand in the Yellowstone ecosystem. The pee had actually called in the animals from far and wide. And, by the way, bears don't eat grass. Bison do.

—Rachel Weaver—

40

Canine Confusion

A smile starts on the lips, a grin spreads to the eyes, a
chuckle comes from the belly; but a good laugh bursts
forth from the soul, overflows, and bubbles all around.
~Carolyn Birmingham

Much to my mother's chagrin, it was not unusual for animals to "follow me home." Cats, dogs, squirrels, bunnies, snakes... I loved them all. One afternoon, when I was out for a stroll, a beautiful Siberian Husky fell in step at my side. I spoke to him and scratched his head. I just did not have it in me to shoo him away. His healthy appearance and friendly attitude were a good indication that he had a loving family, but I had never seen him in our neighborhood.

I decided to keep him secure until we could find his people. This was before you could post a lost dog on the Internet, so I figured he'd be with us a while.

I called the handsome, blue-eyed boy, Czar. He was young, powerful, and energetic. Try as we might, we could not keep him contained. One day, he escaped from our fenced back yard, ran down the street, and was quickly out of sight. The highway was only a couple of blocks away, and I was worried he would run into traffic. Mitch, my boyfriend at the time, took off in his car to search for the wayward canine. Our street was a circle with two roads exiting the neighborhood. Hoping Czar would follow the circle, I set off on foot in the opposite direction. After walking around the neighborhood with no sign of the escape artist,

I made my way back home to see if the dog had returned on his own.

Soon after I arrived at the house, Mitch pulled up and reported happily that he had Czar. He got out of the car and recounted the capture.

"I saw him in front of a house a couple of blocks away, and Czar didn't want to come to me. Every time I got within reach, he would growl and sidestep. I was finally able to grab his collar and wrestle him into the car. He was not happy! He gave me the evil eye and growled the entire ride."

Mitch walked around to the passenger side of the car and struggled to get the dog out of the front seat. I noticed something right away: Czar now had brown eyes! Once he was all of the way out of the car, I saw that he had also gained about ten pounds, and his fur had turned blacker. I don't even think he was a Siberian Husky; I think he was a Malamute. I clapped my hand over my mouth to keep from blurting out an expletive. My eyes must have been as big as saucers. This disgruntled pooch was not Czar!

I was horrified. My boyfriend had dognapped somebody's pet right from their front yard. If he was seen, the police were probably on the way. Also, Mitch could have been mauled by his surly passenger. Luckily, the dog seemed to be all growl and no bite.

As the initial shock wore off, it was replaced by amusement. I covered my face with my hands and tried to contain myself. After a few seconds, I peeked through my fingers to see a confused expression on Mitch's face as he held the large dog by its collar. The pressure of trying to hold it all in proved too much. I erupted in uncontrollable laughter. Doubled over and gasping for air, I managed to inform Mitch of his mistake and that he now had to return this angry beast to his home. I suggested he might want to put the dog in the back seat this time.

We never did see Czar again. Hopefully, he found his way home and lived a long, happy life.

— Debbi Mavity —

41

Wedding Night Blues

Be all in or get all out. There is no halfway.
~Author Unknown

t wasn't supposed to happen that way. On my wedding night, as the drenching rain soaked my ecru lace wedding gown and my carefully coiffed hair wilted in the storm, I ran through the back yards of my neighbors crying, "Honey! Honey, come back!"

I could feel them staring behind their curtains, wondering how what was supposed to be the best night of my life had turned out so badly. I imagined how my carefully applied make-up was probably giving me raccoon eyes and wondered if the grass stains would come out of the bottom of my once-lovely gown.

"Honey!" I was almost screaming now. "Honey, please come back! Please!" I could feel their pitying eyes as my pleas became more desperate, and the rain pounded down on my back.

It was just after midnight on our wedding day.

The minister had declared us husband and wife much earlier that evening inside the small Baptist church where my betrothed had once attended Sunday school. We made it through the vows, and when my new husband gazed at me, there were tears in his eyes. Tears of joy, I assumed. There was a brief moment of concern when we were lighting the unity candle and I caught my veil on fire, but quick action by my betrothed smothered it out.

The typical Florida summer rain had started its drizzle before we even left the church. "It's good luck when it rains on your wedding day," everyone told me as we tried to dodge the rain and headed to the hotel where the reception would begin.

It was a glorious gathering of our closest friends and relatives, with an open bar. We made the rounds of the tables, danced to the deejay's tunes, which we had selected together, and then laughed and cried as we got ready to leave.

My bridesmaids had loaded my car with boxed gifts and cards, and we planned to drop them by my house — now, our house — before we went to the hotel where we would be spending our wedding night. Our flight out to San Francisco wasn't until the next afternoon, and a honeymoon in the wine country awaited us. I looked forward to sleeping in through the morning.

The house was only five minutes away from the lovely, turn-of-the-century hotel where we'd hosted the reception, so we figured we'd leave the gifts there and go home to take out my dog. That would hold the little Australian Shepherd until the next morning, when my friends were coming to take her to their house.

I unlocked the front door and held it open as my husband carried in a stack of boxes wrapped in glittery white and silver paper. As I stood in the doorway, my honey-colored Shepherd dashed past us into the rain.

By the time we put the gifts on the dining room table and ran after her, Honey was gone, nowhere to be found. And that's why my husband and I spent the first hour after our wedding reception — tired, wet and more than slightly drunk — running around the neighborhood, calling desperately for the dog named Honey.

Finally, we cornered her, filthy and wet, and smelling — well, like wet dog — and brought her back into the house. We wiped her down with a towel as best we could and then went on to our hotel. We flew off to our honeymoon the next day.

But from the time we began our married life in the little Lake Worth neighborhood where I owned my first house until we moved together, along with the dog, an hour north to Port St. Lucie, I imagined

I could feel the pitying eyes of the neighbors, who were probably still imagining that I was chasing my new husband that rainy wedding night.

— Sue-Ellen Sanders —

Mistaken Identity

Best Foot Forward

The person who can bring the spirit of laughter
into a room is indeed blessed.
~Bennett Cerf

I t was our first high school reunion. Five years had passed quickly, and it felt like only yesterday we had all been together, enduring the joys and frustrations of dorm life at a private boarding school. We had become like family.

This event would be well attended, and my husband Gord and I were excited. Like us, many couples had been high-school sweethearts, but a few would bring spouses we had yet to meet.

We found the house where the reunion was being held and spent the first hour sharing hugs, kisses, backslapping and introductions. It was wonderful to see everyone again, and it seemed the years of separation fell away like we had never been apart. As more people arrived, the hostess encouraged us to move into the living room, so we made our way into a place set up with chairs positioned around the room in a U shape. Every seat offered a great view of the entire group, and Gord and I took our seats at the bottom of the U so we could enjoy the conversations on all sides.

It was a typical mild winter evening in British Columbia, but the atmosphere in the crowded room was growing stuffy, so someone opened a window to allow a lovely, crisp breeze to blow through. It was refreshing at first, but soon the chill swirled around the room, collecting under my chair. No one seemed to notice, but after leaving my shoes at the door, I did! After a few minutes, I slid my feet under Gord's chair in search of his feet — a familiar source of warmth. He was always hot, and I was always cold, so I often snuggled close, borrowing from his body heat.

His feet were just where I thought they would be, and I gently rubbed my foot on his. It worked like a charm, as always. The cold got worse, though, and I searched for more respite. It took some creative movement, but I finally managed both feet under his chair, sucking heavenly warmth from his long legs. He didn't seem to mind at all, so I traveled farther up his pant leg, tucking comfortably just under his knee where his smooth, warm skin relaxed my frigid toes. I wiggled my toes gently to convey my gratefulness for his compliance.

Thawing now, but still drawing relief from my husband, I was better able to enjoy the evening and share in the conversations around me.

Laughter filled the room, and the evening continued with retold stories of humorous escapades and infamous shenanigans. Although it was great fun for all the classmates, the newcomers still seemed quiet. When there was a lull in the noise, classmates sitting across the room looking at a photo album called my husband to come and see a picture. It appeared to be something hilarious, so he got up and sauntered over.

Watching him walk over to them, I thought again how handsome my husband was. Suddenly, I blanched. A terrible, dreadful realization pinballed through my brain. He was over there, yet… I was still rubbing behind his knee!

Slowly, as in a dream, my head pivoted to where Gord had been sitting. On the other side of his empty seat, a classmate's new husband, Jim, whom I had just met, was sitting in a chair facing Gord's. He sat smiling at me, with arms crossed and feet stretched under my husband's chair. His eyes danced with glee as he watched me realize that my foot rested deep within his pant leg.

There are no words to describe my horror. No words at all.

Instantly, raucous laughter broke out across the room, and everyone was looking at our corner. Gord turned to see the cause of the hilarity and focused on my stricken face.

Suddenly, it became clear.

Sometime during the evening, the others had spotted my foot-warming antics up Jim's leg, and the conniving crowd had contrived a covert operation to reveal all by getting Gord to leave his place.

It was impossible for me to hide, so although my embarrassment knew no bounds, I managed a half-hearted chuckle and carefully withdrew my foot. On the bright side, the entertainment lightened the atmosphere, and that awkward situation actually proved to be an effective icebreaker for the still-shy newcomers. The rest of the evening was wonderful for everyone. Fortunately, Jim found it as funny as everyone else, so I eventually managed to swallow my pride and relax.

But the best part was that the window was closed, and my feet could now comfortably stay where they safely belonged.

— Heather Rae Rodin —

Intentional Coffee With an Unintentional Stranger

If you don't learn to laugh at life it'll surely kill you,
that I know.
~Brom, The Child Thief

"Hey, Laura!" I wrote in my e-mail. "Long time no see. Can I take you out for a coffee date soon to catch up?"

Let me stop right there. Anyone who knows me knows I'm quite possibly the worst ever when it comes to keeping in touch with people. Just ask any of my high school or college friends. What friends, you ask? My point exactly.

What I'm saying is this e-mail was a big deal. I hadn't seen Laura in well over a year and I was trying to turn over a new leaf by reaching out to her.

A respectable twenty-four hours later, she responded, "Are you sure you're e-mailing the right person?"

Ouch. I mean, yeah, I'm a putz at keeping up my relationships, but there was no need to be snarky about it. Still, Laura was known to be a bit sarcastic, so…

"Yes, of course I meant you!" I responded milliseconds later because I never did figure out dating etiquette. I offered up a time and place to meet, and she accepted. Whew. That wasn't so hard.

The day of our scheduled date, Laura sent me an e-mail. "I'll be sitting by the front window, wearing a green vest."

Seriously? It's not like we haven't seen each other in a decade or something. I still remember what you look like. Geez, Laura. Your sarcasm is getting a bit out of hand. Will you be holding a red rose, too?

I showed up to the coffee shop and looked over at the table by the front window. Sure enough, a woman wearing a green vest (no rose) was sitting there. But it most certainly was not Laura.

Turns out, I'd been e-mailing back and forth with a complete stranger! I stared in disbelief at her until she looked up and smiled. I'd been noticed. At that point, I had two viable options:

1. Run like hell out of that place and never look back.

2. Fake my way through a friendly conversation as though I had indeed e-mailed the right person.

But wait, you ask, isn't there another option? Couldn't you just admit you'd made a mistake? To which I say, Are you crazy? She'd already given me a chance to realize my wrongdoing. No way was I owning up to this.

"Chelsea?" she asked, extending her hand to shake mine. "I'm Laurie."

The woman I'd sent multiple e-mails to didn't even have the same first name as my actual friend.

"I know that!" I lied, bypassing the handshake and going straight in for a hug. "It's so great to see you, Laurie!"

Option #2 was now in full play.

Laura-now-Laurie already had a drink, so I excused myself to order some tea. Unfortunately there was a short line at the register, which meant I had approximately forty-nine seconds to do some serious detective work.

I searched Laurie's name in my e-mails and learned that while we'd never actually exchanged personal messages (other than to set up our little date), we were on the same e-mail promo list for a yoga organization I'd done some work with. That's as far as I got before it was my turn at the counter. Begrudgingly, I put away my phone, sending up a silent prayer that my tiny sliver of discovered information could get me through the next hour of my life. I made my way back to the table, repeating the name of the organization over and over again in my head as I walked.

"So," I started, the second I sat down. There was no way I was going to give this conversation a chance to get awkward. "How's the yoga world treating you?"

"Oh, I left that job last year...."

So much for not letting things get awkward. But I didn't give in. Nope, not even a little bit. I rolled with the punches and asked her what she was up to now. She told me, but don't ask me to repeat it because I wasn't listening to a word. I was far too busy making sure I was nodding at the right times and laughing when it seemed appropriate. I even managed to touch Laurie's arm a couple of times, just to really assure her that we knew each other. In other words, I was crushing it.

Finally, after forty-five non-awkward minutes (I know, right?), I finally drummed up the nerve and said, "You're probably wondering why I asked you out to coffee since we don't know each other too well...." (Err, at all.)

Her face relaxed, like she'd been holding in that exact question the entire time.

"It's just..." I came up with the fib one precious word at a time. "I... ever since... we were involved in that organization together... I've always looked up to you as... as a strong woman in the area..." That probably would've been sufficient enough. But, no, I had to keep going. "And I've... made a list of all the strong businesswomen I know... and am asking them out to coffee... one by one... to get inspiration for my own life...."

She was flattered. And rightfully so. My delivery was so realistic that I almost believed my own lie. She asked me if I could please send her that list of strong women. Of course I could, because that's what friends (or people pretending to be friends) do.

We said our goodbyes, and she hugged me like she meant it, as if she finally believed we truly knew each other. It was beautiful. Then I got the hell out of that place and never looked back.

Boy, did I learn my lesson. Sorry to all my old acquaintances, but I'm never e-mailing you again. It's just too risky to try to catch up with you.

And now, if you'll excuse me, I'm off to make up a list of influential businesswomen so I can e-mail it to my new BFF Laurie.

— Chelsea Walker Flagg —

44

Sweet Delusions

If people did not sometimes do silly things,
nothing intelligent would ever get done.
~Ludwig Wittgenstein

On a cold winter morning, we decided to stop for coffee at Panera Bread before heading off to church. We finished our second cup while perusing the *Tribune*. I looked at my watch and said, "It's time to go." Larry promptly refilled his takeout cup of coffee with five creams and five teaspoons of sugar. I followed him to our gold Honda Odyssey where he promptly set his coffee cup in its secure holder. He was surprised that the door was not locked and the rug was moved, but he attributed it to senioritis.

I made my way to the passenger door and noticed two big gashes. I yelled out, "How did this happen?" Larry came over to inspect my door and said, "Someone really banged it hard. Look how deep these gashes are."

I opened the door, sat down and saw an electronic device. "Larry, when did you get this?" I said in my accusatory tone. Larry has a habit of buying things on sale and then sneaking them into the house.

As I lifted the electronic device to examine it more closely, Larry said with a frantic voice, "This is not our van." Quickly, I put down the device and slammed the van door. We scurried off to our vehicle two cars down while looking over our shoulders for the owner or, worse, the police. When we were on Route 14 and safe from apprehension, Larry sighed. "My coffee. I left it in the other van."

Now I imagined the owner, who forgot to lock his door, settling in and being welcomed by a cup of hot, steaming coffee, saying, "Where did this come from?"

I sure hope he likes his coffee very, very sweet.

— Susan Schuerr —

45

Eddie

I was irrevocably betrothed to laughter,
the sound of which has always seemed to me
to be the most civilized music in the world.
~Peter Ustinov

"Welcome to the neighborhood," said Kelsey and Jim, our neighbors who lived across the street from our new house. As we chatted, Eddie, their short, portly, wrinkled Bulldog, sauntered over for an introduction and to check us out. He was slow-moving and mellow but curious. Eddie hung out nearby while we got to know Kelsey and Jim.

Two weeks later, when my husband Paul was working in the yard, I noticed he had gone across the street and was talking to Jim. Soon, they disappeared into the garage for an hour. Turns out, they enjoy a common passion for cycling.

When Paul came home, he said, "I was just talking to Eddie across the street." He started to elaborate about his cycling gear and rides.

As Paul described his visit with Jim, I burst out laughing.

I said, "Eddie is their dog. Jim is the man's name."

"Oh my gosh!" gasped Paul. "I couldn't remember his name but heard Kelsey yelling 'Eddie' from the back yard a few times, so I started calling him Eddie. He never corrected me."

Despite his horror, Paul could see the humor in his mistake and began laughing along with me.

It turns out that Eddie was being yelled at that day for devouring the lilies in the back yard, and then vomiting on the grass and plopping down on the plants for a nap.

Paul wasn't sure if he should apologize to Jim for confusing him with a Bulldog or just ignore it and move on. He decided on erasing any memory of the event by just calling him Jim from that day forward. Nothing was ever said about the mistake, and we are good neighbors to this day. But we still laugh every time we remember Paul addressing Jim as "Eddie" for an evening.

— Gwen Sheldon Willadsen —

46

The Ghost in the Monastery

For when the wine is in, the wit is out.
~Thomas Beccon

The Monasterio de Oseira is a Cistercian monastery that has been in operation since the year 1137. Located in a mountain valley in the Spanish province of Galicia, the huge building complex is comparable in size to the Palace of El Escorial near Madrid. These days, only about a dozen monks permanently reside there.

The accommodations available to pilgrims on their way to Santiago are very basic. There is no hot water, and the building I was directed to was cold, damp and located alongside a graveyard. As the sole pilgrim staying at the monastery that particular day, I was entrusted with the only key.

Opening the huge wooden door, I found myself in a dark, cavernous room. The area was dominated by a huge, amateurish painting of an avenging Christ, which loomed over the few bunk beds. The ceiling was difficult to make out in the gloomy light, but the walls showed their age by the dark stains spreading down from above. It might not have been the best accommodation, but it was the only one available, and after all, it's possible to put up with a lot when it is only for one night.

I dropped off my backpack and, after a cold shower, made my way out into the welcome sunshine. The monk who had greeted me on arrival had suggested that I come back up to the main building once I'd settled in. There was not a lot of settling in to be done. Once again, he apologised profusely for the limited facilities and, as if in justification, pointed out that they did not get many visitors.

The monk offered to give me a tour of the main monastery buildings. As we wandered through the many deserted cloisters, he regaled me with stories of the monastery in its heyday.

He invited me to join his fellow monks for their evening ritual. I agreed readily since there was little to do around the area apart from visiting the graveyard. The church visit was a wonderful experience. I got to sing Vespers with the monks as we sat together in the choir stalls. There was no possibility of joining them for their evening meal, so I made my way into the local village to find a place to eat.

As the sole customer in the restaurant, I received special attention. The lady running the place was very generous with both the food and wine. It had been a long day, so I finished off my dinner and drank a full bottle of wine. That was my way of showing my appreciation for the delicious meal. In the gathering darkness, I made my wine-addled way back to my accommodations located alongside the graveyard.

As I was the only pilgrim staying in the monastery that night, I locked the door behind me and checked to see that the other two doors into the building were similarly secured. One that led out in the direction of the graveyard looked as though it had not been used in many years, so I ignored the fact that it could not be locked from the inside.

Aided no doubt by my wine consumption, sleep came quickly. I had been unconscious for about an hour or so when a noise woke me. A thin sliver of light came in from somewhere high up in the ceiling. I turned in my bunk to face the side where I'd heard the noise. To my horror, I made out a figure lying prone on the bed next to mine. The hairs on the back of my neck stood up. My mind began racing as I tried to imagine how someone, or something, could have possibly come through the locked doors.

I lay still trying to think how best to confront the situation. As quietly as possible, I reached down into my sleeping bag where I kept my headlamp. I managed to steady my shaking hands just long enough to switch it on. The bright white light brought my ghostly neighbour into sharp focus.

It was my backpack, along with the clothes still lying where I had carelessly tossed them on the next bunk. In the dark, they had taken on the shape of a person.

I have never been so happy to see a backpack. There is a lot to be said for not finishing off all of the wine on offer with a Spanish meal.

—James A. Gemmell—

47

I Am Standing Here Not Dead

Absence of proof is not proof of absence.
~*Michael Crichton*, The Lost World

After her husband passed away, eighty-year-old Marian Beckham dutifully wrote the Social Security Administration to notify them that he had died and thus should no longer receive a monthly check. Marian had received her own monthly Social Security check for fifteen years, and after the funeral she was so consumed with grief that she didn't notice her usual monthly bank deposit from the SSA was missing. When a second month came and went with no deposit into her bank account, she noticed and decided to call. After weaving through an intimidating web of voicemail options, she finally reached a live human being.

The employee researched her complaint and informed her, "You didn't get a bank deposit because, according to our computer, you're dead. You died two months ago."

"My husband died two months ago," Marian corrected, "but I'm very much alive, and I need that money to survive."

"Unless you can prove you're alive, we can't reinstate your Social Security deposits," the unsympathetic clerk informed her.

"Prove I'm alive? I'm talking on the phone with you," Marian snapped, disgusted with the runaround. "Doesn't that prove I'm alive? I'm not calling from heaven, you know!"

"I'm aware of that, ma'am. You don't have to get testy with me."

Marian sucked in a deep breath to compose herself. "Look, whoever entered into the computer that my husband died two months ago inadvertently marked me as dead, too. This is obviously a simple human error."

"Maybe, or maybe not. You could be an imposter trying to steal Marian Beckham's identity so you can swindle checks out of the Social Security Administration. Identity fraud. Happens all the time," the clerk retorted.

Marian slammed down the phone receiver, too disgusted to deal with the unsympathetic clerk another second.

"You'll just have to drive there in person to prove you're alive," Marian's daughter told her later that evening. "Your picture is on your driver's license, and you can bring your birth certificate and Social Security card for good measure."

The next day, Marian drove to the Social Security Administration to remove any doubt that she was, in fact, very much alive and who she said she was. "With all these documents, surely they'll believe you and resume your benefits," her daughter said, patting her hand.

After waiting in a line long enough to make her knees need replacing, Marian slapped down her many documents onto the counter of the unsmiling clerk. The clerk flipped briefly through the documents and then shoved them back at Marian. "This doesn't prove a thing. You could have stolen these documents."

"Stolen them?" Marian pointed at the picture on her driver's license. "That's my picture on the driver's license, with my name and date of birth on it. Look!" she insisted, waving her driver's license in the clerk's face. "An imposter wouldn't look like me."

The clerk shrugged. "How do I know you're not Marian's identical twin trying to steal her identity and bilk the system?"

Marian pounded her fist on the counter. "Because I don't have an identical twin. I don't even have a sister." Nerves frayed, Marian snapped, "What is wrong with you people? Obviously, my status got inadvertently changed to dead when my husband passed away two months ago. Now I want it fixed, and I want it fixed now! My pantry is empty."

When the clerk just shrugged again, Marian jabbed her index finger at the clerk. "I need that money. I depend on it to make ends meet."

The hardened clerk arched an eyebrow. "Look lady, all's I know is our computer clearly states Marian L. Beckham is dead. Until you can prove she isn't dead and that you are, in fact, Marian L. Beckham, I can't reinstate your Social Security benefits."

Marian released an exasperated sigh. "Well, how do I prove I'm not dead if standing here in person, with my birth certificate and driver's license, aren't enough to convince you?"

The clerk pursed her lips. "Get your personal physician to write a certified letter testifying you are who you say you are and that you aren't dead. I would consider that proof that the computer made a mistake."

That's when I became involved with this bureaucratic nightmare. As Marian's long-time family doctor, I could confirm she was very much alive and who she said she was.

Marian rushed to my office, explained her frustrating predicament, and asked me to write a letter on her behalf. Below is the oddest letter I have ever written in thirty years of being a doctor:

Dear Social Security Administration,

Marian L. Beckham has been my patient for over ten years. She came into my office requesting a letter stating she is not dead. Therefore, I, Sally Burbank, MD, do hereby legally testify that Marian L. Beckham is not dead, nor has she ever been dead. Please reinstitute her Social Security benefits.

Sincerely,

Sally Burbank, MD

The letter worked. Her monthly bank deposits were reinstated. But, geesh, what a tedious headache for a grieving widow to endure. She and I now laugh about it, but at the time, Marian wanted to wring that clerk's neck!

— Sally Willard Burbank, MD —

48

Down the Hatch

I often laugh at extremely inappropriate times…
Not because I'm nervous or anything. Mainly because
I think inappropriate things are funny.
~Author Unknown

My husband was leaving the country for a week and a half so I invited my sister to spend the weekend. Alike in many ways, there is one major difference between the two of us. My sister is given to grumpiness a) when she wakes up and b) when she feels the tiniest bit under the weather. On the other hand, I have the waking attitude of a puppy and the immune system of a flea, meaning I'll be cheerful even as I catch viruses in the draft of the dawn's early light.

As is usual for me, I was sniffling when my sister arrived. As is usual for her, the tickling itch in her throat the next morning did nothing to aid her usual morning temper.

"You got me sick!" she grumped as she nursed her morning coffee.

I opened the door to the corner cabinet and searched through the cold-remedies section. There'd surely be something in here to restore her mood — and my vacation. "We'll do an immune boost together," I announced. "I'll have you feeling better in no time at all!"

I handed the bottles and jars down to her.

"Six vitamin Cs, 1000 mg. Six multivitamins…"

Then I removed a brown glass bottle labeled Immune Booster, the ultimate panacea for colds.

"Get a spoon," I instructed her. "One, two... fifteen, sixteen... twenty drops!" I handed her what was left of the precious liquid.

She sniffed and grimaced but swallowed it all.

Up until this point, I had matched my intake with hers, and I had swallowed everything except that foul-tasting, puce-colored miracle-liquid. I stuck my head back into the cabinet to look for an alternative, for that special something that might actually cure my cold, too.

That is when I saw it: a bottle similar in shape and size to the herbal remedy. The main difference between the two was the labels. The Immune Booster's label, with as much small print as a dictionary, looked sue-proof, while this vial was a homemade affair with only three words stamped black on its bright green background — tea tree oil.

No dosage. No instructions. No warnings.

Vaguely, I remembered buying it with/for my husband at the local pharmacy/health-food store. For which specific ailment we had purchased it, I couldn't be sure.

"I'll take this!" I said. "If it's any good, I'll give you some, too."

For those who know what tea tree oil is, you know where this is going. For those who don't — listen and learn.

I twisted off the dropper and took a whiff. If smell was any indication of potency, this would be the most powerful cure I'd ever ingested.

I prepared a cup of grapefruit juice to wash down the taste that would most certainly accompany such a pungent aroma.

"One, two, three, down the hatch," I said to myself.

But after four drops, the hatch refused any further ministrations. At this point, I decided four drops must be the proper dose, and I downed the cup of pungent citrus juice.

But it was no match for the tea tree oil. That moldy smell now filled my mouth and nose, and no amount of liquid could chase that taste away.

It got me thinking.

"Okay, Google, what is tea tree oil used for?" I announced into my phone.

Google returned Wikipedia's entry on tea tree oil headed by the following: *Warning! Tea tree oil is toxic when taken by mouth.*

My heart began to pump rhythmically. I felt a distinct numbness about the mouth.

"Toxic," I stuttered. "Tea tree oil is toxic!"

My sister is excellent in stressful situations. She does the absolutely most helpful thing possible. She laughs. Hysterically.

"You're going to be fine," she managed between wheezes of laughter.

"What should I do?" I cried.

"Call the doctor!"

But I was busy checking my vitals. If death were nigh, I would carefully track its arrival.

So my sister dialed. She reached the doctor's gatekeeper, the fabulous medical secretary.

"My sister took tea tree oil, and it says online it's poisonous. Can you ask the doctor what she should do?"

Over the pounding in my ears, I could just make out her voice reciting the digits of my telephone number.

"Why are you giving her my number?" I managed to whisper through numbed lips.

"The doctor is busy now," my sister said apologetically. "The receptionist says she'll call us back."

"She'll call us back?" I repeated incredulously.

Then I took over the call.

"I ate poison," I said, counting out each word as if it was my last. "Are you sure you want to call me back?"

"Uh, hold on." The word poison seemed to have finally sunk in. After a few moments of radio silence, the healthcare operator returned to the call. "The doctor said you'll probably be fine."

I hung up.

"*Probably?*" I said. "What does 'probably' mean?"

Congestion coupled with hilarity, my sister spoke three words: "Poison Control Center."

But I had more pressing matters to attend to. Something in my stomach region didn't feel right. I made it to the bathroom, but I was still in shock when the entire contents of my stomach delivered themselves into the porcelain bowl.

Beside me, my sister laughed like a hyena.

"Are you, ha, ha, ha, okay?"

"Did you reach Poison Control?"

She pointed to the phone. "I'm on hold."

I relieved her of the device just as a Poison Control representative came on the line.

"Poison Control, how can I help?"

"Tea tree oil," I breathed. "I swallowed tea tree oil. What do I do?"

"How much?" the overly calm voice responded.

"Four drops."

"You might experience nausea, but you'll be fine."

Nausea. Well, I had that covered.

"So I don't need to do anything?" I insisted.

"Nope, you'll be okay. Anything else?" the nice man asked.

"That's it. Thanks," I said.

I leaned on the kitchen counter and did a quick body scan. My heartbeat seemed to have returned to normal, and aside from the lingering moldy taste in my mouth, I did feel fine.

And the tea tree oil seemed to have restored my sister's good humor, so it did do something.

Later, during my evening phone call when I recounted the day's mishap to my spouse, he gave me a hearty telling-off. "We should not keep poisonous things in our kitchen cabinets!"

After my experience, I agreed with him heartily.

Right before we hung up, I said, "I don't ever remember seeing tea tree oil in the kitchen cabinet before. How did it get there?"

"Oh," he said breezily, "I cleaned out my drawer before I left, and I put it there!"

— Shayna R. Horowitz —

49

Short-Timer

From there to here, and here to there,
funny things are everywhere.
~Dr. Seuss

Predawn is my favorite time to walk. One day, as I headed out to catch the panoramic sunrise on our road, my husband warned, "Watch out for vehicles. They can't see you in the dark."

Later that afternoon, he came home from town with a smug look on his face. "Honey, I bought you a present."

One glance at the orange bag from our local home-improvement store told me it wasn't flowers or chocolates. The hooded fluorescent yellow coat with silver reflective stripes was so bright it should've come with the warning "Sunglasses Required."

Since my better half went through the trouble of buying it for me, I put it on before heading out the door the next morning. On my five-foot-nothing frame, the men's protective gear jacket came down to my knees, and the sleeves were so long that my hands were swallowed whole.

That morning, the glow of the early light showed evidence of an overnight storm. Leaves and downed branches were everywhere. As I crested the top of a steep hill, a power-company van headed my way. I ducked into a neighbor's lane to let it pass. Instead, the driver pulled up next to me. His eyebrows arched when he took in our matching jackets.

Pointing to a pole in the yard, he said, "This is my grid. Who sent you?"

That's when I realized I looked just like him.

"Don't worry, buddy. You've got this," I said before racing back to the road. That's when the giggles started and lasted until my cheeks were wet.

When I got home, my husband pointed to my tear-stained face and asked, "Sweetheart, what's wrong?"

After I told him, he teased, "Maybe you should've volunteered to climb up the utility pole."

Wrestling out of the oversized coat, I handed it to him. "No, thanks. This needs to go back. I quit."

— Alice Muschany —

50

Out of This World

*Dating a man is like flying a kite. You only need to
know when to wind up the string or let it out.*
~Jenna Alatari

The existence of planet Orat was a well-kept secret. At least, I'd
never heard of it. That is, until a call with my sister Vicki led to
events that changed that. Ever since I'd told her about Frank,
someone I'd met at a singles dance, she'd pestered me about
accepting his dinner invitations. Each time she brought it up, I'd
change the subject, and that night's conversation was no exception.

Vicki was happily married to Jack, whom she'd met at a singles
dance. Believing I would have the same good fortune, she persisted.
"Frank sounds like a steady guy. You said he works where Jack does."

Unswayed, I countered, "Yeah, but that doesn't mean anything.
For all I know, the guy's about to be fired." My caution with dating
was well earned. I'd gone out with too many men who turned out to
be as interesting and fun as scaling fish.

"Listen, Jack may know him. If so, I'll ask him for the lowdown.
Promise me that if Frank is a decent guy, you'll give him a chance."

My misgivings were based on nothing but a feeling, but I wasn't
sure ignoring them was the best option. Still, Vicki refused to back
down, assuring me Jack wouldn't mind dishing dirt.

Reluctantly, I agreed. "But if Jack thinks there's anything weird
about the guy or if he's a jerk, forget it."

About an hour later, Frank called. A few moments into our

conversation, I heard call-waiting beep in. "Hang on a second, Frank."
It was Vicki again.

"Vicki, I'll call you back. Frank's on the other line."

I was about to cut her off when she shouted, "No, wait! Jack says Frank's a great guy, and you should go out with him. Call me back later."

Assuring myself that Jack was the kind of sensible guy who didn't sugarcoat anything, I decided to give Frank a chance. What could it hurt?

Frank and I conversed for another minute. Then he got down to the reason he'd called. "If you're available, how about dinner Friday night?"

I squeezed my eyes shut, squelched the last of my doubts and agreed. Still, experience bred caution. "Let's meet at the restaurant." This way, if the evening was a disaster, at least I could cut it short and get myself home.

All day Friday I had the urge to call Frank and claim illness. Then I'd chastise myself for being so negative. After all, I knew Jack wouldn't steer me wrong.

Frank was already seated when I arrived. Spotting me, he smiled. It was a dimpled, attractive smile that calmed my nervous stomach. When I reached the table, he stood and pulled the chair out for me, impressing me with his good manners.

He had thoughtfully chosen a table away from most of the crowd, presumably so we could talk without shouting. Silently, I scolded myself for unnecessarily fretting about this date.

Our conversation went smoothly, and by the time we ordered dessert, I felt a warm glow and planned to call Vicki and thank her for pushing me into this.

I'd just put down my napkin when Frank glanced from side to side and leaned in. Foolishly, I thought he wanted a kiss and debated on granting it. Instead, he spread open his shirt collar and revealed a thin gold chain with a pendant that resembled a half-moon, except it was jagged, like the teeth of a shark.

He asked, "Have you ever heard of the planet Orat?"

Sitting back stiffly in my chair, I shook my head. "No, I haven't."

He scanned the room again as if he was about to share a national security secret. "It's in another galaxy. They've been observing us for centuries."

My stomach contracted. "Who? What?"

"The Orats. To decide the best way to invade Earth."

Speechless, I took a sip of water to buy time. Then, "Have they decided?"

"They have. It'll be one year from today." He puffed out his chest. "But I'm not worried because they took me up to their planet to make me an ambassador. So when they invade, I'll be spared."

Trying not to let him know I planned to bolt as soon as I found my car keys, I grinned and congratulated him. Unfortunately, my keys must have slipped to the bottom of my purse and remained out of my grasp, so I played for time. "How will they know it's you?"

"This is how." He rolled up his shirtsleeve to reveal a small tattoo on the underside of his forearm. The design matched the charm around his neck. His eyes glowed with the fire of a religious zealot. "Other ambassadors exist as well. We'll rule Earth on behalf of the new masters. First though, the Orats will have to take us back to their planet so we can complete our training."

Without warning, he snatched my free hand. "But you don't have to be afraid. You can also be rescued."

I froze. How could Jack have thought this guy was dating material?

"The Orats only need to know you're on their side."

Enough! I yanked my hand away from him, but he was undeterred. "I can teach you to steer the starship and show you all the wonderful sights. They'll show us how to live longer than we could imagine." With a crafty smile, he added, "But you have to sleep with me tonight."

I popped from my seat so fast that the chair rocked. "Sorry, gotta go."

Before I could step away, Frank tried once more. "You won't regret it."

I sucked in a deep breath. "Not interested." Miraculously, I found my keys as I dashed to my car and floored it all the way home.

Slamming the front door behind me, I grabbed the phone and

punched in Vicki's number. Jack answered.

Before he could say more than hello, I yelled, "How could you have said Frank was a good guy to date?"

"Frank who? I don't know any Frank."

My eyebrows shot up so high I'm sure they disappeared into my bangs. "But Vicki said you vouched for him, and I should give him a chance."

A rustling sound told me the phone was being shifted, and Vicki asked, "How was your date?"

The story of my close encounter with the Orat ambassador tumbled from my mouth. My jaw was so tight that I could barely get out the accusation. "Jack didn't say Frank was a good guy, did he?"

Vicki snickered. "I didn't ask him. I thought you should go out with Frank. And I was right."

My head ached. "Right? How could you say that?"

"Dates are supposed to be fun. And this one sounds like it was very entertaining."

"To you, maybe. Thanks a lot." I slammed down the phone.

But I must say, by the next morning, safely away from Frank and, in spite of myself, I chuckled. And since then, I've trusted my own intuition about people, rather than relying on the opinion of others. So far, that thinking has served me well.

— Carole Fowkes —

Chapter
7

Work Whoops

51

The Klutz

Laughter is the shortest distance between two people.
~Victor Borge

I have always been known as a little awkward and absent-minded. I drop things from my butterfingers or walk into doors because my mind is always elsewhere.

So when my colleague told me that his wife was the queen of klutz, I shrugged it off. She couldn't be worse than me.

"She is so clumsy," he said, "that she tripped over her own wedding gown walking down the aisle when we got married."

I thought he was exaggerating. He was so casual about it.

We were in the staff room that day, chatting about cycling and riding bikes. Marcel expressed the desire to try cycling with his family, so I invited him to come to my house with his family and try out some of the bikes my husband had been picking out of people's garbage for years, rebuilding them or using them as spare parts. It would be a great way to get rid of some of them.

And this was when Marcel warned me about his spouse before accepting the invitation.

" Oh, no worries," I said. "I am pretty clumsy myself, so that will make two of us. We'll just laugh it off. It should make for a fun evening."

We set a date and decided to turn the visit into a barbecue get-together.

He and his wife showed up with their two preteens who connected with our two. And, yes, upon arrival, his wife tripped over the first step coming up the stairs, but it was nothing major. She found her balance in the blink of an eye.

I made the introductions, and we put the cake Marcel's wife had made in the fridge. Then we carried out condiments, glasses, plates, wine and beer to the backyard patio. So far, so good. After a moment, my new "friend" complained that she was a tad chilly, so I ran back in and picked out one of my jean jackets for her to wear over her denim dress.

As she was reaching to take the jacket from me, her arm knocked over the plastic glasses that were stacked on the table, and they all fell to the ground.

"Oh, my," she said. She stepped back, instead of forward, onto the plastic glasses, flapping her arms in order to avoid the fall. The crack was audible. Eight stacked glasses that crack all at once do make quite a sound.

"Oh, my," she said again. We hadn't had a drop of alcohol yet, so we couldn't blame the booze.

I handed her the jacket and then picked up the glasses that were now stacked forever.

"No worries, we recycle," I said, now a bit concerned about bringing out glassware instead of plastic.

The rest of the meal was pleasant and uneventful. We talked about work and raising children.

Then I brought out the huge cake that Marcel's wife had made with loads of whipped cream and fruit. By the time we had finished eating, we were quite full. I got up to start gathering some of the dishes. She offered to help me clear the table.

"Oh, no, that's okay," I said. "I can do that on my own. I…"

But before I could finish my sentence, she had seized the platter that still had half a cake on it, marched up the back steps, and then missed the landing. She tumbled headfirst as the cake flew in the air and exploded all over the back balcony, including the screen door and the kitchen window.

Marcel's wife was on all fours. Whipped cream was everywhere.

Our two kids watched my face in horror, expecting a possible outburst at this point. I was speechless. I had never seen anything like this before. I was already anticipating the ants that would invade the back porch in droves to feast on all the bits of sugar and cream that now sparkled beneath the patio lights. Some of the fruit filling had puddled under the couch, dripping off the sides of the balcony.

The woman kept apologizing, but I avoided her gaze, mumbling beneath my breath, not knowing where to step around the mess or how to start cleaning it.

"I warned you," Marcel chirped from the table while his daughter climbed the tree behind him to catch up to her brother and our own kids.

For a split second, I wondered if this clumsiness could be genetic and thought maybe I should call the paramedics as a precaution. How adept was this child at climbing trees?

My husband, being on the ball as usual, took the hose, closed the inside door to the kitchen, and sprayed the entire back porch with maximum pressure as we all watched the deluge wash away the last of dessert.

"Great cake by the way," he said to our guests, hoping to lighten up the mood. "It must have cost you a fortune in whipping cream."

A few minutes later, there was no sign of the disaster.

Afterwards, Marcel looked at the bikes and agreed to take the four we were offering. My better half insisted on helping Marcel put the bikes on his rack, just in case the clumsiness was contagious, adding extra ties for good measure.

Then, as it got cooler, we moved indoors. When it was time to leave, I reminded Marcel's wife to return my jacket. While we were chatting, I thought I caught a glimpse of the woman's underwear and bra. I shook my head thinking I had gone completely mad, but when I looked up again, she was handing me the jacket in full undergarments, including skin-colored pantyhose. This took the cake!

I stuttered, "Your dress! Your dress!"

Everyone turned and looked at her. Her daughter cried out, "Mom!" and hid her face against her father's chest.

"Oh, my," his wife said.

Not only had this woman unbuttoned my jacket to remove it, but she had unbuttoned her denim dress, which opened onto what would be… a memorable story to tell.

—Julie de Belle—

52

Total Physical Response

A very wise old teacher once said: I consider a day's
teaching wasted if we do not all have one hearty laugh.
~Gilbert Highet

Total Physical Response is a standard Second Language teaching method frequently used with beginning speakers of English. The method has three main parts: The teacher models a series of actions while narrating the actions; the teacher models and narrates the series again with students also performing the actions; and finally the students perform the series while narrating their actions.

A sample lesson might be sharpening a pencil. The teacher says, "I put my pencil in the correct hole of the sharpener. I turn the handle of the sharpener. I take out my pencil and look at the point. My pencil is sharp!" This pattern of actions and narration is repeated frequently until students are able to say the narration alone. It is "old school" methodology that works very well in many different teaching situations and with many different types of vocabulary.

While teaching at P.S. #36, I had kindergarten through grade six, including several special education students. There was also a group of absolute beginners in English who were in the intermediate grades. They came to see me for extra lessons in English. I saw them for about two hours a day, and I often used Total Physical Response, or TPR, in order to push along their vocabulary and spoken English. We had lessons based on science, cooking, art, and even gym. They were in a groove when it came to this kind of lesson. TPR made learning English exciting.

In the spring, I decided to teach my little group of Spanish-speaking beginners how to make a vocabulary collage for the season. I had at least twenty magazines, scissors, glue, and large construction paper on which to mount the chosen pictures. The lesson began. Four young boys and two older girls sat at the rectangular table near my blackboard, and I stood on the other side of the table. "I choose a magazine," I said. "I look through the pictures. Here is a nice one for spring. I take my scissors. I cut it out. Now I put it on my paper." That was the entire narration; there were very few steps to complete. I motioned to the group to do it with me; they stood up and smiled.

"I choose a magazine," I began again. My Puerto Rican students each chose a magazine. "I look through the pictures." We all looked in the magazines. The routine continued throughout the whole narration. By the end of this step, they all had one picture, and I had two. We repeated the routine. This time, a few of my braver students began to echo my narration. "I choose a magazine." We continued without my correcting any language errors; I wanted them to talk, and I was merely modeling, not testing. When we finished this time, they each had two pictures. That was hardly enough to fill up a collage. We repeated the entire routine. Still not enough pictures.

"Let's do it again!" I said. They were delighted to oblige me. I picked up another magazine. "I choose a magazine," we said. "I look through the pictures" was supposed to be my next line; however, when I looked down, I did not see any pictures. I saw a big, fat, ugly, live cockroach in the middle of the magazine. Instead of saying, "I look through the pictures," I screamed, threw the magazine on the floor and jumped on top of the roach to kill it. The entire group followed my lead. They screamed loud enough to be heard in the class next door, threw their magazines on the floor, and pounced on them. Then they all smiled angelically at me. They were wonderful listeners and learners of English, and they were proud of their great skill. Even if I changed the routine, they could not be fooled. My kids knew how this TPR stuff worked.

I looked around at my beaming students and cracked up. My TPR lesson was over for the day. English was over for the class period. I could barely speak through my tearful laughter, and I had to open the magazine, searching page by page in order to show them the squashed roach to get them to understand what had happened. We spent the rest of our class time laughing while Misael re-enacted the roach stomp event for us a few times. Spanish flew around the room followed by hysterical laughter. I did not need a translator to understand what was being said. We laughed through our tears and never finished our springtime collages.

— Melanie A. Savidis —

53

Hold the Phone

Mistakes are a fact of life.
It is the response to error that counts.
~Nikki Giovanni

love to watch bloopers on the Internet. The videos of unexpected or embarrassing events, usually from live television, often make me double over in laughter. I watch them not only because I think they're funny, but also because I can usually identify with the hapless souls who make the on-air faux pas.

I've worked in television long enough to know many people who have fallen victim to an accidental, unforeseen and thoroughly hilarious incident on live TV. For the most part, I have been fortunate to have escaped the hugely embarrassing and mortifying on-air gaffes that bring out the biggest laughs, except for one memorable occasion.

The incident that is seared in my memory, and the one that was hardest to live down, occurred back in the late 1970s when I was a young TV news reporter and not yet accustomed to paying close attention to details. It was election night in Kansas, and I was getting ready to do a live telephone interview with Senator Bob Dole, who had just won re-election. Again, this was the 1970s, so technology wasn't what it is today. Placed beside me on the news desk was an actual corded telephone that I was to pick up at the appropriate moment in order to talk to Senator Dole live on the air. The receiver was hardwired into the TV station's audio system to broadcast our conversation to viewers across the state.

Election nights are always fast-paced and unpredictable, and as I slid quickly into place at the news desk that evening, I concentrated my full attention on my scribbled notes. Distracted, I positioned myself in front of the camera, failing to notice one important detail: Whoever had placed the phone on the desk had set the receiver into its cradle in reverse. This wouldn't have been a problem except that one of our producers had written for me a last-minute and overly complicated introduction to the interview. In order to avoid verbally stumbling my way through it, I had to keep my eyes glued to the teleprompter. As I carefully read the on-camera lead-in, I casually reached over toward the telephone and picked up the receiver without looking at it. Placing it to the side of my head, I began speaking.

"Senator Dole, thank you for joining us on the phone this evening." There was silence. Dead air.

I spoke again. "Senator Dole, are you with us?"

More silence. In my peripheral vision, I saw the floor director standing near the camera waving his arms and pointing violently to his ear. I had never seen such a cue before. Confused, I looked at him and spoke again into the phone, "Are you there, Senator Dole?" All the while, the camera beamed my puzzled expression into thousands of homes as I struggled to understand what sort of audio problem we were having.

The floor director became more animated, holding his fist to the side of his head as if he were holding a telephone and began twisting it, another unfamiliar signal. Not comprehending the code, I looked past the camera at him and shrugged my shoulders, all the while hoping in the next second to hear the voice of the Senator in my ear.

Finally, in a frustrated outburst, the floor director yelled, "Turn the phone around!"

That's when I looked at the receiver. I stared at it a couple of seconds, at first not grasping what I was seeing. Suddenly, the light bulb in my head flickered on, and I realized that I had been speaking into the earpiece and listening through the mouthpiece. As my face filled the TV frame, I slowly turned the phone to its correct orientation and went on with the interview, so red-faced that some viewers at home probably rose from their sofas to adjust the color on their sets once they stopped laughing.

My colleagues didn't stop laughing about it for a long time. For weeks afterward, I was the punch line to everyone's favorite joke. As I walked past their desks, each of my fellow news reporters lifted their phone receivers, holding them mouthpiece-up, and shouting, "Nick, phone call for you from Senator Dole!" Every time, the entire office howled in laughter.

To me, it wasn't nearly as funny then as it is now. But it did make me resolve to pay closer attention to details from that day forward. And to this day, I am forever grateful for at least one thing: In the 1970s, Internet bloopers didn't exist.

—Nick Walker—

54

Vigilante Crossing Guards

I'd rather laugh with the sinners
than cry with the saints.
~Billy Joel

My school's crossing guard was crabbing about commuter traffic speeding through the school zone. "SUVs drive me nuts," Hazel said. "They don't respect the speed limit where schoolchildren cross the street. I need something powerful to slow down traffic."

Tuesday mornings, I sat in our school principal's chair because he was out of the building, and I was the assistant principal. A sub was in my classroom. I took notes on Hazel's complaint and said, "When a person is tired of something, that's when things get done."

Hazel stood up. A short, gray-haired woman in a colorful dress, she said, "Yes, but what can I do to enforce the law?" She held up her little stop sign and said, "This is sort of effective."

She walked down the street from school to her house. Her sister, Joyce, lived next door. They were both widows with grown children.

The following Tuesday morning, before school began, I sat in the principal's chair, sipped tea and looked out his office window. Children crossed the street safely escorted by two crossing guards with brand new, official-looking Day-Glo stripes on their hats, vests and pant legs.

When Hazel turned and aimed a radar gun at one SUV's license plate, I dropped my teacup. Where did a crossing guard get a radar gun?

When the vehicle slowed down immediately, Hazel gave the driver a thumbs-up. Then she turned to the new crossing guard — obviously her sister, Joyce — who appeared to be writing down license-plate numbers on her clipboard.

Next, Joyce aimed the radar gun at a speeding truck, held her hand over the radar gun as if to reduce glare on its screen, watched the truck slow down and gave the driver a thumbs-up.

Joyce and Hazel took turns using the radar gun. None of the cars or trucks pulled over, but traffic was very slow-moving all morning when children needed to cross the painted lines. After the school bell rang, Joyce and Hazel filed into the principal's office, and we all sat down.

"I took your advice," Hazel said.

"What advice?" I said.

"When a person is tired of something, that's when things get done," Hazel said.

"I volunteered," Joyce said. "I didn't want Hazel having all the fun."

"What data did you write on your clipboard?" I asked.

"Data?" Hazel said. She looked at her sister. "We did crossword puzzles when no one was around."

I coughed and said, "Uh, where did you get the radar gun?"

My question caused a fit of laughter.

Hazel wiped her eyes and said, "Out of the wastebasket."

"Which basket — one at the police station?" I said.

The women nearly fell out of their chairs laughing.

Joyce laid a dark plastic instrument on the desk. I gripped it by the handle, looked up, and said, "This is a hair dryer."

"*Was* a hair dryer," Hazel said. "It died Saturday. I threw it in the wastebasket and bought a new one. When the cashier at Walgreens said new hair dryers don't look like radar guns anymore, I knew how to slow down traffic. I took mine out of the wastebasket and cut off the cord."

Joyce said, "The Day-Glo stuff came from my husband's hunting clothes."

"Ladies, I appreciate your creativity," I said, "but you're like vigilantes. You took traffic law enforcement into your own hands."

"We're vigilante crossing guards!" Hazel said.

Joyce said, "Our book club will be so proud!"

The sisters high-fived one another.

"Ladies," I said, "how about if you meet with the principal before lunch duty and find out if your, ah, radar gun is legal?'"

Joyce and Hazel left, but I heard Joyce say, "What if we both had radar guns?"

Hazel was eventually fired for impersonating an officer of the law but it was good while it lasted.

—John J. Lesjack—

55

Professional Jealousy

*What I don't like about office Christmas parties is
looking for a job the next day.*
~Carl Zwanzig

A company Christmas party, dinner theatre, and wine... The atmosphere was festive, the food was delicious, and the actors were fantastic. Our group made sure to claim a table near the front of the room in the "actor participation section" to ensure that we would be fully immersed in the fun.

There was one very handsome, charming character with a velvety singing voice. As the wine flowed, he became more and more handsome and debonair. He was going from table to table, crooning to lucky ladies. My friend Marie and I giggled and swooned, hoping it would soon be our turn. Our husbands were having a wonderful time laughing at us.

Finally, he started moving our way. As he came closer and closer, Marie and I became forty-year-old fan girls, squealing and giggling. Suddenly, with a dramatic swoop, our dreamboat sat at our table, across from Marie, gazing into her eyes and singing to her. Of course, I had to demonstrate my jealousy just a little. My plan was to give her a slight hip bump to move her over and then scoot over into her seat to be across from the dreamy singer — to playfully take her place in our mock rivalry for his attention.

What actually happened, however, was this: I scooted over and gave Marie a little hip bump. Her chair tipped over and dumped her on the floor. The aforementioned wine made me misjudge my center of balance. I went with the chair and landed on top of Marie. Boots flew in the air, and we both landed in an unflattering heap.

Dreamboat took Marie by the hand, helped her up, and sang into her ear as he danced with her. Meanwhile, I picked up myself and the chair, trying desperately and failing miserably to retain a shred of dignity. Our husbands were in paroxysms of laughter by this point, and the actors were wondering if I needed to be removed.

This was one company party that has still not been forgotten! Or I should say, one that I have not been *allowed* to forget!

—Sheri Bertaux—

Stress Test

They whose guilt within their bosom lies,
imagine every eye beholds their blame.
~William Shakespeare

Our family doctor always presented himself as the consummate professional with his tailored shirt, striped tie, and starched lab coat. With every hair in place, every word a cornucopia of wisdom, Dr. Jackson epitomized confidence, intelligence, and grace. Now a primary-care internist myself, I strove to emulate those high standards of professionalism that had so impressed me during my childhood.

Unfortunately, Dr. Jackson proved a tough act to follow, especially after the birth of my first child. I had been taught during my pediatrics rotation that breast milk was the superior nutritional choice for developing brains and immune systems, so I was adamant that I would provide breast milk for my newborn baby until he was at least one year old.

This proved an easy endeavor while home on maternity leave. But what about when I returned to the long, hectic hours of running my medical clinic? "No problem," I informed my husband. "Thanks to this new handy-dandy, double-cupped, electric breast pump, I can still provide the 'liquid gold' our son needs, even when I'm at work." My husband looked skeptical but knew enough to keep his mouth shut.

Early morning and night feedings proved to be a cinch. But carving out the fifteen minutes I needed to use my pump on overbooked clinic days, when every patient I saw yanked out a foot-long list of medical problems to discuss, proved challenging.

On one particularly stressful day, I was already running an hour behind schedule. By one o'clock, I hadn't had a bite to eat and still hadn't completed my morning patients. My breasts, now as engorged as cow udders before milking time, were right on schedule and demanded I take the time to relieve them of their misery. I knew I couldn't delay pumping any longer unless I wanted to win a wet T-shirt — or, in this case, wet lab coat — competition.

What to do? I still had one more morning patient to see: Mr. Simpson, a hunched-over ninety-year-old with umpteen medical conditions. He had come in for his annual "wellness" exam. Wellness, my eye! "The man doesn't have a 'well' bone in his body," I sputtered to my nurse. I released a defeated sigh. I'd never get back on schedule at this rate, but try telling that to my squalling chest!

I told my medical assistant to draw Mr. Simpson's blood, obtain his EKG, and then send him to the bathroom for a urine specimen. That would buy me a little time.

I dashed into my office to relieve "the girls" from their misery. (I now have great compassion for the common Holstein when the farmer is late for milking.)

Since Mr. Simpson moved with a slow, shuffling gait, I figured I had a good ten minutes to pump while my nurse completed her nursing duties, and I would need to begin his wellness exam.

I dashed into my office, shut the door behind me, flopped into my desk chair, and assembled the breast pump. I slipped off my lab coat, tugged up my bra, and connected my now engorged coconuts into the suction cups. I flipped on the power switch, and ah, sweet relief, as my misery drip, drip, dripped into the baby bottle.

I finished pumping and had just pulled off the suction cups when Mr. Simpson suddenly flung open my office door and barged in. (Apparently, he'd gotten confused on his way back from the bathroom to his exam room and had entered my private office instead.)

Talk about embarrassing! There I sat — topless — with my breasts exposed like some floozy in a strip club. Instinctively, I yanked down my blouse, but not before his eyes grew big as moon pies.

I could only hope that he wouldn't go into cardiac arrest!

I don't know who was more embarrassed. I blurted out, "Excuse me — I was pumping!" His brow furrowed in confusion. I then realized a ninety-year-old man probably had no idea what I meant by "pumping." No doubt he thought I was performing some newfangled exercise to increase my bust size — like pumping iron. Oh, dear! Bad, bad, and getting worse!

He muttered a hasty apology, shut my office door quickly, and shuffled back to his exam room with the guidance of my nurse. Unfortunately, since I had not yet performed his exam, I now had to walk back into his exam room and face him again — as his doctor. I eyed my breast pump longingly. If only it could suck me into the baby bottle, and I could swim far, far away from the dreaded encounter. I did not want to face him after he'd just seen me topless, but the poor man had already waited an hour for his appointment, so I couldn't very well cancel.

Reluctantly, I pulled on my lab coat and brushed my hair — anything to delay the humiliating moment when I had to face Mr. Simpson again. Why couldn't he be severely demented and have forgotten all about our little misadventure? But no, Horace Simpson, while decrepit, was sharp as the shards of a broken baby bottle.

As I trudged toward his exam room, I asked myself how I should act. What would Dr. Jackson do?

Curses! As a male physician, Dr. Jackson would never have landed himself in this position.

I decided to pretend it never happened.

I knocked on his door, entered, and completed his exam, avoiding eye contact at all costs. Thankfully, the patient made no mention of our unfortunate encounter. I answered all his questions, updated his pneumonia vaccine, and then nervously dove into a dissertation on the importance of maintaining excellent blood-sugar control. We discussed potential side effects of his new blood-pressure medication. (Hmm. I can't imagine what could have raised his blood pressure....)

I handed him five prescriptions, still avoiding eye contact. Yes, there was a ginormous pink elephant in the room, but no way would I bring it up! Elephant? What elephant?

As I stood to exit the room, Mr. Simpson said, "Hey, doc? You might want to put a lock on that office door of yours. Views like I just saw aren't good for a ninety-year-old heart." He grinned and added, "I hope that new baby of yours appreciates what you're doing for him. In my day, the women all used formula, but I hear breast milk is now all the rage."

As my cheeks turned redder than the sharps container on the wall, I mumbled some lame comment that perhaps we should look at my unseemly exposure as a free cardiac stress test. "Luckily, you passed."

"I nearly passed out," he teased.

We both had a chuckle, and all was right with the world again.

Now my top advice to women who want to combine a career with motherhood is, "Lock your office door!"

— Sally Willard Burbank, MD —

Pierre's Pliers

*At the height of laughter, the universe is flung into a
kaleidoscope of new possibilities.*
~Jean Houston

In our early twenties, my co-worker Pierre and I were telephone technicians working for Bell Canada. One day we were dispatched to a well-known sanatorium in a suburb of Montreal. I had worked there before, but it was Pierre's first time.

Recently, the facility had come a long way in the treatment of mental-health disorders by the successful use of new and improved medications. However, there were still many seriously ill patients confined against their will who were considered dangerous to themselves or others.

When we had completed repairing the phones, we left the premises. Once in our truck, we removed our tool bags and the telephones, which had been hanging from our belts. In those (prehistoric) days, that's what identified us as Bell employees. Believe it or not, even with all the security around the hospital, we were not required to wear our employer's uniforms, nor badges, not even IDs — just the telephones hanging on our belts.

As I prepared to drive off, Pierre realized he had left his pliers inside the hospital.

"I swear you'd forget your head if it wasn't attached," I muttered sarcastically. "You know I have night school! Hurry."

"'Old your 'orses!" he responded, in his French accent, dropping the "h" at the beginning of the words. "I'll be right back."

Everybody loved Pierre. He was a great guy, but sometimes he was a bit immature for his twenty-two years.

He left to retrieve his pliers. When he hadn't returned in a few minutes, I went to look through the window of the building. I could see Pierre strolling leisurely down a long corridor toward the exit. He had his pliers in his right hand and was slapping them against his left, as if keeping time to the music.

Pierre, you knucklehead! Who goes around swinging pliers in a mental hospital? I thought in exasperation. *His action could be perceived as threatening!*

I pounded on the window, but when no one heard me, I rushed to the front door. A security guard I knew was entering the premises and let me in. I was admitted into the front office. By the time I reached the corridor where I had observed Pierre, the situation had changed dramatically. What I witnessed surprised and alarmed me.

The personnel shift had just changed, and since Pierre no longer had the phone hanging on his belt, no one recognized him as a telephone technician. He was suddenly surrounded by a large group of hospital employees: nurses, orderlies and a couple of big, burly security types. They were wrestling the pliers out of his hands.

"Who are you? Why aren't you in your room?" they demanded to know.

Poor Pierre was in a panic. His usually pale complexion was almost the color of his unruly copper-red hair, and beads of sweat were pouring down his terrified face. The nurses were trying to calm him as he kept mouthing, "Pee... Pee... Pee... Pee..."

One of the nurses leaned in closer to him and asked, "What are you saying? Do you need to use the restroom?"

Pierre blushed. Then I remembered he had a tendency to stutter when agitated. I guessed he had been trying to tell them his name was Pierre. When he wasn't getting anywhere, he started pushing everyone away. The men shoved him into a chair and were holding him down by force.

I don't know what it was about the guy, but women found it

endearing when he stuttered. Another young nurse placed herself protectively between him and the security guards and demanded, "He's not doing anything. Go easy on him."

Being unsuccessful in trying to say his name, Pierre stuttered some more: "T... t... tele... teleph..." I guess he was trying to explain that he was a telephone repairman.

Another female staff member said gently, "It's okay. Calm down. You will get a chance to use the telephone soon — after we get you back to your room."

I could see Pierre was scared stiff. But when he saw me coming, his expression lit up with hope. "La... La... La... La... " He was attempting to say my name, Lawrence, but he didn't get very far.

A sympathetic nurse joined him in a sing-song sound. "La la la la la. That's good. We will sing a song together. Nice. La la la la la."

I was startled to see my colleague Pierre in such a predicament, but then, sorry to say, I couldn't help but chuckle inside. After all, he had caused this problem himself. And I owed him for all the pranks he had played on me in the past.

So I joined in the melody, "La la la la la!"

When his captors realized he was trying to call out to me, they asked if he was with me. With a straight face but snickering inside, I exclaimed, "Never saw the man before in my life!"

Pierre's expression reminded me of the phrase, "If looks could kill...!"

I stood there watching the scene, feeling somewhat guilty, but what the heck? Pierre had played a lot of pranks on me. Among other things, he had once planted a dead mouse in my lunchbox.

Finally, I couldn't stand to see him suffer any longer.

"Yes, I know him!" I announced. "He is my associate, a fellow telephone repairman, Pierre! He fixed your phones today. Give him back his pliers." By then, I couldn't control my laughter.

When the group of nurses and even a couple of residents heard me, the giggles began gradually at first but soon spread into full-blown hysterics throughout the corridor and beyond. The young female nurses hung close to Pierre, who no longer felt threatened but continued his charming stutter. Leave it to Pierre to turn what some may have considered a detriment into an asset.

Even patients in their rooms could be seen standing at their windows and sharing in the amusement. Soon, applause for Pierre filled the corridor. Cheerfulness had engulfed the insane institution!

And voilà, Pierre was released. The entire staff of nurses and orderlies apologized and hugged him one by one. Even a couple of doctors and some big security types shook his hand and patted his back in a good gesture. As we were leaving, a cute, little French Canadian nurse called out to him, "Pierre, you can come fix my lines anytime, eh?"

By now, Pierre was not only blushing but laughing. Eventually, he forgave me for not sticking up for him immediately. When we got back to the home office, all of Bell Canada learned about our entertaining escapade. Over the years, we had many laughs recalling the time when Pierre almost got locked up in an insane asylum.

And Pierre, being charming Pierre, made the best of it. After this visit, the hospital mysteriously experienced frequent telephone issues. Calls would come into Bell requesting that Pierre be dispatched to repair the problems. Rumor had it that Pierre and the cute little nurse spent several months seeing each other.

— Larry Carter —

The Toilet Paper Incident

Problems are like toilet paper.
You pull on one and ten more come.
~Woody Allen

What I am about to reveal happened many, many years ago, and I have never divulged my shameful secret to a living soul. I am now over a hundred years old, and I feel my secret really doesn't matter anymore. I'm sure those who might have been a witness to this saga of the errant toilet paper couldn't care less — and have probably all faded away over the course of time anyway.

It happened exactly seventy-six years ago when Britain, my native country, was at war. I had already joined the Army and was serving in the artillery in an anti-aircraft unit in the south of England. The outlook was grim, and we had little time for any kind of frivolities. A little celebration or party of any kind was something to get excited about and looked forward to with great anticipation.

A person of note was about to visit our gun-site, and there was to be a social gathering in his honor, with some dignitaries attending. A few days before this was to take place, I was attacked by a severe bout of hay fever (as allergic rhinitis was commonly known in those days) even though the nearest hayfield was several miles away. It should be noted at this point that in Britain (and I assume the whole of Europe), people blew their noses on handkerchiefs. Little squares of tissue (or Kleenex) had never been heard of on the European side of the Atlantic as far as I know until the American soldiers came, blowing their noses in Kleenex a few days after encountering the traditionally humid English climate.

Today, after more than sixty years of using disposable Kleenex in America, I freely admit that blowing one's nose into a "hanky," which had to be washed afterwards, was a rather barbaric habit. On the other hand, I found that little paper tissues, such as Kleenex, were highly inadequate for a full-blown English cold, unless used by the bushel.

I had already used up what seemed to be a small drawer full of handkerchiefs, and my eyes were still watering and my nose streaming. My only resource was toilet paper, which I was now using by the roll. I was getting quite excited about the coming party, and in spite of red eyes and a nose that continued to leak with unbelievable fury, I was not about to miss this special occasion for a harmless bout of hay fever.

On the day itself, I took special care in my preparation for the party. The buttons on my tunic were polished until they shone like little beacons, my skirt was pressed almost to extinction, and my Sam Browne belt and shoes positively glowed after their extra dose of spit and polish.

By the time I had showered and dressed, I was gratified to find that things were improving. When I looked in the mirror, my eyes didn't appear to be as bleary and bloodshot as they had a day or two earlier, and the small river flowing from my nostrils was clearly starting to dry up. Not wanting to have an unsightly bulge in one of my pockets, I decided that I would secrete the remaining half roll of toilet tissue in the waistband of my skirt for future use. There it would sit, snugly concealed by my tunic, until it was needed.

All of a sudden, I noticed that the officers' quarters seemed to be ominously quiet. Checking my watch, I found that the festivities had already started at least five minutes ago, and it was obvious that everyone else had left in order to be on time. Now I started to panic. It would take me another few minutes, even at a gentle trot, to reach the building where the party was being held, so I quickly put the finishing touches to my uniform and made for the door.

The party was in full swing when I arrived, with everyone congregated at the far end of the room. Feeling embarrassed by my late entry, I sidled toward the milling throng, hoping I wouldn't be noticed.

After dutifully removing my Sam Browne belt and hanging it on the rack at the doorway with a multitude of other belts, I was about halfway across the floor when an older female officer broke away from the gathering of people. Taking me gently by the arm, she whispered into my ear, "Look behind you, dear." I looked, and what I saw was enough to cause a minor heart attack.

Pause for one moment and try to imagine several feet of toilet paper trailing along behind you in a crowded room, emerging from under the back of your skirt. I stood transfixed in horror, unable to move. For one deranged moment, I hoped a German Heinkel would drop a bomb on us. Then my Good Samaritan, with great presence of mind, reached behind me and, in one fell swoop, snatched the offending tissue from the floor together with the remains of the paper still evident under the hem of my skirt. She grabbed the toilet roll and, together with the toilet paper, secured everything under one arm. By this time, everyone else in the room was so engaged in earnest conversation and dedicated drinking that no one seemed to notice the little drama being played out in the center of the room. Or if they did, after ten minutes of imbibing, Army-style, probably no one could have cared less.

How this wonderful lady officer disposed of the cause of my embarrassment I never knew. At the time, the whole thing became a blur in my mind, although I do remember being piloted — mildly protesting — to the end of the room on her other arm in order to mingle with the crowd. Here I found, to my great relief, that everyone was so happily preoccupied that they didn't even notice me.

So, over a span of a hundred and one years, I have learned two important lessons in life: First, don't stuff toilet paper in your waistband. Second, don't ever blow your nose on a "hanky." Use a bushel of Kleenex instead.

— Monica Agnew-Kinnaman —

Chapter
8

Laughing at Ourselves

59

Looking Good

*To make mistakes is human; to stumble is
commonplace; to be able to laugh at yourself
is maturity.*
~William Arthur Ward

t was "Hairdo Day." As a teacher and a mom, these kinds of days
are big doings. I don't get out a lot, so I had big plans: hairdo,
Home Depot, Dollar Tree and Walmart. It was going to be a leisurely day without kids.

I chose decent clothes, not my typical sweats and sweatshirt, as I
would actually be seeing humans above the age of seventeen. I chose a
nice blue shirt and white shorts because I had done a spray tan, and I
was actually feeling like showing my forty-five-year-old legs in public.
I was living on the edge, but I threw caution to the wind.

I showed up at the beauty salon, and my hairdresser worked her
magic. I returned to the car and put my face together as I wanted to look
decent for those on the outside world. I didn't use too much make-up,
but enough so that people would not stop me and ask if I was sick
or something. I applied a little eye shadow, mascara, and some black
eyeliner. With the summer heat, the eyeliner had gotten a little soft,
and a large portion of the crayon broke off in my attempt to line my
lids. So much for perfection. People were going to get what they got.

I visited Dollar Tree and then continued on to Home Depot. As I
approached the building, a large spray-painted sign jumped out at me
(an English teacher). To my horror, a large word was spelled wrong.

Yes, I am *that* teacher.

As I entered the building, I casually grabbed one of the associates and quietly explained that they might want to check the sign as a word was spelled wrong. The gentleman was sweet and explained that they were in the process of getting it changed, but I was the first customer who had noticed it. I was feeling pretty good about myself. I had righted the world's grammatical wrongs. All was right again with the universe. A little part of me knew that many people had probably noticed it but didn't really care. Nevertheless, I wore my honor with pride.

Then on to Walmart I went. Long lines. Lots of people. As usual, it was the gathering place of all of those who work during the week. I saw several people I knew and made conversation. I did my shopping — enough groceries so I would not have to return any time soon.

I returned home, dreading the lugging of the groceries into the house. As I pulled in the driveway, I jumped out of the car to call my minions for the great unloading. Sliding out of the front seat, I noticed a black smear down my hand. *Hmm…* I wondered where in the world the black mess had come from. I went into the house and studied the black mark. I could not remember rubbing up against anything.

Returning to the car, I opened the front door, only to notice more black streaks on the side of the driver's side seat. Slowly, my brain began to replay the events of the day. It was like a bad movie. Hair done. Check. Make-up done… make-up done… MAKE-UP DONE! That little black piece of crayon that broke off had apparently made its way into my seat. Coupled with the rising temperatures and the heat radiating from my rear end, it had effectively smeared a big poop-looking stain right in the crack of those white shorts that I had so bravely put on that morning.

And then the darkness got darker… How proud I had been to be the spelling Wonder Woman at Home Depot, only to walk away from the kind gentleman, and him, quite possibly, being less impressed with my ability to wipe my rear end than with my English skills! Then there was Walmart! How many people had passed me? How many people had I come in contact with who saw my smeared bum and didn't know the truth? I was shaken.

So I did what any self-respecting person does: I took a picture of my soiled back side and put it on Facebook. I needed to tell my story, to get it out there and explain why I looked like a toddler who had spent too long on the playground before making it to the bathroom. And you know what happened? People laughed. They laughed and laughed. I had people stop me over the next couple of days cracking up about my eyeliner fiasco. Apparently, looking like you pooped yourself as you make your way through shopping centers makes for lots of "likes."

In full disclosure, ten years ago this event would have devastated me. But with age and experience, I have learned to laugh at myself. If white shorts, a broken eyeliner pencil, and a smeared rear end are enough to break me, I have real problems. But if those three items can make for a great story that will bring joy to the hearts of others at the expense of my dignity, then so be it. I am happy to be a part of that. Life is too short to take ourselves too seriously. We are all a mess, so it's a lot of fun to be able to know that we aren't alone in our mishaps.

I still keep the picture on my phone so that I can hang with the best of them when people are telling their tragic stories, because my story of woe from the blasted eyeliner is enough to make people laugh or cry or both. But either way, it's a great reminder that humanity is about loving yourself, laughing at your mistakes, and the very little things, like a piece of eyeliner pencil, that can certainly keep you humble.

— Corrie Lopez —

60

Gobble, Gobble

I believe that the ability to laugh at oneself is
fundamental to the resiliency of the human spirit.
~Jill Conner Browne

won a writing contest last week. It was a 100-word short story for the local paper. The editor, who called to tell me I'd won, interviewed me over the phone. Just as we were finishing the call, he added, "And we'll need a picture."

"Of me?" I asked.

"Yes."

"How about someone related to me?"

"Nope."

"Or a middle-aged actress who resembles me?"

The editor was probably wishing he had selected a sane person.

"Fine," I said.

Frantically, I began searching through my phone and computer for one decent picture. I e-mailed my daughter, asking her to send a good photo of me.

And she did.

But who was this less attractive, older version of myself? Oh, the horror!

Finally, I found a picture that was flattering. It was far away and blurry, and the person next to me partly obscured my face.

Jackpot!

The editor was less impressed. "We need a clear, solo, unfiltered photo."

A clear picture? Since when is clear better? For a glass of water, perhaps. But for pictures, let's not discount hazy.

And a solo picture? Who has a solo picture of themselves, besides real estate agents and convicts?

An unfiltered picture of myself? Filters were invented for a reason.

After not finding a single clear, solo, unfiltered picture of myself, I realized I would have to take a selfie. I examined my middle-aged face. Not bad. But really my face wasn't the problem.

It was my neck.

I didn't even know necks could be a problem until one of my friends (who will remain nameless, but we'll call her Carrie) recently told me about her neck woes. "I hate my neck," she said. "It's gotten so saggy, like a turkey."

That didn't sound like fun. I felt sorry for "Carrie" until I looked at my own neck in the mirror. Maybe it wasn't full-blown turkey, but it was turkey-esque.

Now I had to take a clear, solo, unfiltered photo that didn't involve my neck.

And then I remembered. Carrie once told me how she used tape to lift her eyebrows and soften the lines in between.

But tape on a neck? Wasn't that going too far?

I cut a piece of red duct tape, and while holding the tape in one hand, I pushed the left side of my neck back with the other hand. Carefully, I tucked the loose skin under the tape on the back of my neck. This stuff was amazing. My skin was firm, taught, years younger. Perfect.

Uh oh.

I could see red on one side, which could make one ponder, Is this a vampire story?

I started over, and it was going well until I ran out of tape. One side was smooth. The other, saggy. I was a before-and-after advertisement for duct-taped turkey necks.

I found more tape and finally got it on my third attempt. The skin was pulled back evenly on both sides without a hint of vampire or sag.

Just right.

After make-up and hair, I went in search of the best possible lighting in the house and snapped six selfies. Within minutes, I had made my selection, and one picture of a middle-aged neurotic writer, with a good neck, was en route to the editor.

His response? "Thanks."

The following week, my story, a short article on me, and the picture came out. My family, friends and colleagues had many kind words.

"What a great story."

"I love the ending."

"The imagery was powerful."

I thanked them politely, feeling a sense of pride. Still, it would have been nice if just one person had commented, "You know what was even smoother than your transitions? Your neck."

— January Gordon Ornellas —

61

Seeing Double

*Life literally abounds in comedy if you
just look around you.*
~Mel Brooks

It's referred to as the world's largest moving automotive event: the
National Corvette Caravan. And we were fortunate enough to
be part of it! Every five years, there is an anniversary celebration
of the National Corvette Museum in Bowling Green, Kentucky.
Between 3,000 and 5,000 cars converge on Bowling Green for a
three-day celebratory event. Corvettes from all over the United States
travel thousands of miles to attend. Some drivers even have their cars
shipped from other countries!

My husband and I (in a beautiful blue C-5) along with my in-
laws Frank and Barbara (in a sexy, sleek yellow C-6) and our friends
in the Corvette Club of Santa Barbara began the journey at our local
Chevrolet dealership. They saw us off with music and a BBQ lunch.
How exciting!

Corvette aficionados really love their cars. Most people have their
cars customized with souped-up engines, fancy paint jobs, custom rims,
tricked-out interiors, after stock exhaust systems, window decals, and
ghost flames painted along the side. Some even have murals painted
on the hood. It's very rare to see two Corvettes that are exactly alike.
Corvettes are truly beautiful works of art on wheels.

Because the cars are so individualized and personal, Corvette
owners are very attached to their cars. They lovingly renew, restore,

wash, wax and pamper their cars. Some drivers wash them each night after a long day of driving! Everyone gets to know his or her car so well that it becomes a part of the family. Some are even given names.

Our cars were no exception. We both had Corvette Club of Santa Barbara window decals going across the front windshield, custom license plates and American flag stickers on our side windows. We could take one look at our cars and know they belonged to us. And, yes, we named our cars — Bluebird and Woodstock.

Each day, we drove quite a distance, stopped for lunch, and continued driving until we reached our next destination. Bowling Green or bust! At each stop, more and more cars would meet up, join in our caravan and drive together to the next event. We'd continue in that fashion until we reached the final destination.

At every evening destination, my husband and father-in-law would park our cars next to each other, and Barbara and I would go check us in to the hotel. We'd eat, party, sleep, wake up very early the next morning, drive for hours and repeat.

By the time we got to Tucumcari, New Mexico, our caravan had so many cars that the townspeople lined the streets with banners and Corvette flags, watching as our parade of cars drove through town.

That night, the town had a giant welcome BBQ for all of us with live music, wonderful food, and dancing. It was really a night to remember.

Waking up the next morning was tough. All the excitement must have been wearing us down. Rock stars, we are not.

My husband and his father went downstairs to load the luggage while Barbara and I checked out of the hotel. When we finished checking out, Barbara and I went outside to meet our husbands. What a beautiful sight to walk out into a sea of bright, shiny fiberglass!

We found Bluebird and Woodstock immediately, parked right next to each other, and wondered how we beat Frank and Mike to the cars. Nevertheless, we decided to make good use of our time by taking photos of me in front of my car and Barbara in front of hers. We asked a stranger to take photos of us together in front of our cars parked side by side. Satisfied with our photo session, we couldn't help but wonder what in the world was taking Frank and Mike so long.

Finally, we saw Frank, Mike and another gentleman walking toward us. All three of them stopped at our cars at the same time. I was just about to open the door of my blue car when I realized the man was waiting patiently. I asked him if he needed something.

In unison, Mike and Frank said, "These aren't our cars." At the same time, the man said, "This is *my* car." Barbara and I stopped cold. We took one quick glance at the cars and realized that, in fact, they were *not* our cars, but two very similar blue and yellow Corvettes parked side by side.

Maybe it was the sleep deprivation or too much fun from the night before, I'm not sure. Barbara and I took one look at each other and doubled over with laughter. To this day, when Barbara and I go somewhere and park side by side, we double-check that it's really our cars before we get in.

— Crescent LoMonaco —

62

The Bell Ringer

God invented mankind because he loved silly stories.
~Ralph Steadman

I had been waiting patiently for several years to move up the list of bell ringers at my church. It is a well-known fact that the only way to move up the list is if someone retires from ringing or passes away.

Finally, I received the prized e-mail. Two old souls had passed away, so I moved up to "active ringer." I received the new schedule with my name written in black ink, just like everyone else. I checked the dates where my name was listed and wrote them on my calendar so I would remember. Then I waited for my first bell-ringing Sunday. I knew it would be magical.

The Sunday morning before, I sat in the pew downstairs and listened to the melodious ringing of those beautiful bells. What poise, what élan that bell ringer had. I knew I was up for the task. It never dawned on me to go upstairs to the balcony and watch what he was doing. That afternoon, however, it hit me: I had no idea what I was supposed to do.

Quickly, I e-mailed the fellow who was in charge of the bell ringers. I reminded him that I was to ring the bells the following Sunday, but I had not had any lessons or even an introduction to bell ringing. I impatiently waited for his response.

Finally, on Tuesday afternoon, he e-mailed back. He said it was fairly straightforward, no big deal. The bells were located in the north tower. Just go up to the balcony, he explained, release the rope, pull on the woolen pad evenly until there is momentum, then check and pull for about thirteen to fifteen minutes. Remember not to look up or I might get dizzy or get dust in my eyes.

Okay, I knew I could do this. It didn't sound very difficult — as soon as I figured out which of the two was the north tower.

On Wednesday, I spoke with a friend who is a bell ringer at her own church. She told me about the class she and her husband had to take. They learned how not to step on the rope or put the loop at the end of the rope around their arm or foot. They were taught how to move with the bell pull to keep the momentum going. I could feel the panic welling up once more.

By Thursday, total panic had set in again. How often was I supposed to pull the "sally" (woolen pad)? How would I know when it reached the proper momentum? Then the really big questions came: What would happen if I pulled too quickly? Would I end up swinging by the bell pull and flailing around as the bells rang crazily? What would happen if I pulled too hard? Would I have to chase the bells down Meeting Street because I managed to pull them out of the bell tower?

I knew I was not ready for this.

Inevitably, Sunday dawned pure and clear. I had been hoping for a hurricane. No such luck. My beloved husband bravely went with me. We climbed the north tower; thankfully, an usher knew which one it was. We found the bell pull. I untied it from the exquisite filigree cast-iron holder. I gave it a pull, and the bells rang out bravely in the hands of one so unworthy.

Yeah, right. I wish that is the way it went.

Truthfully, the usher did know which tower housed the bells, but when we climbed the tower, I discovered that the bell pull was right at the edge of the wide, stately, carpeted stairs at the top of the balcony. I had to stand near the edge, looking down the stairs. That was a problem because I have a little issue with heights. If the entire world were completely flat, it would be a perfect world. As it is, I cannot even drive to Ohio to visit family because I have to drive over the mountains in either West Virginia or Tennessee, so I just fly.

I knew that I had to ring the bells, so I looked around for something I could use for ballast. Then I took a deep breath, wrapped my left arm around the water pipe that was painted to blend in with the wall (good thing I have sharp eyes), and started pulling the rope and ringing the bells with my right arm. It almost killed me. No one had told me I needed to do weight training before ringing the bells. Those bells were so heavy, and my beloved husband was absolutely no help at all. He was sitting in the chair on the balcony landing with tears streaming down his face because he was laughing at me!

Then I saw the loop at the end of the rope. I couldn't remember what my friend had told me to do with it, so I just stayed away from it. Several people came up the balcony stairs and said how nice it was to have someone ringing the bells by hand. I hadn't a clue what they were talking about.

Finally, one lady came by and said I was so brave to ring the bells manually. She'd always just pushed the button beside the organ.

What button?

I smiled sweetly and thought dark thoughts about the fellow in charge who had not told me about The Button. The one beside the organ. That I could push. That wasn't up here.

Well, I did get through it. No falling down the stairs, no flailing around at the end of the rope, no chasing bells down the street. I had done it. I was ready for my next turn at ringing the bells.

On Monday, I received an e-mail from the fellow in charge of bell ringing. He said he heard I did a great job, but to remember that we only ring the bell for three to five minutes. Seriously, three to five, not thirteen to fifteen? I went back to his original e-mail and, sure enough, it said three to five minutes.

It also stated where I could find the button.

—Kaye Lucas—

63

Number 7

*Anyone who takes himself too seriously always
runs the risk of looking ridiculous; anyone who can
consistently laugh at himself does not.*
~Vaclav Havel

was delighted to be invited to one of my fifteen-year-old nephew's
soccer games. This game was pretty special because it was for a
spot in the semi-finals, and it was a night game! The park was
packed, so I was glad I had arrived early to stand in line at the
concession stand. I was surprised to find that they had one of my
favourite snacks — nachos — and grateful because I had missed dinner. I ordered the nachos and took my seat in the stands.

I found my nephew on the field and waved to him. I assumed he
didn't see me because he didn't wave back. I figured he was just focused
on the game, but he would notice me the next time I waved. I stood up
and called his name, "Mason! Number 7! Hi!" Still nothing. He didn't
acknowledge me, so I thought I'd better not embarrass him further.

The whistle blew, and the game started. I watched him run up and
down the field while my chest filled with pride. I dipped a tortilla chip
in the cheese sauce, and a huge glob of it fell onto my pants. Shoot! I
stood up and was about to venture back to the concession stand when
the soccer ball flew into the crowd and hit my plate of nachos! It sent
me flying backward in a mass of cheese sauce and chaos.

I landed flat on my back, and that's where I wanted to stay. I
knew that people were laughing, and those who tried to keep it in

finally broke down. The referee called a stop on the play while several gentlemen helped me to my feet. I was covered with chips and cheese from my head to my toes. I was mortified for my nephew to see his auntie this way, so I hung my head and crawled back to my car. I went home and washed off the nachos.

The next day, I called him to apologize. "Honey, I'm so sorry if I embarrassed you last night at your game! I'm such a klutz, but this was a freak accident."

The phone went silent for a beat. "What are you talking about? My game is tonight."

—Lacey L. Bakker—

64

Almost Taken

I like being absurd.
~Jimmy Fallon

Last week, after getting my car detailed, we decided it was time to sell it. And when I say *we*, I mean my husband. He advertised it on Craigslist, and within minutes, the calls were pouring in. Who knew a banged-up Honda Pilot with 175,000 miles would solicit so many admirers? One such admirer was Lenny from Long Beach, who insisted on seeing it that night.

"Should I have him come here?" my husband asked.

"If you want him to murder us," I replied.

"He's not going to murder us. He just wants to buy a car."

"Don't you remember in *Taken*, when the girl's dumb friend tells the bad guys where they live?"

My husband, not wanting to hear the entire scene, held up his hand.

A few texts later, my husband agreed to meet the murderer at the Target parking lot.

"I'll follow you there," I told my husband.

"Why?"

Here's what I was thinking: After Lenny abducts you, I'll need to describe him to the police.

Here's what I said: "If you sell the car, you'll need a ride home."

"True," he said, picking up the car keys. "But don't park too close."

"You won't even know I'm there," I said. "And remember to observe any distinct features, so when he takes you, you can yell them out. Tattoo on shoulder! Scar on wrist! Unibrow!"

"What are you talking about?" he said.

My husband's knowledge of cinematic abductions is embarrassing.

My husband arranged to meet his abductor at 9:00.

At 9:05, I pulled into the Target parking lot. I spotted my husband next to our car, talking with two men. That made sense. If you're going to kidnap somebody, best to have backup.

I pulled into a space two rows over and turned off the car.

The stakeout had begun.

The younger of the two looked to be about six feet, bearded, and in his thirties.

The other one was a few inches shorter, bald and around sixty.

Perhaps a father/son team?

The son bent down to inspect the tire, running his left hand over the rim.

He was left-handed! Was it too late for me to join the FBI?

My husband popped the hood, and the sinister duo checked out the engine and some other stuff.

My husband walked away from the car. Why was he walking away? He pulled something out of his jacket pocket. Oh my gosh he was calling the police. He needed help.

My purse vibrated. I ignored it. I was on a stakeout.

It continued to vibrate.

My husband looked in my direction.

I pulled out my phone.

"I see you," I said in my best undercover voice.

"I see you, too," he said. "Your lights are on."

Oh, crap!

I flipped the switch, and the parking lot dimmed. No wonder I could see them so clearly.

The assassins continued to inspect the car and got into the front seat a few minutes later. My husband slid into the back without yelling out one distinct character feature.

It was almost like he wanted to be taken.

I called him on the phone. "Where are you going?"

"For a test drive," he answered. "It's cool."

"It's cool?" He never said, "It's cool." Was that code for, "I AM BEING TAKEN. CALL THE POLICE?" Why didn't we agree on a "safe word" ahead of time? What sort of FBI agent was I?

I made a mental note to come up with a really good code word for my next husband.

Lenny started the car and pulled out slowly.

I waited until the car was halfway down the row before I turned on my engine.

The Pilot disappeared behind a sea of minivans. It wasn't clear which way they went.

My keen tracking skills said to go right, so I edged forward.

I looked right. No Pilot.

I scanned left. No Pilot.

Did they just disappear?

I started driving, and then realized with a jolt that perhaps they didn't go right or left. Maybe they went to the loading area behind Target, where it was dark and deserted and more conducive to murderous activity.

I drove slowly, looking for clues.

Nothing.

I returned to the front of the store, and drove up and down the rows in the lot. My stomach was in knots.

Finally, I headed back to where I started. As I prepared to turn right, a car made a left turn in front of me. It was them!

They parked, and three bodies emerged, none of which was bound or gagged.

I found a spot, partially hidden, but close enough that I could see everything.

I turned off the engine *and* the lights — a good agent learns from her mistakes.

Lenny's dad hung back while Lenny and my husband talked.

My husband seemed to have all his limbs.

The talk escalated to an argument. Lenny gestured with his hands.

My husband shook his head.

Lenny was probably saying, "I should have taken you when I had the chance."

My husband folded his arms. He was probably thinking, I wouldn't try it, buddy. My wife is practically FBI.

Then, with a final shake of the head, Lenny and his dad walked to their car, one row over from me.

I slid down the upholstery, holding my breath as they passed.

Miraculously, my cover wasn't blown, and my husband escaped death.

I reminded him of this when I arrived home.

"They just wanted to buy a car," he said.

"Then, why didn't they?"

"They thought it was too much," he answered. "They were trying to lowball me."

Lowballing sounded dangerous. I made a mental note to look it up later.

"And by the way," my husband added, "Lenny has a mole shaped like Florida on the back of his neck."

I gave him a hug.

Maybe there's hope for him after all.

—January Gordon Ornellas—

65

Snaccident

I believe in a benevolent God not because
He created the Grand Canyon or Michelangelo,
but because He gave us snacks.
~Paul Rudnick

My sister's holiday feast was to die for. A cousin's delicious Death-by-Chocolate Fudge almost killed me. Starving, I sampled one piece after another. Then I recalled the trick of drinking lots of water to quell hunger pangs. Three glasses later, I helped myself to my uncle's homemade peanut brittle. Might as well enjoy. Who knows? This grandma might get run over by Santa and his sleigh on the way home.

Despite the munching, I found room for the main course, where even the vegetables were fattening. Who could resist sweet potatoes buried under mountains of marshmallows, broccoli smothered in cheddar cheese sauce, and homemade rolls dripping with honey butter? And then dessert came along and one sliver of my favorite homemade coffee cake topped with maraschino cherries quickly turned into three.

So stuffed that I could do Santa's suit justice, I was grateful when we finally moved away from the grazing table. While my elderly aunt entertained everyone with stories of the good old days, I absentmindedly reached over and grabbed a handful of nuts from the candy dish on the coffee table. When I bit down, there was a horrible crunching sound. I swallowed and worried I'd chipped a tooth. My throat burned, and tears streamed down my face.

Mustering a weak cry, I whispered, "Water! Hurry!"

My brother-in-law raced over, ready to perform the Heimlich. Waving him away, I pointed to the potpourri centerpiece as I continued to cough and sputter. To be honest, the cinnamon flavor wasn't all that bad, but I'd recommend savoring the aroma instead.

When we got ready to leave, my sister held up the potpourri and giggled. "Would you like me to package the leftovers for later?"

"No thanks. Guess I'll never live this down."

The following afternoon, my husband walked into the room just as I lifted a floral centerpiece to dust beneath it and snickered, "Snack time already?"

— Alice Muschany —

66

Out of the Closet

Nothing feels as good to me as
laughing incredibly hard.
~Steve Carell

t was a sad time for my family, but I was all right. Dad and my
brother were holding up as well as they could, and I was relieved
about that. Both of them had tender hearts, and I was more concerned about their level of grief at the loss of their wife and mother
than about my own.

I had always been the brave one in the family, so I quickly volunteered to take over the funeral arrangements for Mom. Thankfully,
Mom had spelled out her final wishes with crystal clarity down to
the last detail, including her decision for cremation. This was a first
in our family, and while I supported this decision, Mom had had a
harder time convincing Dad. Though he struggled with mixed feelings,
Dad did start to become more agreeable about the idea when Mom
framed her decision by saying that he could keep her urn at home so
she would always be near him. As far as such things go, he said he
found it a sweet thought.

While I expected to feel overwhelmed at the prospect of planning
such an event, the director at the facility we chose was so kind and
compassionate that I traded any jitters I may have had for complete
and total trust in his capabilities. So, when the gentleman told me that
our home church pastor was attending the same out-of-town confer-
ence that all Lutheran pastors in our area were attending, I had full

faith that the replacement pastor he enlisted to speak would be fine.

I was correct. Pastor Pam, a lovely Methodist minister with warm eyes sat with me prior to the service and listened as I told her about all the things that made my mother special. We spoke a bit about my home congregation and hers as well. Then I suggested some favorite scripture to be read, and she agreed to include the passage in her eulogy.

We started into the main area where the mourners had gathered. "I just want to tell you," I explained to Pastor Pam, "that my mother has been cremated. She thought it would be a comfort for my dad to have her urn nearby."

She looked at me with her understanding eyes. "Yes, we all find comfort in different ways. My husband is in the closet."

I took my seat in the front row between my brother and Dad while mulling over her comment. What a weird time to tell me her husband was in the closet. I know we had been speaking personally, but was it really the appropriate time for her to share with me that her husband was gay?

About halfway through the service, sometime during her reading of Ecclesiastes, I realized my error. Pastor Pam's husband wasn't gay. He had been cremated, too. His urn was in her closet.

I tried to force down my smile. My shoulders started to shiver. Within seconds, all the pent-up emotions I had been holding for the past week came out in a very inappropriate, uncontrollable laugh. Pastor Pam stopped. I grabbed some tissues and placed them in front of my face. She continued. Behind me, I could hear the mumbling of the other mourners.

"Oh, she's taking it hard."

"They were very close."

"It's been a tough loss."

It was awful. And it was wonderful. It felt good to know that I could still laugh.

— Monica A. Andermann —

67

Miracle at Split Rock

*Never be afraid to laugh at yourself, after all, you
could be missing out on the joke of the century.*
~Barry Humphries

S everal years ago, when the Red Hat craze was at its height, 685 Red Hatters converged on Split Rock Resort in the Pocono Mountains of Pennsylvania for the annual regional Red Hat Runaway. My best friend Peggy and I were the only ones in attendance from our chapter, the Red Hat Rascals.

In the lobby, glittery, boa-feathered women pressed ever tighter against rows of registration tables. The sponsoring chapter, Bordeaux Chapeau, was overwhelmed with the crush of red and purple womanhood.

"We need a volunteer!" shouted one of the harried Bordeaux ladies. "Help!"

I can help, I thought. *I worked registration dozens of times before I retired.*

"Me!" I cried out, waving frantically from the back of the crowd. "I'm experienced in registration. I'll help."

"I'll help, too," added my friend, Peggy.

"Hurry! Can you get through?" came the fastest job offer following the shortest job interview in history.

Peggy and I squeezed through the crowd, careful to step over the assortment of luggage, handbags, hatboxes and totes. Peggy was directed to another section of the lobby. I was placed behind the G–K registration placard.

As I welcomed each weekend celebrant, I checked her name off my master G–K list and issued her a complimentary Runaway tote bag and name badge. Throughout the afternoon, I welcomed, smiled, checked, and handed out. And I loved every second of it.

Once the crowd was processed and the stream of registrants slowed to a trickle, the grateful Bordeaux Chapeau women expressed their gratitude. I was thanked, hugged and kissed, and asked if I could come to the ballroom an hour before dinner to help set out favors, balloons and centerpieces.

How thrilling, I thought. *I'm not only attending the Runaway, but I'm helping!*

"Sure," I said.

Flushed with the excitement of the registration experience, I reunited with Peggy, who had received, numbered and arranged the huge influx of donated gift baskets that would be raffled off that weekend. Peggy and I bubbled over with stories to share about our morning's volunteer experiences. We were both psyched to be invited to help out prior to the dinner.

I noticed a crush of women in and around the bar area, each with a colorful cocktail in hand.

"Let's go to the bar," I suggested.

"Whoa," said Peggy. "You don't drink!"

"I know, but I'm so revved up," I insisted. "I think a drink is just what I need to help me relax."

"But you can't handle liquor! You never drink!"

I insisted, using the logic that since I wouldn't have to drive, one little drink couldn't possibly do any harm. My dear friend just shrugged and gave me a "we'll see about that" look. I ordered a Kahlua and Cream, a drink that does not taste boozy to me. In fact, that afternoon the mocha liquid tasted so refreshing, so cool and delicious, that I chugged it down like it was chocolate milk. Peggy was horrified.

Still thirsty, I wanted to order a second drink, but Peggy reminded me that we both had promised to help set up the Purple Pajama Party Dinner. Time was short, and there was barely time to shower and dress. *I can handle another drink!* I thought. *The first one didn't affect me in the least!* Peggy persisted. I relented. I dropped a tip on the bar, stepped off the barstool, and the room began to spin. I grabbed Peggy's arm as she shot me an "I told you so" look. With patience born of deep friendship, she took my elbow and guided me to my room. She took the key from my fumbling fingers and kindly opened the door for me.

"Don' look s-h-o worried," I slurred. "A hot s-s-s-hower, and I'll be my old s-h-elf again."

Peggy gave an encouraging smile and promised to return in forty-five minutes.

Alone in my room, I laughed at myself. *Drinking! Me? Just imagine!* I hadn't had a drink in decades—maybe twenty or thirty years. The severe dizziness had passed, but I still felt light-headed as I began to peel off clothing. I made my way into the bathroom, stepped inside a steaming shower, and pulled the glass door closed. "Ahh, a nice sh-sh-sh-shower is just what I need!"

As I lathered up, I noticed something was not quite right. I wasn't sure what it was, but everything seemed, well, brighter, lighter. I washed my arms. Things were getting... whiter! The maroon tile design was fading. *Oh my! My sight is going. There's something wrong with my eyes. I'm losing my vision!* By leg washing time, all I could see was a wall of pure white. *I'm blind, I'm blind! What did I do to myself? I had one little drink and now... I'm blind!*

I was frightened... really... seriously... genuinely frightened. *Look what I did to myself. I'm blind!* Sobs choked in my throat; tears ran down my cheeks. My hands flew up to cradle my ruined eyes.

Glasses! I was still wearing my glasses!

I wasn't blind! Miracle of miracles! My glasses had fogged up from the shower steam. I wasn't blind, just tipsy! And then the big picture hit me, and I convulsed with laughter. That one little drink *had* affected me — so much so that I'd forgotten to take off my glasses before stepping into the shower.

I was still laughing when Peggy returned. I couldn't wait to share the story with her. All weekend long, Peggy and I would break into laughter suddenly over the shower debacle. Eventually, the story of my brush with alcohol made its way around the convention crowd.

Strangers insisted I retell the story, complete with a dramatization of the fear, sobbing, and final crescendo of understanding as my hands cradled the fogged-up glasses. Everyone laughed... especially me.

It turned out to be a funny experience, but I learned a good lesson, too. Actually, I relearned an old lesson: I can't hold my alcohol. At the following year's Red Hat Runaway, I passed when everyone ordered drinks. And I had a marvelous time anyway!

—Lynne Daroff Foosaner—

68

Jazz Fans

*Passion is universal humanity. Without it religion,
history, romance and art would be useless.*
~Honoré de Balzac

I was in the parking lot of a restaurant when I overheard the conversation. "Wait a minute," said one man. "You're a jazz fan? I'm a jazz fan, too!"

"Yeah! I am a jazz fan," gushed the other. "It's so nice to meet another jazz fan. There aren't too many of us in Wisconsin!"

On and on it went, the words spilling out of their mouths like the jittery syncopation of a 1930s drummer.

"I have a jazz hat and jazz shirt at home," said the first one. "Gaaa! I wish I had worn them tonight."

I knew what "jazz hands" were. And a jazz hat was probably a fedora, I surmised.

I wondered what a jazz shirt would look like. Didn't most jazz musicians wear regular clothes?

"You know," continued the first man, "people around here don't like that I'm a jazz fan. I get a lot of grief about it."

If the place I live is particularly hostile to jazz, it was news to me. Maybe people were a little more enthusiastic for goofy polka, but were they really bullying this guy just because he liked Louis Armstrong? How awful.

"I've been following the jazz since I was a little kid," added the other guy. "Since before I could talk, I think. My whole life!"

"Me too! We should get together sometime and just talk jazz. We could have a party for jazz fans!"

That sounded awful, but I couldn't help being swept away by such passion for the arts. I've always found jazz to be the most difficult music to appreciate, with its heavy riffing building a formidable aural barrier between me and any real enjoyment of the music. But these guys were so excited! Maybe I needed to give jazz another chance.

I wondered how I should go about doing that. Were there jazz clubs in Madison, Wisconsin? Should I listen in the privacy of my own home first, just so I wouldn't be in totally over my head when I start listening to jazz around other people? Did this mean I would have to watch that 1,140-minute Ken Burns documentary about jazz in America?

The arts are like that. They can inspire and connect us. They can empower who we are and help us to become something greater. In this case, I realized that an art form had created a magical spark between two Midwesterners standing in a restaurant parking lot. It was inspiring, I thought, to see this kind of passion for music. After all, Americans these days seem to talk about only two things with any real emotion: politics and sports. It was refreshing to find this level of enthusiasm for something else.

"I love all the old jazz greats," said the first man, smiling from ear to ear. "Who's your favorite?"

I was betting he'd say something about Miles Davis. I considered walking over and telling them how much I love listening to Billie Holiday. I guess I did like some jazz, after all. Maybe I could go to their jazz party, too. Maybe we could all be friends.

As I imagined how cool I would be with my new friends and maybe even a jazz nickname the other guy responded, "It's really hard to pick just one. There are so many greats. But, of course…"

"Of course," the first guy agreed, somewhat somberly.

"But my favorite has to be 'The Mailman,'" he continued. "He was one of the all-time greats."

The Mailman! Another amazing jazz nickname, dripping with aura. And I hadn't even heard this one before. It was slightly less regal-sounding than some of the others, admittedly, but still pretty cool. He must have been some obscure bass player who performed in smoke-filled Harlem clubs full of happy, drunk people wearing pinstriped suits. Prior to this, the only Mailman I'd ever heard of who wasn't an employee of the United States Postal Service was a power forward who played basketball for the Utah Jazz when I was a kid.

Oh. Wait a minute.

"Yeah, Karl Malone was one of the best," said the other guy. "He was a scoring machine. But you can't even mention him without talking about John Stockton, too. I think he was the greatest point guard of all time."

In that moment, I realized everything I knew about their conversation was wrong. They hadn't been talking about music at all. They'd been talking about the Utah Jazz. They had been sharing their special moment about a professional basketball team.

I stood there for a moment, dazed by how endlessly wrong about the world I am. As I walked away, I burst out laughing, so happy to be alive, and pleased to be mystified and surprised at every turn.

— Matt Geiger —

Chapter

9

Child's Play

69

Going Commando

Fathering is not something perfect men do, but
something that perfects the man.
~Frank Pittman

heard the sudden crying from behind the bathroom stall. I had hoped that my then four-year-old son was ready to handle things on his own. It turned out that we were a little premature.

"What's wrong?" I asked from outside the stall door.

"My pants." He cried louder.

"What's wrong with your pants? You can't pull them up?"

More crying before the answer came. "I pooped my pants."

I started asking more questions. "Did you take off your pants before pooping? How bad is it?"

There were no answers, only wailing. "Open the door, and I'll help you." He did, greeting me with streaming eyes. I looked down. The pants and underwear were a total loss. Thank goodness we were in a bargain department store.

"Stay right here," I told him and turned around.

He started to cry harder. "Don't leave me."

"I have to go find something you can wear out of the store. You don't want to leave the store naked, do you?"

"No."

"Okay, I'll be right back with something to wear. Don't open the door for anyone but me." I raced out, trying to find the boys' department. Then I started to think about how his mom never let me pick out his clothing and how picky she was about what he wore. In fact, I didn't know what size he wore and couldn't imagine this was the time to make multiple trips in and out of the bathroom. With a beach-towel display right in front of me, I rethought my strategy, selected one with Batman on it, and raced back to the restroom entrance. The sign said, "No unpaid merchandise in the restroom," but I was certain that this was a reasonable exception.

By the time I returned to my son with the towel in hand, the crying had stopped. I announced my arrival, and he unlocked the stall door. We wiped his bottom and gathered up the clothing to throw in the trash. I showed him Batman for his approval, wrapped him in the large towel, and then lifted him in my arms while he grabbed the bundle of soiled clothing. I walked to the trashcan. "You can just throw them in," I told him.

"Can't we bring them home and wash them?"

I looked at them and tried to figure out the logistics for transporting the soiled items to the car. "No, we just have to throw them away." He dumped them in the trashcan and started to cry. "It's okay, honey," I said softly. "It's just clothing. We have more at home."

"But I'm not wearing any underwear," he sobbed. As a parent, I knew this was one of the smallest problems he would ever face in life. But for him, at that time, this was big. And my son was crying. It broke my heart to see him so upset. So I thought up a solution.

"Would it help if I took off my underwear and threw it away?"

His sobbing stopped suddenly and he nodded with tear remnants still running down his cheeks. So I put him down, kicked off my shoes, yanked down my pants, stripped off my underwear and redressed. I held the underwear out over the trashcan and asked, "Is this better?" He nodded again.

Just before I was able to release my hold on my tighty-whities, a guy about twice my size entered the bathroom and stared at me holding my underwear over the trash can as I announced, "Bye-bye, underwear." He rolled his eyes and walked toward an empty stall.

"He had an accident and…" I started to explain, but he walked quickly into the stall and engaged the lock. I realized that I was now one of those "People at Walmart" stories everyone shares over the Internet.

"Come on, we need to go," I said. I lifted my son into my arms again and headed for the checkout register. I set him on the conveyer. "We're buying the towel," I told the cashier. She gave me a look to which I felt obligated to reply, "We had an accident."

She smiled at my son. And for the first time since the incident, he smiled back. "We're both commando," he informed her. "My daddy threw away his underwear, too. We had an accident."

Her smile faded quickly, and I realized that using the royal "we" is a habit both he and I needed to end immediately. I grabbed my son and walked quickly out the door.

While I was strapping him into his car seat, he said, "I was sad about throwing away my pants, but now I'm okay. Can I keep the towel?" I told him he could.

He smiled again and got past the embarrassment much faster than I did. I am still wondering how many months it will take before the cashier won't recognize me when I set foot in the store again.

And then, without warning, I heard the four words that make my day magic. I will remember them far longer than the embarrassment from the bathroom or at the register. "I love you, Daddy."

— Gary Zenker —

70

The Family Business

A cousin is a little bit of childhood
that can never be lost.
~Marion C. Garretty

While I was growing up, my cousin and I always spent the month of August at our grandparents' cottage on the shore of Lake Ontario in upstate New York. Throughout the summer, the whole family — uncles, aunts, spouses and assorted cousins — would converge on the cottage at various times. My father always avowed that my mom's family was like an old string of Christmas lights: "Half the time they don't work, most of them are pretty dim, and they just keep getting all tangled up together." However, I always remember my visits being full of adventures, especially one hot, muggy Saturday morning in 1970.

Sitting on the porch, my cousin and I complained we were bored. We wanted to ride our bikes to the movie theater in town to see the newly released cinematic classic, *Beneath the Planet of the Apes*. Unfortunately, between us we had a total of forty-seven cents. Back in those days, a matinee movie cost seventy-five cents — a deal compared to the $1.75 price of an evening show — but still unaffordable with our feeble finances.

"You could earn some money," suggested Grandpa. "When I was your age, I sold bait to the fishermen. There's bound to be fishermen going down the road to the marina. They'll need bait."

"You mean bait… like worms?" I asked.

"Not worms, tadpoles." Grandpa pointed to the east side of the cottage. "Over in the marshy area, beyond that willow tree, there used to be swarms of tadpoles in the muck. I would scoop them up, put them in cups and sell them at the end of the driveway to fishermen."

"People paid you?" my cousin asked, disbelieving.

Grandpa nodded. "Yep, fishermen told me tadpoles made the best bait. Better than worms."

My cousin and I were desperate, so we donned our boots and headed out beyond the willow tree. Gently, I scooped an old butterfly net through the murky water, capturing a surprising number of tadpoles with each pass. Then I dumped the tiny, squirming creatures into a water-filled bucket held by my cousin.

"Yuck," he whispered, being quiet so as not to startle our prey. "It's hard to believe these gross things turn into frogs."

"Well, for us," I replied, "they're going to turn into money."

After we had captured what we thought was a good supply, we took the bucket of tadpoles back to the garage. We set out Dixie Cups on a tray, filled them with murky, brown water and carefully dumped a few tadpoles into each one.

Then we set up a card table and two folding chairs at the end of the driveway. Carefully, I carried the tray full of Dixie Cups out to the table.

With some paint and an old piece of cardboard, my cousin created a sign: 10 CENTS A CUP. He taped it to the table.

We were open for business.

We sat together at the table as the sun beat down and the dark, brown water in the cups grew still — though not as still as the traffic on the road. After a half-hour, not one car had passed by.

"Where are all the fishermen?" grumbled my cousin.

"Probably at the theater watching *Beneath the Planet of the Apes*," I answered sarcastically.

Another thirty minutes crept past. One pickup truck passed by, but it didn't even slow to inspect our merchandise. It just sped along, showering us with dust.

We both sighed loudly.

Just then, we heard something coming down the road. Not a motorized vehicle, it was a man on a bicycle.

Smiling at us, the man stopped and straddled his bike.

"Got a little business going here, huh?" he said.

My cousin and I nodded.

"Ten cents a cup, huh?" the man asked.

We nodded again.

The man reached into his pocket, pulled out a dime and handed it to me.

"You want a cup?" I asked. I had no idea what a man on a bicycle was going to do with a cup of fishing bait. Was he riding to the marina to fish?

"Sure, one cup," the man responded.

Still straddling his bicycle, the man reached over, picked up a cup and held it up in front of him for a moment.

Then he tipped the cup to his mouth and drank the contents in one large gulp.

My cousin and I were speechless. We stared silently, wide-eyed.

The man smacked his lips and shook his head. "Wow," he said. "You need to add some more sugar or something. That's lousy iced tea."

"Okay," I said.

"Have a good day," he shouted as he rode away.

Within ten minutes, we had put away the table and chairs, dumped what was in the Dixie Cups back into the swampy area, and tore up the 10 CENTS A CUP sign, stuffing it in the trashcan.

My cousin and I never did see *Beneath the Planet of the Apes* that summer.

— David Hull —

71

Sunday Morning Smiles

*Laughter is, after speech, the chief
thing that holds society together.*
~Max Eastman

Every Sunday morning, I enjoyed attending religious services at a small chapel located in a nearby hospital. It was quaint, quiet and beautiful. Magnificent stained-glass windows and stately life-sized statues encircled the sanctuary. I knew the people who attended on a first-name basis, including the chaplains on staff. It provided me with comfort and a sense of wellbeing.

Our firstborn, Danielle, accompanied us to mass, attended weddings, and delighted in looking at all of the artistry throughout the chapel. After her little brother, Zachary, was born, he accompanied us on many of our religious outings as well.

One Sunday morning in May, Danni and I prepared to attend services. Zack was not feeling well, so he had to stay home with Dad. It was a mother/daughter adventure! She had just turned four, and little did I know that even though the terrible twos had passed rather uneventfully, I was about to be introduced to the formidable fours!

The chapel was unusually crowded that morning. All of the seats were taken, so we stood in the back. For some reason, the service was longer than usual, and I could tell that Danni was starting to get fidgety. I picked her up, hoping that she would be more comfortable in my arms. She curled up against me and laid her head on my shoulder. Her sweetness always warmed my heart.

I just happened to be standing directly in front of an exquisitely sculpted, life-sized figure of Jesus on the cross. Danielle had been fascinated by it on previous visits to the chapel. Now she was in a position to examine it more closely.

I felt her reaching out to touch it. At first, she seemed to be fascinated with the slick texture as she gently slid her tiny hand back and forth on the base of the statue. Then she leaned her head back, gazing up at it. I heard her mumble, "Hi, Jesus!"

I thought about what a little darling she was, giving her an extra squeeze. But then her inquisitive nature took charge. She wriggled in my arms, so I readjusted my stance. I could feel her reaching out with a fierce determination. Since I did not want her to interrupt any of the prayers and thoughts of the nearby worshippers, I held her a bit tighter. Big mistake! She had her own agenda.

"Mommy!" she said in a commanding, but still adorable, voice. The woman standing next to me smiled warmly at her. "Mommy, look!" I turned to see what was on her mind while fruitlessly asking her to whisper.

She seemed to be trying to lift something. But what was it? Suddenly, it hit me! The intricately carved cloth draped over Jesus was filled with ridges and rivulets that mesmerized her. She wanted to rearrange it, or so I thought.

At that moment the music stopped playing and the congregation became silent. That was the perfect time for my precocious daughter to ask in her loudest voice: "Mommy! Is Jesus like Zachary? Mommy, does Jesus have a penis?"

All heads turned in our direction, including that of one of my favorite chaplains, Brother Matthew. I panicked, attempting to shush Danielle and fade into the background as much as possible.

However, my determined daughter was not to be ignored. "Well, does He?" she blurted out. "Mommy, DOES HE?"

I looked sheepishly toward Brother Matthew, silently praying for immediate forgiveness. A compassionate smile appeared on his face. He knew our family well, and we had received personal blessings from him in the past. Boy, did I need one now!

I glanced around and realized that most of the people were making a valiant effort to control their laughter, including the chaplain. His smile grew even bigger as he spoke directly to me.

"Gail," he quipped quietly, winking at both of us. "Your daughter is waiting for an answer."

Breathing a sigh of relief and giving my strong-willed firstborn a hug, I whispered in her ear, "Yes, Danielle. I suppose He does."

— Gail Gabrielle —

72

The Revolving Door

Luck's a revolving door. You just need to know when it's
your turn to walk through.
~Stan Lee

We were living in Istanbul because my dad worked as a financial advisor for the United States Agency for International Development. It was the early 1960s and there were no telephones or televisions. One of the ways I kept busy was collecting autographs. With my sister Sue's help, I had collected autographs from six of the seven original U.S. astronauts, a U.S. five-star general, and Turkey's famous singer at the time, Zeki Müran.

When we learned that Vice President Lyndon Johnson and his family were visiting Turkey and staying at the Istanbul Hilton, Dad suggested we greet the Vice President on his arrival. Securing Vice President Johnson's signature in my 4½x6-inch brown autograph book would be a thrill.

We arrived early to get a good spot from which to see the Johnsons. Diplomatic ties between the United States and Turkey were strong, and crowds gathered in front of the Hilton to see the American dignitaries. Turkey's fourth president, Cemal Gürsel, greeted the Johnsons at Yeşilköy Airport that morning, and then their motorcade paraded through Istanbul's cobblestone streets.

Later in the afternoon, the Johnsons arrived at the hotel on schedule. I watched as the Vice President's open green Cadillac convertible pulled up to the front entrance of the Hilton.

The driver hopped out, ran around to the back right door and helped Lady Bird Johnson out of the limo. The Johnsons' two daughters, Luci Baines and Lynda Bird, were next, followed by their father. The tall, lanky Vice President waved as he stepped onto the sidewalk.

Mrs. Johnson, dressed in a light blue suit with a white blouse, strolled by, and I managed to squeeze my arm through the crowd and shake her hand. She waved and smiled, but moved a little too fast for me to ask for an autograph.

Mrs. Johnson impressed me. She enjoyed greeting and talking to those who had come out to say hello. Her two daughters were behind her, smiling and waving.

"Here comes Vice President Johnson. Get up close for his autograph," said Dad.

The Vice President looked like a giant to me. For such a tall man, he radiated a certain grace. Dressed in a black linen suit, white shirt and tie, he gave his trademark wide smile as he approached the hotel's revolving doors.

Just as Vice President Johnson pushed on the revolving glass door, my dad shoved me between Secret Service agents so I could get his autograph. Not prepared for the unexpected push from behind, I tripped and stumbled directly behind the Vice President. As I tumbled into the revolving door area, my back foot kicked up a small hotel welcome mat behind me. Somehow, the welcome mat wedged itself under the revolving door. The door jammed in such a way that it was impossible for me to squeeze back outside or into the lobby. LBJ and I were trapped inside the revolving door together.

As I gazed up at the Vice President, he looked exactly like his pictures in newspapers and magazines. His long, lined face was dominated by a rather large nose, a strong cleft chin, and oversized protruding ears.

I looked behind me past the glass doors outside. Sue stood on the sidewalk, with her mouth open and her hands smashed up against her cheeks. She looked like she was in a trance, staring directly at me with wide eyes and raised eyebrows.

Ahead of me in the lobby, Luci Baines and Lynda Bird laughed while Lady Bird smiled and shook her head. As Secret Service agents yanked at the mat and pushed against the revolving door, I asked LBJ for his autograph.

"Well, sure, honey," the Vice President said. "You certainly have a way of making an entrance."

I handed him my autograph book. He began to sign his name, but my pen ran out of ink about halfway through his signature. He pulled out his own pen from an inside jacket pocket and started over.

"There you go," said Johnson. "Looks like we might be stuck in here for a while. We should have brought a snack."

As I looked out over the crowd through the revolving glass doors, Dad was nowhere to be found. The Secret Service managed to dislodge the welcome mat from underneath the revolving door, but not without tearing it to shreds. The revolving door spun around, opening into the hotel.

"Well, you have a real nice day," said Vice President Johnson, shaking my hand. "And you might want to stay clear of revolving doors," he added with a laugh. The Vice President had the biggest grin on his face as he gave me a wave and was escorted away with his family.

If that had happened today, my family would probably be thrown in jail. But in 1962, life was good, security was lax, and everyone had a good laugh. I still have LBJ's autograph — written one and a half times.

— Maureen C. Bruschi —

Busted

Heredity is what sets the parents of a teenager
wondering about each other.
~Laurence J. Peter

I was bored, immature and a little mischievous. Inevitably, if you mix those three qualities within one teenage boy, his mind will travel to inappropriate places. At least, mine did.

It all started one day when I came home from school and found a brand-new set of license plates on our kitchen table. Dad had recently bought a car, and the plates had come in the mail. I scanned the bold, black letters and chuckled to myself.

TTT 8039. I wondered what it would be like if that middle "T" were actually an "I."

As soon as the idea hit me, I made a beeline for the junk drawer. I grabbed black duct tape, a ruler and scissors.

First, I measured the top part of the letter T. Then I cut the tape to the exact size. Finally, I positioned the small piece of tape under the middle letter T. I smiled, admiring my workmanship. Leaving the plates on the table, I looked forward to my dad's reaction.

That night, we went to church — a requirement for all pastors' kids. Afterward, we went out for pizza. Meanwhile, I waited for Dad to comment on my handiwork. He never did.

A few days later, I noticed the license plates on the car, but the tape had disappeared. I could only assume one thing: Before Dad had a chance to see it, Mom had spotted my minor modification, ripped off the tape and prayed for her poor, wayward son.

Eventually, curiosity got the best of me. I questioned my mom.

"I did something to Dad's license plates. Did he ever say anything about it?"

Her eyes widened, and her mouth dropped. "You did that?" She bent over with laughter.

I nodded, perplexed. Why was she laughing—and not yelling—at me? She struggled to catch her breath.

"Your dad came home, glanced at the plates and was completely horrified. He scooped them up, drove across town and marched into the DMV."

She dabbed at her eyes as she continued. "He told the man at the counter, 'I can't accept these. I am a pastor. I can't drive around town with this on my car.' Finally, the DMV guy took a closer look and discovered the tape."

Uh-oh. I was busted, at least I thought I was. But Mom was still laughing. "So your dad asked the guy, 'Who in the world would put tape on my plates?'"

The DMV guy came up with the only logical explanation. "These license plates are made at the prison. I'm sure one of the inmates was messing around and thought it would be funny."

My dad didn't think it was funny, but Mom found it hilarious. Meanwhile, some poor prisoner got blamed for my mischief.

—Curt Zeck—

Just Wondering

*There are no seven wonders of the world in the eyes
of a child. There are seven million.*
~Walt Streightiff

One Easter, my husband and I were feeling brave... or was it adventurous? We had accepted an invitation from his parents for an Easter family gathering that would begin with taking our four sons to their very formal church.

With four boys, church was always interesting, even with our church's laidback worship service and children's church, which was in the basement. Taking them to my in-laws' church was daunting. Their service was so different from ours.

Our church was open and airy, with chairs; theirs had dark, polished wood with detailed carvings and wooden pews. In their service, congregants stood and sat, stood and sat, and then repeated. The choir had robes, as did the pastor. While Mitchell, Andrew, and Jacob had seen this before, my youngest, Frazier, who was four, couldn't remember attending there. I was sure he would have lots of questions. I began prepping Frazier because I wanted to make a good impression on my mother-in-law and her friends.

All we had to do was get through an hour. One hour. It started out well. During the children's part of the service, all four of my spit-shined boys walked down the aisle in their Sunday best and took a seat in the front row with the other children. The pastor sat down in his long, black robe.

My guys were great. They listened to the story, answered questions, and were very gracious when the pastor gave them a treat. Then the pastor held the microphone and asked, "Did all of you understand the lesson?"

Heads bobbed in affirmation.

He spoke into the microphone again. "Does anyone have any questions?"

All the children shook their heads, except Frazier. His little hand shot straight into the air.

"Yes, son?" The pastor seemed genuinely thrilled that someone had a question. He held the microphone in front of Frazier.

Frazier leaned in to the mic. "Are you wearing pants under that robe?"

The church fell silent for a moment, and then exploded in laughter.

The pastor didn't miss a beat. "Yep, I sure am."

The children walked back. My four slid into the pew, including little Frazier who still had the church laughing with his innocent question.

I sneaked a glance at my mother-in-law. She, too, was laughing. She turned around, ruffled Frazier's hair, and said, "That was the best children's message ever. I've always wondered the same thing."

— Lisa McCaskill —

My First Confession

The innocence of children is what makes them stand
out as a shining example to the rest of Mankind.
~Kurt Chambers

"Bless me, Father, for I have sinned. This is my first confession."

"What sins do you wish to confess?"

After a long pause, "I broke the Seventh Commandment."

"Do you know what the Seventh Commandment is?"

Father Murphy is trying not to laugh. A child's first confession is serious business.

He waits and listens.

"Yes, Father, I do."

"Whom did you break the Seventh Commandment with?"

"Oh, Father, it wasn't a 'who.' It was the gumball machine outside Sam's candy store on Rogers Avenue. The penny was stuck in the slot; I just turned the knob, and out came a red gumball. It wasn't exactly stealing, but I don't think I have broken any of the other commandments. I'm only seven years old. I haven't lived long enough. Maybe as I get older, I'll have more sins to confess. But right now, the Seventh Commandment is the only one I've broken."

Behind the sliding door of the confessional, I hear Father Murphy laughing, and I'm sure that the people waiting in line for confession can hear him. He gives me absolution and tells me, "For your penance, say three Hail Marys and one Our Father… and you might want to review the Ten Commandments."

I leave the confessional and can still hear his laughter. I should have asked him what was so funny, but I'm shy. I replay what I said to Father Murphy in my mind, but I don't find anything laughable about what I confessed. I dip my index finger into the holy-water fountain, genuflect and exit the church. I thought I would feel different after my first confession, closer to God, but the only thing I feel is hungry.

When I get home, my mother asks me, "How was your first confession?"

I tell her proudly, "I told the priest that I broke the Seventh Commandment with a gumball machine."

My mother's eyes get very large, and she asks me, "What Commandment did you tell Father Murphy you broke?"

"The Seventh Commandment. You know, the one that says, 'Thou shalt not steal.'"

When I tell my mother, she smiles and begins laughing but hugs me immediately. "Did you get absolution?"

"Yes, and for penance he only gave me three Hail Marys and one Our Father. He also said I should study the Commandments. I even remembered to go up to the altar to say my penance."

"That's great. I am so proud of you. But I think Father Murphy may be right — you need to brush up on the Ten Commandments."

Later, I hear my mother talking to my father.

"I can't imagine what Father Murphy thought."

"Shush! Lower your voice. She'll hear you."

He continues, "I'm sure it was the most original first confession he has ever heard. I think we should tell her."

"I don't have the heart to tell her. She is so proud of herself, even if Father Murphy couldn't stop laughing. No worries… He gave her absolution, so she'll make her First Holy Communion tomorrow morning. Everything is fine. Promise me, Al, you won't say a word."

"I promise."

Later, I ask my mom, "Why do you think Father Murphy was laughing?"

"I have no idea. Finish your snack, and I'll set your hair for tomorrow."

It's Sunday morning, the day of my First Holy Communion. I put on my white lace dress and veil. My parents take lots of pictures, and I feel like a princess. The church is crowded and filled with flowers. The choir is singing, and the sun is streaming through the stained-glass windows.

The First Holy Communion wafer — the body of Christ — sticks to the roof of my mouth and takes forever to melt. It is a strange sensation.

We have a small party with all the relatives. It is a great day.

A few years later, I realized I had confessed to breaking the Seventh Commandment — Thou shalt not commit adultery — with a gumball machine. It was violating the Eighth Commandment — Thou shalt not steal — that I should have confessed. I was so nervous that I got confused.

I am grateful now that I was too young to know what I confessed and that my parents never told me.

No wonder Father Murphy couldn't stop laughing!

— Phyllis Reilly —

76

Do You Have Jesus?

Simple moments with your grandchildren
often become priceless moments.
~Author Unknown

"**G**rammy, do you have Jesus?"

The question came from the mouth of my two-year-old grandson. I paused, thinking of a correct way to answer him. I was especially concerned with the repercussions from his non-churchgoing parents. Avoidance was my immediate choice.

"Does Daddy have Jesus?" I asked.

"No, he does not." (Samson always spoke in complete sentences.)

"Does Mommy have Jesus?"

"No. She says she is 'piritual.'" (Samson did not pronounce "s" blends.)

Then, thankfully, his two-year-old mind was off to another venture. I had successfully diverted the Jesus conversation.

That evening at dinner with his parents, I spilled the Jesus story, indicating my complete innocence. I definitely did not introduce the topic. Peter and Jessica laughed, telling me that Samson had been saying parts of prayers and blessings. Maybe he'd learned them from a friend or the playgroup he went to once a week. They said he's been asking them about Jesus, too.

Several days later, I saw Samson again.

"Grammy, do you have Jesus?"

Knowing I was off the hook with his parents, I decided to do some investigative questioning.

"Do you have Jesus, Samson?"

"No, I do not."

"Do you know someone who has Jesus?"

"Yes, I do, Grammy. Maggie has Jesus."

"Where would Jesus be?"

I expected him to say "in my heart" or something profound. (He was a most intelligent two-year-old.) He slid off my lap and went to the kitchen. I followed.

"Jesus might be there," he said, pointing to the breadbox. "Or there," he commented, pointing to the cupboard.

I was onto something now.

"What does Jesus look like?"

He paused.

"Jesus is orange and… quare." (Missing the "s" on square.)

I paused and smiled. Mystery solved.

"Cheez-Its?"

"Yes, Grammy. I would like Jesus. Do you have Jesus?"

"No, but I have some Goldfish crackers. Would that work?"

— Joan Dubay —

Chapter 10

Not What I Meant!

77

Kauai Kaffee Kaper

There's nothing like coffee to help you espresso yourself.
~Amy Newmark

W e were living on the island of Kauai, part of the Hawaiian Islands and known for its endless natural beauty. People from all over the world travel there to hike its trails, see its natural waterfalls, and enjoy the secluded beaches. "It's so beautiful and feels like paradise!" they say.

Many visitors to the island say they could live there forever. That's how we felt, too. When we became empty nesters, we moved from Chicago to invest in and manage a small, oceanfront hotel on Kauai. We were living out our dream — "in paradise" — from a 700-square-foot manager's apartment.

Having never managed a hotel before, we were in for a lot of surprises. Ours was the oldest operating hotel on the island. Its two-story main building had sixteen guest rooms and was constructed of solid cinderblock. It had withstood two hurricanes over its sixty-year lifespan.

After two months as on-site property managers, we began to look for hidden cameras throughout the property, as we honestly thought we were part of a television reality show. In the first two weeks, the pool pumps failed, the hot-water tank stopped working, and we learned there was a gas leak in the electrical room adjacent to our bedroom! Despite the initial challenges, we prevailed and celebrated the re-opening under new management with a native "blessing ceremony."

The traditional island language and culture were getting easier to understand and respect.

Because Hawaii is a destination for travelers from all over the world, we realized quickly how much we had in common and yet how much there is to learn from one another. On occasion, we would have guests with limited knowledge of the English language visit the island. At the time, we relied upon the universal "mimicking" gestures of sleep, eat, swim, boat, plane, tummy, vomit, bandage, fork, knife, soap, shampoo, hair dryer, towels and, most importantly, toilet paper.

We took great pride in understanding the needs of an international guest, but from time to time, it wasn't easy and could easily turn into a comedy of misunderstandings.

On one such occasion, I was standing outside the front office door as a guest came toward me with a concerned look on his face.

"*Esgibteinhamburgerinderkaffeekanne*," he said in German.

I returned his look of concern and said, "Pardon?"

He repeated the sentence and then seemed to think if he slowed down and said it louder, I would naturally understand. "*Esgibteinhamburgerinderkaffeekanne!*"

At this point, I thought I was clearly hearing "hamburger," and I was pretty sure that I was understanding the word "café," so I replied, "Ah! Sooo, hamburger and café?"

He nodded his head up and down, so I assumed he was looking for a café that served hamburgers. "Oh, yes, of course!" I smiled and then pointed to a restaurant across the street from the hotel while I said, "Hamburger café over there!"

"No, no!" he replied in a tone that, if translated, might have meant, "No, that's not what I'm saying, and is there anyone on this island who might possibly understand me?" This time, he repeated it more fervently, "*Esgibteinhamburgerinderkaffeekanne*." He made an even more pointed gesture toward his hotel room. Clearly, he did not want a café that served hamburgers, but he was still pointing toward his hotel room. Did his wife want some coffee with her hamburger?

Wanting desperately to help this poor man, I was fairly certain I now knew what he wanted and said, "Ah! You need coffee for your coffeemaker!" Hoping that we were getting closer to understanding what he needed, I mimicked a coffeepot being poured, along with a hopeful expression on my face.

"No… no…" he said in an even slower voice, but this time it appeared he might have a slight smile on his face. He said, "*Esgibteinhamburgerinderkaffeekanne*" and slowly repeated the word "hamburger" while mimicking eating a sandwich, followed by the word "*kaffeekanne*" while mimicking a coffeepot being poured, and again pointed to his guest room.

Now staring at him with a hopeful expression, I said in a slow voice, hoping that I was translating correctly, "Hmmm… so… hamburger (as I mimicked a sandwich) and café?" (as I mimicked sipping a cup of coffee).

"No…" he said as he now mimicked a coffeepot being poured, "*Kaffeekanne, kaffeekanne!*" He then repeated, "Hamburger" followed by "*kaffeekanne*" while mimicking a sandwich going into a pot of coffee.

This is crazy, I thought. Is he telling me he wants to pour coffee on his hamburger?

Just then, the housekeeping supervisor walked past and overheard our conversation. After a few minutes, she was scratching her head in disbelief and suggested that we all go to his room and solve the mystery.

The man agreed quickly and led us to his room. After opening the door, he pointed to his coffee machine. I walked over to see a perfectly normal hotel coffeemaker. Seeing that we were both still very confused, he walked over and opened the lid of the coffeemaker's water reservoir. Much to our surprise, there was a half-eaten McDonald's hamburger in the reservoir. It had been left by the previous guest, who was traveling with a mischievous toddler who was probably trying to hide his half-eaten dinner!

We all had a good, hearty laugh, and the guest slowly repeated "*Es gibt ein Hamburger in der Kaffeekanne*," which we finally understood means "There is a hamburger in the coffeepot."

— Karen Blair —

78

Not So Reserved

It's clearly more fun to make the rules
than to follow them.
~Seth Godin

I was excited that our library had finished installation of a drive-up window. Now I could reserve books online and then drive up and have them handed to me like fast food. It would be a great timesaver, especially since I spend way too much time browsing when I go inside.

I had a couple of books reserved, so I drove up alongside the library to the window and pressed a button to alert the library staff I was there. A young male librarian came to the window.

"Hello," I said. "I have some reserves to pick up." I held out my library card to the guy. He took it and scanned it.

"Did you call in advance?" he said.

"No."

"You're supposed to call in advance if you want to use the drive-up window so we can have your items ready." He handed my library card back to me. Then he just stood there looking at me. He was definitely not getting my books.

"I was unaware of that policy," I said. "Could you make an exception for me today?"

"I'm sorry," he said. "I'm supposed to follow policy. There's a flyer inside, and an e-mail was sent out for the proper procedure for using the drive-up. You have to call the number." He handed me a flyer with the information.

"Call this number on here?" I said, pointing to the sheet.

"Yes."

I picked up my cell phone and dialed the number. The telephone right inside the drive-up window rang. The young librarian picked up the phone.

"Hello," he said, staring directly at me.

"Hello," I said. "My name is Justin Hunter, and I would like to use the drive-up window to pick up my library reserves."

"I will have them ready for you," he said. "Goodbye."

"Goodbye," I said. I ended the call on my cell. He hung up the phone.

I reached over and pushed the drive-up bell.

"Hello," I said to the librarian's unsmiling face. "I'm here to pick up some reserves." I handed him my library card again. He scanned it.

"Did you call in advance?" he asked.

"I sure did."

He left and came back with my books, scanned them and handed them to me.

"Have a nice day," he said.

"Thank you!" I said and drove off.

I went to the library the next week, and there was a large sign with bold red letters under the drive-up window. It said: ALL PATRONS MUST CALL THIRTY MINUTES BEFORE PICKING UP RESERVES AT DRIVE-UP.

The same librarian and I had another genteel run-in about a month after that. I had a book that I wasn't quite able to finish before its due date. I tried renewing the book online, but I wasn't allowed to. I went to the library and brought the book to the counter. My nemesis was there.

"Hello," I said.

"Hello."

"I have a book here that I want to check out again," I said, handing him the book.

"I see," he said. "This book is part of our 'Most Wanted' selection.

It cannot be renewed. I have to check it back in."

"Okay," I said. "How about you check it back in and then check it right back out to me?"

"I can't do that. I have to check it in and put it back on the 'Most Wanted' shelf."

"Okay," I said.

He checked in the book, tucked it under his arm, and began walking to the "Most Wanted" shelves. I followed him. He looked over his shoulder every few steps. When we arrived at our destination, we just stood there for a moment. Then he put the book on the shelf. I took it off and walked back to the checkout.

"This is an egregious use of the 'Most Wanted' section," he said.

"I am a bad man," I said.

—Justin Hunter—

79

Booking Fiasco

Thank you for calling customer service. If you're calm
and rational, press 1. If you're a whiner, press 2.
If you're a hot head, press 3.
~Randy Glasbergen

I was going to a seminar about five hundred miles from my home and was making a reservation with a large hotel chain. I wanted to guarantee the room with a credit card so they wouldn't give away my room if I arrived late.

I had just applied for a Visa card, and I had to call the issuing bank to activate the card. The card company asked me questions that only I knew the answer to so that if the card was stolen, the thief wouldn't know the answers. They were questions like, "What is your mother's maiden name?" "What was your first car?" and "What is your pet's name?"

Later, when I got on the phone with the lady who was taking my information for a room reservation, she had her own questions for me.

"How many nights will you be staying?"

"Two nights."

"Do you want a poolside room?"

"That won't be necessary."

"Would you like your room guaranteed for late arrival?"

"Yes, please."

"I will need a major credit card for the guarantee, sir."

"Of course. My card number is 1234-5678-9012-3456."

"What is the expiration date?" I gave her the expiration date, and then she asked, "What is the name exactly as it appears on the card?"

"Douglas D. Sletten."

So far, so good. But then our conversation began to deteriorate. Her next question was, "And you're Doug?"

What I heard, however, was, "And your dog?"

Instead of answering, "Yes, I am Doug," I thought she was asking one of those questions to which only I knew the answer, so I gave her the name of my dog.

So, let's pick up the conversation where it started to go wrong:

"And your dog?"

"Oscar."

"Oscar who."

"Oscar Meyer."

"Well, who will be staying in the room?"

"I will."

"Well, then, will Mr. Sletten be in the same room?"

"Of course. That's why I am calling."

"Well, then, Mr. Meyer, will you be sharing the room with Mr. Sletten?"

"What are you talking about? I am Mr. Sletten."

"Then who is this Mr. Meyer?"

"There is no Mr. Meyer."

"If you and Mr. Meyer are going to be sharing a room, I have to let the hotel know that it is double occupancy."

"What Mr. Meyer? Do you mean Oscar?"

"Yes."

"Oscar is my dog!"

"Well, what does your dog have to do with this?"

"Not a #%#&!#* thing, lady! You're the one who asked about the dog!"

"I could care less about your dog, sir. And on second checking, I find that we have no rooms available. We are booked solid. Good day, sir."

I skipped the seminar.

— Doug Sletten —

Trick or Treat

You don't stop laughing because you grow old.
You grow old because you stop laughing.
~Michael Pritchard

n the early 1990s, Central Washington University was filled with students sporting perfect skin, gel-spiked hair, and high hopes. And then there was me, a single mom pushing forty, striving for a degree that promised to pay the bills.

College life as a mom with a full-time job and a long list of creditors was not exactly social. And I grew used to the groans and eye rolls when the professors would slide me into a group project. I learned to show grace when asked the burning question on my classmates' minds: "How old are you?"

I didn't have time to bother with their issues concerning my age. Thus, we settled into our roles, side by side, avoiding contact beyond a polite nod. Normal days dragged on with deficits of sleep, money, and time for taking care of myself. Extraordinary days, like mid-finals, left me vulnerable to the flu of the moment. One such day, I landed in the on-campus free medical clinic.

I was ravenously hungry and so grateful when I saw a huge bowl of colorful cellophane-wrapped candy in the center of a table in the lobby. I grabbed fistfuls of the rainbow of choices: red, green, blue, yellow.

Back in my chair, I placed the pile of candy in my lap, choosing red for my first indulgence. Fumbling with the package, I felt stares, the kind that make one check for open buttons or trailing toilet paper.

Victorious over the stubborn packaging, I popped the promise of sweet in my mouth. I was expecting hard candy, but I found it was chewy like a gummy bear. A few chuckles rose as I spat out the flavorless, rubbery candy.

That's when I realized what I'd done. There in my lap was a pile of condoms. Now the unnoticed sign on the bowl flashed like a Vegas billboard.

"FREE Condoms — Safe Sex."

I heard my name. I stuffed the two dozen condoms in my pockets and followed the nurse from the lobby. Before disappearing, with no way out of the embarrassing dilemma, I decided to own it, shooting a smile and a wink to my mesmerized fans.

— Deb Palmer —

Love Thy Neighbor

The embarrassment of a situation can, once you are
over it, be the funniest time in your life.
~Miranda Hart

It was early, and I hadn't had my coffee. I stood barefoot on the front step of my home, looking to the driveway as my husband loaded our three kids into the car to head to school. I called out last-minute encouragement to the kids to do their best and have a good day.

Meanwhile, my next-door neighbor of eleven years — Jim, a nice man with two grown children — started backing down his driveway, presumably headed to his job as a physician's assistant. As Jim pulled into the street, I did the neighborly thing and waved to him. At the same time, I called out loudly to my husband and kids, "Bye! I love you!"

I smiled as my neighbor turned to look at me and waved. Then my stomach sank, and my face grew hot. The window of his blue minivan was open. Embarrassment turned to a good laugh as the lesson sank in: Always be friendly, but be more careful with multi-person farewells.

Then again, maybe Jim needed a loving send-off, too.

— Heather Norman Smith —

Shortcut to Disaster

When we can begin to take our failures non-seriously,
it means we are ceasing to be afraid of them. It is of
immense importance to learn to laugh at ourselves.
~Katherine Mansfield

In 1974, my college campus was filled with uniformly "nonconforming" males and females clad in T-shirts and worn jeans. Against that backdrop, Luis's entrance into my film class was nothing short of revolutionary.

With all the confidence of John Travolta's swagger in *Saturday Night Fever*, Luis invaded my world. His thick, dark hair had an impressive sheen that hinted at professional care, and his bright hazel eyes offered intensity rarely glimpsed in the frat boys who surrounded me. He offered his 500-watt, whiter-than-white smile like a movie star.

His starched white shirt seemed tailor-made and his slim black pants and leather shoes completed the outfit that set him 180 degrees apart from his classmates. I found myself staring helplessly. He looked like the hero from the cover of a romance novel. Instantly, I decided that I would become his real-life love interest.

After class, I managed to "accidentally" bump into him in the quad. He seemed as eager as I was to begin a conversation. Over an orange freeze, I learned that he was a foreign-exchange student from Guadalajara, Mexico.

His family owned a plantation there. This explained his style of dress and added one more thing to my list of adorable Luis traits: his softly accented voice.

All went well between us, and soon we were dating steadily. Language was no barrier as he was determined to perfect his English.

We might have lived happily ever after if his three sisters, who spoke little English, hadn't decided to visit. By that time, I was madly in love with Luis and determined to make a good impression on his family. The only problem was that I was too busy with my classes and part-time job to take a Spanish class. Instead, I decided to take the Spanish-English cognate shortcut.

I discovered that I could add a vowel to the end of many American words and voilà! Instantly, it became Spanish. Thus active was *activo*, ranch was *rancho*, habit was *habito*, and abrupt was *abrupto*. I should also have known that stupid was *estupido*, and I was about to become an *estupendo estupido* very *rapido!*

When his sisters arrived, I was invited to dinner at Luis's apartment. I thought the dinner went well since the three girls continually returned my friendly smiles. Little was said, and no one seemed to find the silence awkward.

Then Luis excused himself from the table to go to the restroom. Though his absence couldn't have exceeded two minutes, the companionable silence we'd enjoyed throughout the meal took an ominous turn. With three sets of eyes focused on me, I felt compelled to speak.

I chose to play it safe by simply complimenting the fine meal they'd made. "*Me gusta dinero*," I said, beaming at each girl in turn.

The gentle traces of their former smiles completely evaporated with my final syllable. The oldest folded her arms across her chest in the international symbol for contempt.

Confused, I decided to try again. This time, with feeling and enthusiasm, I repeated in a slightly stronger voice, "*Me GUSTA dinero!*"

Three pairs of angry eyes stared me down as Luis re-entered the room. Loyal to his family, he looked at me suspiciously.

"What did you do?" he asked evenly.

"I just complimented your sisters on this delicious dinner," I uttered weakly, suddenly questioning my limited Spanish vocabulary.

"¿Cuál es el problema?" Luis addressed his sisters.

All pretenses of quiet, serene, demure little ladies were gone now. The three spoke at once, each managing to point an accusing finger at me to punctuate some aspect of their diatribe.

Near tears, I pleaded with Luis to tell me what I'd done to offend his sisters.

"You told them that you like money. They say you're a gold miner."

"That's gold digger," I corrected lamely as if this minor distinction would win anyone over to my side.

I can't say that this ended my relationship with Luis, but things were never quite the same between us after that fateful night. My social faux pas may have robbed me of my fairy-tale ending, but it also served as a valuable lesson. It was always the shortcuts that got me in trouble.

—Marsha Porter—

83

Chicken Soup
for the Soul

Just a Bite

Weirdism is definitely the cornerstone
of many an artist's career.
~E.A. Bucchianeri

When I was a freshman in college, a group of friends and I went out to eat at IHOP. We were seated in one of those corner tables: half booth, half chairs. I sat in the chair next to the wall, and we were all talking, laughing, and enjoying each other's company.

I paused for a moment, listening to the song playing over the speaker. I don't remember which song it was, but I remember thinking it would be funny to sing dramatically to my friend sitting next to me.

The song was at an instrumental interlude, and I was waiting for the moment to burst into song when the lyrics came back on. Right when they did, I turned to face my friend, leaned in, and opened my mouth. However, at that exact moment, the waiter reached in between us to clear the plates off the table. Shocked, I shut my mouth, biting down on our waiter's arm!

My face flushed tomato red. I turned away and tried to melt into the wall. My friends all turned and stared at me. "Sara, what just happened?"

Still trying to hide behind the wall, I said, "Well, uh, the song was playing... and I thought it would be funny to sing... but then... the plates... and his arm..." I was embarrassed and frazzled. I truly believed in that moment that I could die from embarrassment.

The waiter, still standing behind me, and unsure what to do next, said, "It's cool. Don't even worry about it. I'm a theater kid. Weirder things have happened!"

Now, I'm genuinely curious to know what this guy considers weird, but then it was honestly the best outcome given the predicament I had put him in.

Flash-forward a couple of years.

I was at a Halloween party accompanied by the same friend I attempted to sing to when, lo and behold, IHOP Guy came waltzing in!

Panicked, I froze. My friend asked, "What's wrong?"

"Remember IHOP Guy?"

"Yeah?"

"He's here."

She looked up at him and turned back to me. "Sara, I don't think that's the same guy."

"I'm sure it's the same guy! You don't just bite a guy in the arm and forget who he is!"

"Hold on. I'm gonna ask him."

"What? No! Wait! Don't!"

Too late.

"Excuse me, did you ever work at IHOP?"

IHOP Guy looked at her and said, "I did! Why do you ask?"

At that moment, IHOP Guy made eye contact with me — and he knew.

Apparently, he, too, never forgot the stranger who accidentally bit him.

— Sara Escandon —

84

Textarmageddon

My entire life can be summed up in one sentence:
Well, that didn't go as planned.
~Darynda Jones

One hot summer day, I stopped by my daughter's house for a quick visit. When I got ready to leave, my grandson Clayton begged to come with me. He loved swimming in our pool. It had been a busy week, and I had lots of errands to run, but who could resist those pleading brown eyes? I promised I'd pick him up on my way home from the store.

After my last stop, I texted Clayton before leaving the parking lot to tell him I was on my way. I chuckled when his reply popped up: "Who is this?"

Silly boy.

As I pulled out of the parking lot, my cell started ringing non-stop. Everyone in my family knew I didn't answer while driving, so I ignored it. Already clad in his swim trunks, Clayton was outside shooting baskets when I pulled in his driveway. He raced inside to let his mom know we were leaving.

My phone continued to ring as we headed to my house. When I parked in the garage, Clayton bolted from the car before I turned off the motor, yelling, "Hurry up, Grandma!" In record time, I changed into my suit and followed him down the deck steps, leaving my cell phone on the kitchen counter.

A few minutes later, my husband walked outside shaking my

phone. "Now what have you done?"

Apparently, my cell had rung over and over until my better half finally answered it, only to be verbally accosted. A very angry man on the other end accused him of threatening his girlfriend and warned, "You better hope I don't find out where you live." After denying posing any threat, he said he hung up on the irate caller.

Grabbing my phone, I scrolled to the text I'd sent Clayton and read my message out loud.

COMING TO GET YOU!

Clayton overheard our conversation and chimed in, "Grandma, I don't have a phone anymore. It got run over."

Oh, no! My message had gone to whoever had been assigned Clayton's old number. I pressed redial, but before I could say a word, a man yelled, "Stop harassing us!"

Stuttering, I apologized. I explained that the text was meant for my grandson, and that I wasn't aware he no longer had his cell phone. "I'm really sorry, sir," I added sincerely.

"You should be. My girlfriend called me and told me about the menacing text she received from this number. She's terrified. I'm on my way to her house now."

After a long pause, he chuckled. "Guess it's kinda funny now that I know she's safe."

Although I was still embarrassed, relief flooded over me, and I joined in his laughter.

Before hanging up, the man said, "No worries, Grandma. You're forgiven. But do me a favor: lose my girlfriend's number."

"Consider it done!"

— Alice Muschany —

85

One Sec!

Life is better when you're laughing.
~Anna Nielsen

Whenever my five-year-old daughter was called, she would say sweetly, "One sec!"

"Hurry! We're going to be late for school!" I would call out.

"One sec!" she would reply.

"Your snack is ready," I would say.

"One sec!" she would say.

"Time for your shower," I would tell her.

As expected, the response was, "One sec!"

As a mother of two children, I was busy keeping track of their schedules, driving them to activities, making sure everyone finished their homework and practiced their music, and keeping the house orderly. Most importantly, I was carving out time for family fun. To do all of this, I had to be on my game. But occasionally (my family would say "often"), I became impatient.

One day, I was preparing dinner. The lentils and rice were done, and I finished cooking a vegetable dish. I plated the children's dinners and placed them on the counter.

"Come for dinner," I called.

"One sec!" a young, carefree voice responded.

I must've been frazzled because I stormed out of the kitchen into the hallway.

"No more secs!" I yelled.

I paused long enough to catch my husband stumbling out of our bedroom and laughing uncontrollably.

I was annoyed. "What's so funny?" I demanded.

He could hardly speak. "Did you hear what you just said?" he sputtered.

When I repeated myself, I heard what he had heard.

I could not help but crack a smile.

—Viji K. Chary—

Chapter
11

Innocently Inappropriate

A Scene from *Psycho*

*Life isn't like a box of chocolates. It's more like a jar
of jalapeños. What you do today might burn
your butt tomorrow.*
~Larry the Cable Guy

My husband and I were so consumed with food that we sold
our home, bought an abandoned mom-and-pop grocery
store in an old, up-and-coming neighborhood, and built a
cooking studio with a bedroom. Thus, our adventures in
the kitchen began.

One of our missions was to master the art of pepper jelly. We
had been purchasing the spicy condiment from a local deli, but at
four dollars a small jar (fifteen in today's dollars), we felt we should
try it ourselves.

The art of making jelly is totally dependent on the pectin content
of the fruit and the correct temperature while cooking the mash. We
knew the science but were unclear on the proportions. After some
experimentation, we came up with a recipe.

During this time in food history, the "hottest" condiment available
on grocery-store shelves was Tabasco sauce. There were very few fresh
hot peppers available. We managed to find some jalapeños, procured
some Certo liquid pectin, and set off to "the lab."

Bill, the knife master, volunteered to chop the jalapeños. With
the deft strokes of a Ninja, the small, green peppers were soon a pile
of finely diced bits. They were scraped from the cutting board into the

stovetop cauldron along with the sugar and vinegar. Before long, the mass was a living, breathing, burbling coagulate of bubbles and steam. I stood back as tears began to roll down my cheeks from the spicy mist.

While the jelly belched and brewed, I began to flip the sterilized jelly jars upright. Finally, Bill ladled the amber, seed-flecked liquid into the waiting jars. I capped them quickly and tightened the lids. Our pepper-jelly mission was complete.

We had a dinner date planned for later, so Bill went off to shower.

As I stood and admired the fruits of our labor, I heard a blood-curdling scream emanating from the shower. It sounded like Bill was being murdered. Images of Norman Bates and *Psycho* flashed in my brain. I dashed to the bathroom.

"What's wrong?" I shrieked.

"I'm on fire!" he wailed.

What we hadn't learned in our research was that when you chop any type of pepper that has capsaicin, you must wear plastic or rubber gloves. Otherwise, the capsaicin-laden oil of the pepper will be absorbed into the skin. Washing your hands will not eradicate it! You may feel only a warm glow in your hands, but if you touch your eyes, you will definitely feel the burn. Bill was soaping his privates, and as he applied the soap, the capsaicin from his hands transferred to his delicate parts.

I turned off the water and ran back to the kitchen. I yanked open the refrigerator door and scanned for an antidote. Beer! Beer is what you're supposed to drink with spicy foods. I decided beer must be a neutralizer.

Bill stood in the shower, his body trembling in pain, as I poured beer onto the affected area.

"Oh, my freaking gawd," he howled, "you're making it worse!"

I reached into the medicine chest and found Ozonol — "cream for relief from burns," the label read. I squeezed the tube, and a blob of the cream landed on target. As I began to spread the goo, he screeched, "Ow, ow, ow, it's not helping!"

I headed back to the kitchen. Dairy, I thought. Many spicy Mexican dishes are served with sour cream. I grabbed a tub of sour cream and scurried back to the shower. I began to splat dollops of sour cream onto the fiery blaze.

He raised his hands to assist, and I hissed, "Don't touch! Whatever is burning you is coming from your hands."

So he stood with his hands in the air as I flung dollops of sour cream at his raging rash.

After a few seconds, the decibels of the shrieks dropped, and his teeth began to chatter. The sour cream had worked.

He looked a sight coated in sour cream, with soap bubbles sliding and popping. His body was now cold and shivering as evaporation took over from the once steamy bathroom.

"We will never speak of this again," he said through clenched teeth.

Oops.

— Sheryn Smith —

87

I'm Going Straight to Hell

I don't see a glass as half full or half empty. I see it
as a glass somebody has put his lousy germs on.
~Maxine, John Wagner

Cold and flu season was at a peak. Public schools closed throughout the nation by the hundreds. People lined up at clinics for vaccines like they were giving away tickets to a Rolling Stones tour.

"Maybe we should skip church today," I said to my husband. "You know, more people seem sicker than usual."

"I'm sure it will be fine," he said, grabbing our coats.

At church, even the pastor suffered a malady. "Good morning everyone," he coughed. With watery eyes, he continued, "Let's stand for a prayer."

I struggled to hear the service above all the hacking, sneezing, and throat clearing. Lozenges were passed around like Jell-O shots. It was a veritable witch's brew of germs, and I searched frantically for a way out before the sign of peace. When the pastor announces, "Let us offer one another a sign of peace," each parishioner extends his or her hand to the closest neighbor, usually within a four-foot radius.

But lately, it had gone well beyond reasonable limits. I had been at services where people practically hopped over each other and jumped into the aisle to say "Hi" or "Good morning." If offering the "Peace of Christ" takes longer than the actual service, it's time for someone to call "uncle."

But that's not my point.

Typically, to avoid contact, I will pretend to pick up something from the floor right before the sign of peace — or read the Bible, fall asleep, act engrossed in conversation, even fake a faint, whatever it takes.

During this service, I planned to bolt to the restroom. Mentally, I prepared my stealthy exit right after the children's service.

"Get ready to move over a bit so I can squeeze by you," I whispered to my husband.

"Where are you going?" he asked.

"You'll see."

I waited like a teenager for a text message, but that day the church was packed, stuffed like tamales in a jar. I ended up trapped, miles from the end of the pew.

And then the unthinkable happened. The parishioner in front of me had a violent coughing spasm. Afterwards, he wiped his nose across the top of his hand and spit into a tissue. At that precise moment, the pastor addressed the members, "Turn to your neighbor for the sign of peace."

I tried to claw my way past ten other people, but it was too late. The Cough turned around and snatched my hand faster than I could say, "Holy moly!"

"Peace be with you," he murmured.

I stood paralyzed. My husband asked, "What's wrong? You look like you've seen a ghost."

I remained frozen to my seat the rest of the service. As the pastor wished us farewell, we lined up to shake his hand. That's when I wondered how he could do this every Sunday and survive.

Like a politician, he grabbed my hand from behind my back and squeezed my sweaty palm. I walked like a robot to the car for a bottle of hand sanitizer, trying to not even breathe.

— Stacey Gustafson —

88

How to Impress the In-Laws

Sometimes crying or laughing are the only options left,
and laughing feels better right now.
~Veronica Roth, Divergent

Nothing in life prompts anxiety like the anticipation of that first meeting with the soon-to-be in-laws. I wanted my moment to be perfect so I bought a new outfit, and had my hair styled and nails manicured.

Eric came to my church with me on Sunday morning, and he wanted to bring me to his house afterward to meet his parents. I knew it would be stressful because I didn't match any of their expectations for who his wife would be. I was not from their church, did not speak German, and wasn't a good cook. Worst of all, I was a single mom.

I was nervous as we walked through the front door of his parents' house. Surprisingly, they had company, so the focus wasn't on me as much as it was on their guests. I was introduced to them, and his father was pleasant and chatted with me for a few minutes, but his mother was not gracious toward me at all. The visit was short, but there weren't any incidents, so I assumed that I'd passed the test.

However, it wasn't over yet because I learned that Eric still hadn't told his mother that I was divorced. His father knew and accepted me for who I was. Dealing with his mother, though, would be very difficult as she wanted Eric to marry someone from her church, not someone like me.

Fortunately, I was given another opportunity to impress them. His parents owned a vineyard, and it was the grape-picking season. Eric suggested that I come the following Saturday and show my enthusiasm for their family business by joining them in picking the grapes. He assured me that his parents would love me once they got to know me. His words were convincing, but as the old saying goes, "Actions speak louder than words!"

It was late September, but the weather was still balmy, so they planned to start shortly after sunrise and work only until mid-afternoon. This would be my chance to prove to his parents that I was the right girl for Eric.

When I arrived, my make-up was perfect, and my hair was tied back stylishly. I was dressed in gray track pants with a pair of shorts underneath in case it got hot. I wore a light pink hoodie over a discreet white T-shirt, and I felt good about myself. I knew that I'd impressed Eric, but I wasn't sure about his parents.

Picking grapes was not new to me as I'd worked in vineyards before. I hoped that my experience would work in my favor. What I forgot, though, was that the vines were surrounded by grass that was often inhabited by insects ready to pounce on humans!

Eric's father smiled as he handed me a set of clippers, but his mother was still standoffish and mumbled that I'd probably damage her plants. Eric told me to ignore her and work with him on one of the rows while his parents took the one beside us.

The first couple of hours were actually fun. Eric and I worked and chatted together. His father came over a few times, and we talked and joked around, so I began to relax. I felt as if I would fit in, which meant that I could soon bring my daughter to meet them — the ultimate test.

By mid-morning, it was getting hot, so I took off my hoodie, leaving my arms exposed, which meant two things: mosquitoes and dirt. Before long, I was using my hoodie to wipe the dirt from my face and neck, not realizing that my make-up was running and blending in with the sweaty mess on my face.

Eric's mother checked my work often to see if I was doing it right, and I could feel her beady eyes piercing through me each time. His dad would come over periodically and say with a big grin, "You're doing a good job." So that, along with Eric's constant praise, made me think that I'd get through this day with no issues and maybe even win the hearts of both of his parents. Then, suddenly, the unexpected happened.

Something creepy began to crawl up the inside of my pant leg. I gasped and jumped to my feet. I shook my leg frantically, but nothing came out from the bottom of my pants. Instead, the invader crept up to my knee and then above my knee. Without realizing it, I began to dance around and scream in my effort to get the thing out of my pants, but it continued to move upwards. Eric stopped working and his father came over to see what all the commotion was about.

I could tell it wasn't something small like an ant because I could feel its prickly feet crawling up my leg, and it was freaking me out! I began screaming at Eric to get it off me, but he said that he couldn't see anything. That's when I did what came naturally — totally forgetting that my purpose for being there was to impress his parents. I spun around in circles, screaming hysterically, as I yanked my pants down to my ankles and slapped at my legs, finally sending a praying mantis flying!

My heart was pounding, but I was able to settle down and stop squealing and shaking after a few seconds. That's when I was overwhelmed with the sounds of laughter coming from Eric and his dad. I looked through my tears and saw them both doubled over in hysterics. His mother stood there with her hands on her hips as she shook her head and grunted. So much for an excellent first impression!

There I was, pants pulled down to my ankles, eye make-up mingled with tears, and sweat dripping down my face. My hair was a tangled web of sweaty, dirty strands dangling onto the white T-shirt, which was now covered in grape stain and dirt! To top it off, I'd just finished my hysterical panic dance. I was so embarrassed that I just bowed my head and let the silent tears flow. Eric was still bent over in uncontrollable laughter, but his father stopped laughing and put his arms around me.

"I hope our new granddaughter is as much fun as you are," he said.

— Ronnie Dauber —

89

The Grammar Lesson

Being a teacher is not a 9-5 job.
~Heidi McDonald

I shoved an invisible handout at my boyfriend Paul, who lay asleep in bed beside me. It really annoyed me that he was sleeping through my class! I shook him hard and urgently until he woke up. I watched him stir, blink and look up at me.

It was time to start class. I climbed out of bed and walked over to the bedroom's blue wall, which was wide enough to hold a school-sized whiteboard. I grabbed a nonexistent marker from the nonexistent ledge and announced, "So today we're going to learn about adjective clauses."

In big letters, I wrote in the air, "Adjective Clauses," before turning around to face the class. I began my lesson with, "Okay, first of all, let's recap. What is an adjective?"

Silence. A familiar sound. In teachers college, they taught us not to panic during silence. In fact, allowing students an extra thirty seconds more than we'd naturally be comfortable with in regular conversation could actually be beneficial. It would allow the students to process the question and come up with a better answer. So I waited. Still, silence. Stunned silence. I took another approach. "Can anyone give me an example of an adjective?"

Finally, I got a response. It was Paul's groggy voice. "Daniela... What are you doing?"

What was I doing? What was Paul doing in my class? I rubbed my eyes. No, wait, he was right. We weren't at school. There was no whiteboard, no students. It was my bedroom. It was pitch-black outside. The alarm clock on Paul's bedside table read 4:26 a.m.

Sheepishly, I explained, "I'm sleep teaching."

I got back into bed, my cheeks flushed pink. I was such a weirdo. On rare occasions in my life, I had sleep talked, maybe even sleep walked, but this was the first and only time I ever sleep taught.

We could barely contain our giggles the next morning.

— Daniela Trivino —

90

A Nun Walks into a Library...

God has a smile on His face.
~Psalm 42:5

The nun, a petite, gray-haired woman, came up to the circulation desk and handed me a video. It was *Streisand: Live in Concert.*

"I have a little problem," she said. "I purchased this video for our convent at your library last week."

Our patrons often donate used video tapes to the library. We no longer include videos in our collection, so we put them out for sale.

"I paid a dollar for this," she said.

"And it didn't work?"

"It worked just fine," she said dryly. "That's the problem."

"I don't understand."

"Once a week, my convent screens a movie for all the sisters. It's my job to select the films. We've gotten some great movies from your sale table. Many of the sisters are Streisand fans. So when I saw this, I thought I'd picked a winner."

"A lot of people like Streisand," I said noncommittally. I still didn't know where this was going.

"We all gathered in the convent library. I inserted the video and pressed play. And... " She leaned forward and lowered her voice, "The screen filled up with naked people!"

"What?"

"We're all sitting there, watching these naked men and women cavorting around on screen, doing… well, doing some very surprising things. Sister Mary Kate finally asked, 'When's the singing going to start?' That's when I grabbed that video right out of the player and took a good look at it. On the label, it said, 'Swedish Erotica'!"

"I'm very sorry, sister," I said.

I knew what must have happened. Somebody had taken their erotic movie out of its original box and hidden it in what they thought was a safe place. What could be more innocuous than a Streisand concert?

Somehow, that very special "Streisand concert" ended up being donated to our library, probably by a family member doing a little spring cleaning.

"I'd like my dollar back, please," said the nun.

Although library policy is to sell videos "as is" and not issue refunds, I handed that dollar right over — along with a sincere apology.

"Please choose another video for your convent's library, free of charge," I told her. "In fact, please take several."

"Thank you," she said. "I believe I will." She headed off to our sale table with an acquisitive gleam in her eye.

From time to time, the image of that room full of nuns watching Swedish erotica pops into my head. And, God help me, it always makes me smile.

— Roz Warren —

91

Kiss of Peace, Italian Style

Anything awful makes me laugh.
I misbehaved once at a funeral.
~Charles Lamb

My husband Tom and I were on a Mediterranean cruise with his cousins Jack and Marilyn. We had visited the Acropolis in Greece, shopped for carpets in the Grand Bazaar in Istanbul, explored the ruins in Ephesus, and were now docked in our last port, Naples. We decided to search for a Catholic church so we could attend Sunday mass.

It was a hot afternoon, and we were tired, having roamed the hilly cobblestone streets for a couple of hours searching for a church that wasn't locked up tight. I had this romantic vision of us all going to mass together, and then finding some quaint ristorante and ordering a big bowl of Pasta alle Vongole and sharing a bottle of Chianti at our last port.

"There are over five hundred churches in Naples. You'd think one of them would stay open all day," Jack said.

"Apparently, the entire town rolls up after noon on Sundays," Tom said. "They're all home preparing a Sunday family meal. I can see them now, three generations sitting around the table sharing family stories...."

"And a big bowl of pasta, which is what we should be doing," Marilyn said as she rested against the brick wall outside one of the locked churches. "I'm starving. What say we call it quits and go back to the ship? I'm sure they're still serving lunch."

Jack wiped his moist forehead. "Look, we've come this far. Just a few more streets, okay?" A devout Catholic, Jack never missed a Sunday mass.

Tom unbuttoned his sweat-stained shirt and studied the map in his hand. "I get the feeling we're not in a great part of town. Remember what the cruise director told us? Watch your valuables. Take a look around. There are no other tourists from the ship, right?"

We glanced around. Garbage cans were overflowing, piled high with empty wine bottles from Saturday night. Perhaps this port was not considered a safe harbor, but it certainly ate and drank well.

Suddenly, there was a noise in the side alleyway, and a wiry young man with thick, slicked-back hair appeared.

I smiled. "Excuse me. Do you happen to know where there is a church… a Catholic church?" I pointed to the sky and pantomimed a door opening. "One that is open?" I asked.

The kid stared at me blankly and then said something I couldn't understand in Italian. He held up his hand, his fingers indicating five blocks. We thanked him and kept walking. I hoped the kid wasn't sending us to a five-star bar.

At the top of the hill of Pizzofalcone, we found the church of Santa Maria Egiziaca a Forcella and went inside. The mass had already started, and the church was packed. It looked like the entire city went to only one church, and we had found it by sheer luck.

One by one, we genuflected and squeezed into the last open pew, crossed ourselves, and knelt down. The ancient church was dimly lit by stained-glass windows and ornately decorated with statues of saints and the Madonna. But we were so far back that I couldn't get a clear view of what the altar looked like.

Nonetheless, I was thrilled to be inside celebrating a mass in Italian. "This is fabulous," I said. "Just look at these faces. They're so… authentically Italian."

"I'm happy to get off my feet and sit someplace where it's cool," Tom muttered, his voice loud enough for us all to hear.

A grandmother-type dressed in a black shawl and black veil, kneeling in the pew in front, turned to inspect us. She narrowed her eyes at me. I gave her my best perky tourist smile. She returned it with an icy glance and looked away.

I felt I was intruding on her thoughts. I turned to my left and smiled at the man sitting next to me. He put his head in his weathered hands and covered his face.

Maybe he was praying that the Americans would disappear.

I elbowed Tom, who was grinning as he watched me fail to connect with the locals.

Tom whispered, "Maybe the people in this town aren't that outgoing."

Jack grumbled for us all to be quiet, which made Marilyn burst into a fit of giggles.

I nudged Tom again. "I'll win them over. Watch."

The choir in the front of the church sang something I didn't recognize, heavenly voices lifting with the organ music. I was swept up in the bliss and transcendence of a world traveler, feeling connected to these worshipping strangers.

The priest continued his speech from the altar, and although I couldn't see him or understand a word he was saying, I knew from my Catholic-school days that the priest had arrived at a part in the mass called the kiss of peace. Caught up in the spirit, I turned to Tom, lifted my chin and kissed him. Then I tapped my elderly lady's shoulder and held out my hand. She held up her bony hand in protest. I grasped her fingers, gleefully. She jerked back and gave me a horrified look. I turned to the older gentleman and, swept up in the moment, almost high-fived him. I slapped Jack's hand and high-fived Marilyn, who was now chuckling.

I was enjoying this mass.

The mass ended. And for the first time I could see the old priest as he tottered down from the altar, coming toward us. There were four men dressed in black, preceding the portly priest, carrying a large black box. Suddenly, I realized in horror that it was a casket!

Jack leaned over and said, "Don't look now, Perky, but I think we've just crashed a perfect stranger's funeral. And you just high-fived everyone in his family."

Once outside the church, we couldn't control ourselves. We knew that we shouldn't be laughing, but we couldn't help ourselves. We laughed all the way back to the ship. In the dining room, we raised our wine glasses and toasted our unknown deceased relative.

"I'm going to bet Grandma is still trying to figure out whose side of the family we were from," Jack said, "and who invited us." And even though we were sympathizing with those grieving, knowing it was wrong, we could not stop laughing.

"Well, he certainly got an American send-off," Tom said.

—Joyce Newman Scott—

92

Bavarian White Elephant

I can no other answer make but thanks, and thanks;
and ever thanks.
~Sebastian in Twelfth Night, *William Shakespeare*

The hostess peered into the gift bag and carefully peeled away the paper. She looked up at us, her guests, and giggled.

"A small bottle of Champagne!" she said, holding it up for us to see.

"You didn't want this anymore?" one woman asked.

"No," the gift giver answered. "I didn't have space and thought it would be a shame to throw it away."

Several nodded in agreement, as if we all had items like that in our pantries.

This was the first Bavarian White Elephant Party I'd attended in my fifteen years living in southern Germany. I looked around at the other guests. Everyone beamed at each other, waiting for the next woman to open her present.

Suddenly I knew I was in trouble. This was not how we did things back in Ohio.

A tall thin woman ran a manicured nail under the taped paper. "Look!" she exclaimed. "It's a mini espresso maker!"

The photo on the box depicted a blue, stovetop espresso maker.

The previous owner laughed. "I love the color, but it doesn't fit my new kitchen scheme."

My throat tightened, my armpits stuck together, and my heart pounded — signs of an impending panic attack. To calm myself, I joined in the *oohing* and *aahing* over the gifts and murmured agreeably that, of course, I completely understood the burden of one piece of glass too many in my cupboards. I made a mental note to never, under any circumstances, allow any of these women to set foot inside my house.

Two more gifts preceded mine. There was still hope that someone had done this properly, the true "white elephant" way.

A boisterous, red-haired guest grabbed her gift — a one-and-a-half-meter by one-meter rectangle. She'd campaigned for this gift when she saw who brought it — the woman who lived in the largest farmhouse. She had schemed and worked the rules to steal this prize away from the rest of the ladies. Now, she tore open the newspaper like a toddler at Christmas.

"Wow!" we all exclaimed in unison.

It was a framed map of our village.

"It was a lovely gift from an acquaintance, but I didn't have a place for it," the farmhouse woman explained. "I think the frame is from IKEA."

"Most of my house is from IKEA," someone muttered from the corner.

Several of the ladies eyed the print with jealousy.

This couldn't be. Mentally, I scrolled through the invitation messages. The hostess had clearly said "White Elephant." To my American mind, this meant wrapping whatever junk you had and bringing that to pass on to the next unfortunate victim.

Maybe Bavarian women neither buy crap in the first place nor receive anything awful as gifts. Or they are so good at tidying that they dispose of anything tacky or unwanted immediately. I, on the other hand, held on to items purposely for White Elephant Parties. At least that was my excuse for my borderline hoarding.

The next guest opened her gift. I choked on my sparkling water. It was a white Villeroy & Boch ceramic terrine with blue, wide brushstrokes across the side and a red ceramic-apple grip on the lid. It was absolutely charming, something I would buy in which to serve festive, colorful summer casseroles or apple crumble. How was this a White

Elephant?

"It was from my mother-in-law," said the gift giver.

My gift was next. I started to sweat. I had wrapped the parcel in heavy paper and added a gold-and-silver bow, even using the ribbon-shredding tool for dramatic fringe.

The participant eagerly started opening the pretty package, then screamed and covered the items again quickly. "I can't open this!" she cried.

"Do it!" they rest of the women chanted.

She opened the paper and held up the prize: his-and-her red satin Christmas thongs — never worn. (I included a note in German stating the fact.) "Jingle Bells" for Her and "Jingle Balls" for Him.

Time suspended for a minute as the women glanced at each other. It was make-or-break time for me. Either I'd ruined the tea party, or I'd turned it into a disco. Tears from my White Elephant anxiety and suppressing my laughter slid down my face.

Then the victim discovered the music sensors above the pubic area of each panty.

"They're placed so the music starts when you..."

The women howled and smacked the table, joining my own shrieking.

"Where did you get these?" one woman asked between gasps.

"My husband got them from a patient," I answered.

"Male or female?"

"Female," I said.

Silence.

"She's over sixty," I explained quickly, "and her brother owns a sex shop."

I'm not sure that made the situation any better.

"Why didn't you get rid of them?" asked a woman.

"I was saving them for a moment like this." Why else, really? Unless I wanted to admit my problem with throwing away things.

Thankfully, Oregon is nine hours behind Bavarian time, so I could debrief with my sister the second I got home.

"I hear you," she commiserated. "I went to a White Elephant

recently. I picked the nicest wrapped package."

"Never do that," I said. "What was it?"

"A super-sized bag of tortilla chips, salsa, and a can of guacamole."

"Well done," I said.

"Right? The tortillas weren't even the store brand."

— Christina Tolan —

93

Family Viewing

Scientists now believe that the primary biological
function of breasts is to make males stupid.
~Dave Barry

When *Titanic* hit the movie theaters, the whole world was mesmerized by its grandeur and magnificence. The music. The photography. It was totally amazing. It was also one of the few movies our whole family could agree to see.

With three older sisters, my eight-year-old son was always being outvoted when it came to entertainment. The girls wanted love stories and drama, while he wanted action and adventure. *Titanic* fit the bill on all accounts. It was perfect.

Loaded up with popcorn and candy, we found our seats right in the middle of the theater. For once, everyone was happy. We settled in to watch the movie.

As soon as the previews ended and the spectacle of the movie began, we were enthralled. Occasionally, I'd steal a glance at my children, delighted to see them captivated by the story unfolding before them. The theater was quiet, with each moviegoer pulled into the scenes.

I'd managed to find something they could all enjoy! I can still feel the joy that oozed through me.

Then the scene changed. Jack was creating a portrait of Rose, who was nude. The entire audience drew a collective breath and grew completely still. Silence absorbed us as we all watched the artistic scene unfolding on screen.

Then a young boy's voice rang out, "Look at the boobs!"

The words seemed to hang in the air, growing and expanding with each syllable. I recognized the voice instantly. This was not some boy — it was my son. Mortified, I turned crimson, practically illuminating the darkness with my shame.

A ripple of laughter rolled through the room like a wave, gathering speed and volume as it went. It wasn't funny. I didn't want to laugh, but I couldn't help it.

Not surprisingly, this has become a frequent tale shared at family gatherings in our house. I find myself wondering how many other families who were there are still laughing about it, too.

It's still my son's favorite movie.

— Debby Johnson —

Chapter

12

Family Fun

Excuse Me?

*Obviously, if I was serious about having a relationship
with someone long-term, the last people I would
introduce him to would be my family.*
~Chelsea Handler

As a new member of the Sienes clan, I was just starting to understand the personalities and dynamics of my husband's family. My husband's brother-in-law, Jim, who looked like a member of the Hell's Angels with his long, gray beard and his Harley, was more like a gentle giant. He just looked scary. He did the majority of holiday cooking and could rival the talent of any foodie. And my father-in-law, Dan, a take-charge kind of man who was always ready for the next adventure, loved nothing more than to travel with his family.

So it was, on Christmas Eve, at my sister and brother-in-law's home, that we were discussing an upcoming trip to Spain. I was beyond excited because I'd never traveled any farther than Canada and Mexico.

"You have to learn how to pack for this sort of trip, young lady," Dan instructed. As a retired schoolteacher and principal, he never tired of educating me. We were all standing around the kitchen island — the proverbial gathering place anytime we got together. "You don't want to travel around Europe with more than one suitcase, so you need to pack light. There are tricks of the trade."

"Like what?" I slid onto a barstool and leaned my elbows on the counter. I was ready to take whatever advice this seasoned traveler had to offer.

He cleared his throat. "You gotta think outside the box. One thing I do is take women's underwear."

I blinked. *Did I misunderstand him?* Ignoring my husband's snicker, I looked at Dan. "Excuse me?"

"They're easier to wash out in the hotel bathroom, and they dry overnight. I get the same kind your mother-in-law wears. Except..." he held up a finger to make a point, "...I get them in a much larger size."

Diane, my sister-in-law, laughed, probably at the expression on my face. The last thing I wanted to visualize was Dan wearing Pat's underwear. I looked at Chris, my husband, with raised eyebrows.

"Hey, you wanted to know his traveling secrets."

"Do *you* wear women's underwear when you travel?"

"Not on your life," he assured me.

Well, that was a relief.

The next morning, as I was still processing the previous night's lesson, we gathered again in the kitchen, this time for breakfast. Jim was manning the stove, whipping up pancake batter. My mother-in-law, Pat, wandered into the room, still in her bathrobe. She's a tiny woman with twinkling green eyes and a ready smile.

"How'd you sleep, Mom?" Diane asked, setting a stack of plates next to the stovetop.

"I slept great, sweetheart." She readjusted her robe and sat at the barstool Dan pulled out for her. "The only thing is that I forgot to brush my teeth, so I had to get up after everyone else was asleep. When I got into the bathroom, I realized I left my toothpaste in the bedroom. I figured you guys had some in one of the drawers."

Diane set a cup of coffee in front of Pat. "Did you find it?"

"Well, I thought I did. I didn't want to wake you guys up, so I just used the nightlight. I found a tube of something and put it on my toothbrush. But it tasted funny. So I turned on the light. It wasn't toothpaste at all but Vagisil."

There were gasps and "oh, nos" as all eyes turned to Diane.

"Don't look at me," she said with a straight face. "It's not mine."

A heartbeat later, Jim's deep voice cut through the confusion. "It's mine." He flipped a pancake as if he didn't just open the door for a barrage of jokes. "It works great for chafing," he said matter-of-factly. Who knew bikers had such challenges?

I looked at Chris. "What in the world have I married into?" But I couldn't contain the smile that bubbled up. There wouldn't be a shortage of laughs with this family.

—Jennifer Sienes—

What Could Go Wrong?

Our grandchildren accept us for ourselves,
without rebuke or effort to change us,
as no one in our entire lives has ever done.
~Ruth Goode

t was Labor Day weekend, the last weekend in a summer full of outdoor adventures with my grandsons. Twelve-year-old Noah and I headed up north to go white-water rafting. It was my idea. I'd gone rafting dozens of times. Who cared that the last time was almost thirty years ago? What could go wrong?

We arrived at the meet-up spot near Pembine, Wisconsin. Our guide, Derek, fit us with life jackets and helmets. Along with the other six rafters, two women and four men, we boarded the bus with our driver, Bill, who took us to the launch spot on the Menominee River.

The first section of the trip was flat water, and Derek used the time to review the safety instructions and practice paddling in unison. We all listened carefully.

The next section was class 2 rapids, which I now know means "some rough water and rocks, some maneuvering." Only a basic skill level was required. Yahoo! We got wet. Everyone was laughing. We gave a high-five salute with our paddles.

The next section was class 4 rapids, which I now know are waves, rocks, sharp maneuvers, and a considerable drop. "Exceptional" skill level is required.

Off we went. Derek was calling out paddling instructions. However, the people paddling on the left were paddling way harder than the people on the right, so we smashed straight into a giant rock face. The force bounced us into a ricochet, which catapulted me into a backward somersault out of the raft.

My helmet popped off, and I was trapped underneath the raft. I was really, really scared. After a death-defying amount of time, the raft and I drifted apart. But now I was going down the "considerable drop" all by myself. Whitewater crashed over my face. I thought I was going to drown.

Noah was screaming, "Grandma! Grandma! Grandma!" That really drove home the point that I was out of my league. Derek was shouting at me, "Nose up, toes up!" He yelled at the rafters to paddle hard, and they finally got close to me. Derek reached over and grabbed the shoulders of my life jacket. "One, two, three," he said and hauled me into the back of the raft. The bottom of my suit fell down to my knees. I was facedown, bare keister up. As I wriggled around to pull up my suit and find a more comfortable position, Derek said, "Sorry, ma'am."

We got through the rest of the rapids and glided to the riverbank. No one was laughing. "Grandma, are you okay?" asked a wide-eyed Noah. My heart was pounding out of my chest, and my hands were shaking, but I did my best to keep my composure.

We hiked a little way to rendezvous with the bus driver. Bill said, "Wait until you see the video! Some of you are really going to want a copy."

I had forgotten about the video. Bill had been perched above the falls recording.

I rationalized it away. How close could he possibly have been? Plus, the mishap was in the back of the boat. Only Derek really saw it. I told Noah about it just in case and he thought it was funny, but he wasn't concerned. "They would probably fuzz it out anyway," he says.

Back at the meet-up spot, everyone gathered around a small, flat screen to view our exciting journey. Sure enough, there it was — my big, white derriere for the whole world to see. Noah shook his head and said, "Oh, Grandma."

The two other women in the group realized how awkward this was and yanked the men away. I threatened to stalk anyone who wanted to buy the video. Noah consoled me, "It's okay, Grandma. It's not that bad. Everyone has a butt."

I gave Noah a big hug. I'm so grateful that our memory of this trip will be a really funny, embarrassing thing that happened and not something horrible. He tells me that rafting was the most fun he had all summer.

—Elaine Maly—

96

Round Trip

How do people make it through life without a sister?
~Sara Corpening Whiteford

've had a weight problem since I was a child. One of my closest friends is chocolate. Even pronouncing the word makes me salivate. Chocolate has been a pure, constant and delicious companion.

My chocolate cravings have led me down some challenging paths. At sleep-away camp, I led a late-night raid on the canteen by the junior counselors, making everyone sign for the candy they took. I needed extra lines in the ledger to record my variety of chocolates.

On the home front, my poor mother would think she was defrosting a whole chocolate cake from the freezer, but when she opened it she'd find one slice left. The cake had been devoured by my sisters and me, who then closed the box and put it back.

Sugar is our nemesis. My sister Linda and I have an ongoing joke that we have never been thin at the same time. We are always giving each other pep talks about losing weight. We try our hardest to motivate one another without creating resentment.

One winter, I was on yet another diet. I had called Linda and told her that I had given up chocolate. I needed someone else to keep me accountable.

To my surprise, four weeks passed and I did not cheat even one time. But then, one day I decided to run some errands from work. As I was walking down the main boulevard of downtown Chicago, I realized that I was right in front of a Fannie May candy store. This was my favorite chocolate in the world next to Cadbury. And I was stopped and waiting for the walk light right outside the store.

As I looked in the window at the boxes filled with chocolate buttercreams, turtles and fudge, my knees started to buckle. I almost had to hold on to the side of the building. I could feel my resolve dissolving. "One month," I kept saying to myself. "You have gone without chocolate for one month. Keep walking. Cross the street. Now."

I was not listening. The imagined taste of the chocolate on my tongue had taken over. My brain had disengaged. Only my taste buds were operational, anticipating the reward for what I was about to do.

I entered the store's revolving door and pushed it hard to make the door go as fast as I could. As the door started its circular path I prepared to exit and race toward the counter. But the door kept going; it wouldn't stop! Before I knew it, I was outside on the street again. I looked back in shock to see my sister Linda behind me, pushing that door with all her strength.

I had pushed myself into the store, and she had pushed me right out.

Linda happened to be passing by at the moment I weakened. She saw me start my journey toward chocolate cheating and moved as quickly as she could to save me. And she did. We laughed so hard that my need for a chocolate fix passed… for the moment.

— Elynne Chaplik-Aleskow —

97

Gram's Pie

Shared joy is a double joy;
shared sorrow is half a sorrow.
~Swedish Saying

"Did you hear what Grandma did last week?" Grandpa asked with a chuckle.

Gram said, "Now, Delbert. They don't need to hear about that."

"What'd she do, Grandpa?" I asked.

He grinned and said, "She hid the last piece of pie in the microwave so she could have it all to herself. Then she forgot about it until she opened the microwave a couple days later. When she saw it, she got a fork and started eating quickly. She was afraid I'd come in and see her with it. She was so busy watching out for me that she wasn't paying attention to what she was doing."

"Now, Delbert," Gram inserted, but she might as well have saved her breath. Grandpa was not about to be stopped, no matter what Gram said.

He continued, "I came out here to the kitchen and there stood Grandma. The pie was on a plate on the counter in front of her. As soon as she saw me, she put her arm around the plate possessively and said, 'Delbert, this is mine, and I'm not sharing it!' Then she shoveled a bite into her mouth."

"Gram!" I exclaimed. "You weren't going to share with Grandpa?"

"No, I wasn't. I'd saved that piece for myself."

Grandpa continued, "I looked down at the pie and something didn't look right, so I told her to stop eating it.

"Well, you know how stubborn Grandma is. She thought I was trying to trick her into sharing it with me, so she said, 'Delbert, I told you I'm not sharing this,' and took another bite.

"By then, I was close enough to know there really was a problem. I raised my voice and said, 'Edith, put your fork down right now!' She finally listened to me.

"I said, 'I think you might want to take a look at that pie before you eat any more of it.'"

Grandpa started laughing so hard that he could barely get the words out.

"You should have seen the look on her face when she saw it. The top was covered with ants!"

"Ew! Yuck!" I said, and then started laughing.

I looked at Gram. She looked more sheepish than indignant.

"So, Gram, are you going to stop hiding things from Grandpa from now on?" I asked.

"No, I'm just going to find better places to hide them."

— Maureen Longnecker —

98

My Hallmark Moment

Because I am still a little girl who believes
in Santa and the tooth fairy and you.
~Laurie Halse Anderson

Our dad grew up during the Great Depression with nonexistent dental care. Since both my sister and I chose careers in dental hygiene, we constantly had Dad in a dental chair, cleaning his remaining teeth and trying to teach him better oral hygiene.

Dad and my sister, Dee, lived in Buffalo, New York, while I lived in Rochester about eighty miles away. Our employers were alumni of the same dental school. These dentists had served in the military themselves and wanted to give back to Dad, who was a highly decorated WWII veteran. Dad traveled back and forth between the two cities, and the two dentists restored his mouth free of charge.

One day while Dad was with my sister, she phoned me. "Dad's teeth are really starting to take shape, but there are a few that are beyond saving."

Dee made the appointments, and a plan was coordinated between our two employers. I felt bad that Dad was losing his teeth and fretting about it.

"Dad, they'll make you great-looking partials, and you'll be all set." I tried to reassure him.

He looked at me with sad eyes. "Honey, I have been trying so hard to take care of my teeth."

Dad's comment gave me an idea. He would be at my sister's for the extractions. As a grandmother of four little boys who are constantly losing teeth, I knew that Hallmark has a card for just such an occasion because I'd purchased four in the past. The card has a huge alligator with a string tied to a tooth on it and a cheery caption: "You're losing a tooth. Don't be sad."

My hunt began. After checking three Hallmark stores, I was about to give up. I decided to try one more place. As I entered, I asked a saleslady, "Do you have the card with the alligator on it for losing a tooth?"

With her assistance, I hit the jackpot. Triumphantly, she held the card and exclaimed, "I don't believe I've ever seen this one. It's so cute."

We chatted, and when I got to the register, I told her I had purchased it before so I knew it existed. She and her co-worker were talking with each other as I was leaving the store. Just as I got to the door, the saleslady shouted out, "By the way, how old is the little darling?"

Oh, I couldn't resist! I had a grin from ear-to-ear. Without hesitation or explanation, I answered as I walked out the door, "Oh, he's eighty-four."

— Terry Hans —

99

Uncle Ed

No family is complete without an embarrassing uncle.
~Peter Morgan

Way back in high school in the mid-1970s, I was on the wrestling team. A demanding sport requiring hard work, dedication, and self-discipline, wrestling was in its infancy in rural, southern Ohio.

Enter Uncle Ed. My dad's older brother was in his mid-forties and a dues-paying union plumber in Columbus. Uncle Ed had facial skin like a catcher's mitt, a huge Roman nose, and only one eye. The latter was the result of an errant rock thrown in Uncle Ed's youth. God love Uncle Ed.

Unfortunately, Uncle Ed had no clue about wrestling. He was only familiar with what he called "rasselin'." Dad's brother was a huge fan of Big Time Wrestling, the predecessor to today's World Wrestling Federation. Every Saturday at noon, Uncle Ed planted himself in front of a black-and-white television and watched grown men in tights execute moves like the Tilt-a-Whirl, Mongolian Chop, and Cactus Clothesline.

Thus, I dreaded Uncle Ed's visits.

He always dropped in on Sunday afternoon. His first words to me were always, "Are ya still rasselin'?"

"Yes, I am, Uncle Ed, but it's called wrestling. And it's not what you think it is."

"Then let me show you a move called an Indian Burn."

"No, Uncle Ed, it's not like that."

"You can use it in your next match."

Then right there in the middle of the dining room, he grabbed my forearm with both hands and subjected it to a tortuous twisting.

"OUCH!"

"HAHAHAHAHA," Uncle Ed laughed.

"Now let me show you the Sleeper Hold."

"No, Uncle Ed, we're not allowed to…"

He thrust his right arm around my neck and began choking me.

"AAAUUUGH!"

"HAHAHAHAHA."

"Edward, stop it," Mom commanded.

The following Sunday afternoon was more of the same.

"So, are ya still rasselin'?"

"Uncle Ed, it's wrestling. And I am, but…"

"Then let me show you the Bronco Buster."

"No, Uncle Ed, it's illegal to…"

"Here it goes!"

"OOOOF!"

"HAHAHAHAHA."

"Edward, stop!"

By the end of wrestling season, I'd had it.

One cold Sunday afternoon in March, Uncle Ed visited again.

"So how is rasselin' goin'?"

"Uncle Ed, the season is over."

"Well, still, let me show ya the Flyin' Lariat."

"No, Uncle Ed, let me show you a Wedgie."

As Uncle Ed approached me, I leapt up from my dining-room chair. Then I ducked under his outstretched arms to arrive at a position behind him. With both hands, I reached down to his "plumber's butt," grabbed the waistband of his underwear, and yanked it up toward his shoulder blades.

Then I stepped back while Uncle Ed froze in his tracks. The look on his face was priceless. A grown man with a wedgie is no laughing matter.

This time, the "AAAUUUGH" came from Uncle Ed.

This time, the "HAHAHAHAHA" came from Mom, Dad, and my family. They couldn't stop laughing.

And there never was another Big Time Wrestling session in our dining room.

—John M. Scanlan—

Tread Lightly

Progress not perfection.
~Kimberly Snyder

"**A**re you sure you want to come with me?" My fifteen-year-old daughter couldn't miss the doubt in my tone. Nikki thought exercise was on par with slow death by torture.

My weekday trips to the gym were always a lone experience. I taught the 5:00 a.m. aerobics class at the gym before I went to my job as a middle-school teacher, and no one wanted to join me on those early mornings.

But this was mid-morning on a Saturday. "Yeah," she said. "I haven't spent much time with you lately." She shrugged into her sweatshirt, snatched up an oversized water bottle and looked at me expectantly.

"Okay, let's go then." Doubtful or not, I was grateful my teenage daughter still wanted to hang out with me. I had assumed that when she hit high school, I would no longer be considered cool.

Suddenly, I had visions of Nikki becoming my new workout partner. We'd become mother/daughter gym rats and build a whole new relationship based on our mutual love of exercise.

The ten-minute drive to the gym went without incident. Nikki chatted about a school assignment and her classes.

As we entered the two-story structure, I noticed it was fairly crowded, as expected. Universal machines, racquetball courts, aerobic classrooms and the administrative office were on the first floor. "I'm going to head upstairs to the treadmills," I said. "What do you want to do?"

"Treadmill, just like you." She headed for the stairs, and I followed.

The treadmills were lined up around the perimeter of the loft-like second story, overlooking the first floor. Behind the treadmills, weight machines, dumbbells and weight benches were set up in front of the mirrored wall — congested, mostly with men. I always found it a little intimidating to lift weights in that atmosphere, which is why I preferred the treadmill on busy Saturday mornings. As long as the men were behind me, I could ignore them.

We found two treadmills, side by side. I placed my water bottle in the holder, hung a face towel over the handrail and took off my sweatshirt. Nikki's water bottle was too large to fit into the holder, so she set it on the floor and climbed onto her treadmill, confusion knitting her brow.

Stepping over to her, I gave a quick rundown of the controls. "You might want to clip the safety key to your shirt," I instructed her.

"Why?"

"It'll stop the treadmill if you fall."

She rolled her eyes. "That's not going to happen."

I knew from experience that it was useless to argue with her. And really, I'd never actually seen anyone fall off the treadmill, so I figured she had a point. I eyed her sweatpants. "Do you have shorts under those?"

"Nuh-uh." She fiddled with the controls.

"You're going to get pretty warm," I warned her as I climbed on my own machine.

"I'll be fine. How fast do you go?" She watched me set up my workout.

"Just start slow, kiddo. You're not used to working out."

Nikki wasn't very competitive, so it surprised me she was trying to mirror my workout. When I increased my speed, she increased hers. Sweat began to pop up on her forehead and upper lip, and her cheeks were turning a bright shade of red. Then I noticed her eyeing the water bottle she'd set on the floor.

"Don't do it," I warned.

She looked at me. "What?" she managed to huff out.

"Don't reach for that bottle while you're moving. If you need a drink, stop the treadmill first."

With an eye roll and headshake, she ignored me. She managed to snag the water bottle, if not gracefully, at least competently. Maybe I wasn't giving her enough credit.

I increased my speed to a running gait and focused on measured breaths. In through my nose... one, two, three; out through my mouth... one, two, three. I tuned out the weight clanking behind me and my daughter's pounding footsteps beside me. Then I heard a loud thump followed by a rhythmic thump, thump, thump. It took a moment for me to realize that the noise wasn't coming from behind me but beside me.

Looking over at my daughter, I was struck by the bizarre sight of her running on her knees. Thump, thump, thump... She had one hand clutching the handrail for dear life and the other holding the water bottle. Panic filled her eyes as she looked at me while desperately attempting to keep up the pace on her knees. If she let go of the handrail, she'd take quite a tumble.

I jumped off my own treadmill and rushed to hit the pause button on hers. The treadmill slowed, and Nikki's knee-run slowed with it until it finally stopped. I helped her stand as she hugged the water bottle to her chest.

"Are you okay?" I took her free hand and looked down to inspect her knees.

"I'm fine," she said with a grimace, her face beet red, probably a combination of exertion and embarrassment. "Guess I should've listened to you about the water bottle."

A grin split my face, and laughter bubbled up from my chest. I tried to stop it but couldn't. It gained momentum, and the harder I tried to contain it, the worse it got.

"Seriously?" Nikki said, her own lips twitching.

"I'm sorry," I choked out. "But if you could've seen yourself running on your knees..." After a few moments, I was finally able to control myself.

"That was quite a move," said a male voice behind us.

We both turned to look at the young bodybuilder sitting on the weight bench behind us.

"What do you call it?" he asked with a good-natured grin.

Nikki had a pained expression on her face as she ignored the question. "Can we go home now?"

That was the last time Nikki ever joined me at the gym. My dreams of having her as my lifetime workout buddy dwindled in one moment of mishap. Her exercising days were over.

—Jennifer Sienes—

Backseat Driver

When your mother asks, "Do you want a piece of
advice?" it is a mere formality. It doesn't matter if you
answer yes or no. You're going to get it anyway.
~Erma Bombeck

She couldn't drive. Well, maybe that's being unfair. In reality, she never tried to drive. She was too afraid. She never even sat in the driver's seat of a car. She was always the passenger in the front seat.

But not knowing how to drive did not stop her. She was full of advice for the driver.

She was my mother-in-law. She was old school, from the old country, and she didn't trust anything much. That included cars — and me. She understood that cars were a necessary part of living in California if people wanted to go somewhere and didn't want to be stuck in their houses. But she didn't like them.

One time, she was invited to her friend's birthday luncheon. Her friend lived over an hour away, and my mother-in-law was really torn about going because it involved traveling. In a car. In the end, her desire to go to the party won out over her fear of getting there. Everyone else in the family was busy, so guess who was "volunteered" into taking her?

The day of the party came. I told her I would pick her up at 11:00 a.m. to get her to the party by 12:30 p.m. As I pulled into her driveway at 11:00, I noticed that she was already out on the front lawn pacing back and forth — hat on her head, purse over her arm and purpose to her movements.

"Where have you been? You're late. The party starts at 12:30, and I just know we'll be late."

"Don't worry. We have plenty of time to get there. Please, just get in."

Before she could get in, she had to check the tires. Check them for what, I don't know. To be sure there were four of them? That they were round? She wouldn't know if anything was wrong unless the tires were completely flat and the treads were gone. She circled the car, leaning down at each tire to assure herself that all was well. I guess they passed the test because she got in the car.

She buckled her seat belt and then unbuckled it. She buckled it again and asked if I had filled up the car with gas. Yes. Had I checked the oil? Yes, it had been checked. Does the horn work for emergencies? Honk, honk! Did I know where we were going? Yes. Did we have to go on the freeway? Yes. Finally, she announced that she was ready.

I looked over my shoulder as I backed out of the driveway. She looked over her shoulder, too. After she gave me the all clear, she told me to turn the wheel to the right and drive down the street. She told me to be sure to stop at the stop sign. She then directed me to turn right at the corner and to make another right at the next corner. Wouldn't it have been easier to go in the other direction instead of going around the block? Oh, I forgot... She didn't like left turns!

As we entered the freeway on-ramp, the fun really began. Now, in all fairness, I must admit that I like to drive fast — not faster than is safe, but I don't drive in the slow lane either. And maybe, just maybe, having my mother-in-law in the car made me drive even a little faster just to annoy her. After entering the freeway, I put on my blinker to change lanes, and you would have thought my mother-in-law was watching a tennis match. Her head moved from side to side, back and forth, checking the traffic in the next lane over, both behind and in front of me. Then she gave me the all-clear message. Thank goodness she was alert and guiding me. How would I have known when it was safe to change lanes without her help?

The traffic slowed, and I braked. So did she. Although she had no brake pedal on her side, she stomped her foot down hard on the floorboard as if applying the brake. How helpful. She clutched her purse and held it tightly to her chest. I'm not sure what that was supposed to do, but I guess if she were ejected from the car, she would have her purse with her ID in it when they recovered her body from the ditch she was sure to be found in.

And then there were the noises she made. There was the sharp intake of breath at every bend in the road, the little grunts and gasps and whistles as we passed another car or another car passed us, and the shrill *Eeeeeek!* as we came close to and passed any semi-trucks. She didn't like semis and never wanted me to pass them. I had to explain that it was the law to keep up with the traffic, and I couldn't just stay slower than a semi. But she didn't want me to stay behind a semi either—that just wasn't safe. She knew that the semi would suddenly switch into reverse, crash and roll over us, and we would be dead. That was a given. Semis were murderous machines.

I am happy to report that we did make it to her friend's birthday luncheon—and on time. (And back home, too.) We were not hurt, did not crash, and were not dead. I am positive that the only reason we made it there and back safely was because of her assistance. I never could have driven there without it.

— Barbara LoMonaco —

Meet Our Contributors

Monica Agnew-Kinnaman was born in England 102 years ago and came to America after serving in a British anti-aircraft artillery regiment during WWII. She has written a nonfiction book about rescue dogs and her *Sampson* series of children's books, as well as short stories, including three in previous *Chicken Soup for the Soul* anthologies.

Monica A. Andermann lives and writes on Long Island where she shares a home with her husband Bill and their tabby Samson. Her writing has been included in such publications as *Woman's World*, *Guideposts* and *Ocean* as well as the *Chicken Soup for the Soul* series.

Born and raised in northern British Columbia, **Marty Anderson** has raised four daughters and now currently resides with his wife in a remote community where the Wi-Fi is slow so no one is tempted to move back home. His hobbies include hiking, dog walking, shoveling snow and listening to his wife.

Lacey L. Bakker has written over a dozen children's books, two middle grade novels, and one psychological thriller. She has two cats, and loves being in nature and spending time with her best friend.

Kerrie R. Barney lives in Albuquerque, NM, where she attends the University of New Mexico (Go Lobos!) and loves to play with her beautiful Border Collie, MacKenna. Kerrie's book *Life, the Universe, and Houseplants*, about her inspiring adventures growing common houseplants, is for sale online.

Tracy Beckerman writes the syndicated humor column, "LOST IN SUBURBIA," which is carried weekly by Gannett newspapers. She is also the author of the books, *Lost in Suburbia: a Momoir* (2013), and *Rebel Without a Minivan* (2008). She is Vice President of the National Society of Newspaper Columnists Education Foundation.

Sheri Bertaux appreciates every moment of her life in rural Nova Scotia with her husband, three children, cats, rabbits, guinea pigs, chickens, ducks, turkeys, geese, quail, and one huge dog. She is grateful for her Circle, the crew of incredible women and their families who lift each other up every day.

A native Missourian, **Linda Bittle** now blogs from Council, ID. She enjoys tracking wildlife, photography, and growing things. Eliza Jane, the cat, and Sammy, the dog, are her best reading buddies. She is a 2007 graduate of the Anake Leadership Program at Wilderness Awareness School.

Karen Blair studied improv at The Second City in Chicago, which proved invaluable as the operator of a boutique island hotel! After graduating from her Master's program in San Diego in 2020, she plans to write more real-life adventures of small business owners to encourage, entertain and empower aspiring entrepreneurs.

Barbara Bondy-Pare has four children from her first loving husband, Ronald M. Bondy. After Ron's passing from lung cancer, she remarried Eddie Pare, a classmate who had asked her out in high school. Their fourteen adorable grandchildren keep them young, active and entertained. Barbara is all about love, family and hugs.

Christy Breedlove is the author of the *Dixie Days Mysteries* series as well as a frequent contributor to magazines. She works in a public school and is married to her best friend, Dave. She has two teenage children and two dogs — an Aussie and one who thinks he is a goat. Learn more at www.christybreedlovewrites.com

Maureen C. Bruschi's stories have appeared in numerous publications including *GoNOMAD* and *inTravel Magazine*. She received an undergraduate degree at Long Island University Post in Greenvale, NY and a graduate degree at Hofstra University in Hempstead, NY. Learn more at mbruschi305.wordpress.com.

Sally Willard Burbank has practiced internal medicine in Nashville for thirty years. Her books include *The Alzheimer's Disease Caregiver's Handbook* and *Patients I Will Never Forget*. Check out her two new Christian romances: *Can You Lose the Unibrow?* and *More Than a Hunch*. She loves to garden and write.

Terry Burnett graduated from the University of Victoria in British Columbia, with a Bachelor of Education degree in 1971. There, he met his wife, Alice. After pursuing teaching careers, they are now retired and enjoy tennis, birding, hiking, and traveling together. Alice put his funny experience into words.

Larry Carter, a Canadian by birth, is still in the telecommunications business, running a telephone systems company in Dallas, TX. His wife Eva is the ghostwriter for his story.

Elynne Chaplik-Aleskow, Pushcart Prize-nominated, is founding general manager of WYCC-TV/PBS and distinguished professor emeritus of Wright College. Her stories have been performed throughout the U.S. and Canada and are published in anthologies and her book, *My Gift of Now*. Her husband Richard is her muse.

Viji K. Chary has a B.A. in Genetics from the University of California, Berkeley and a Master's in Public Administration from California State University Hayward. She is primarily a children's writer but occasionally writes for adults too.

Linda Carol Cobb taught English electives at the same Virginia Beach, VA high school for thirty-seven years. She sponsored award-winning forensic teams and newspapers. Unwilling to retire, she teaches seminars, copyedits and coaches public speaking. She writes true stories about her Tennessee family and personal experiences.

Homeschool mom of four, **Shannon Cribbs** enjoys traveling and adventures with her children and husband. Shannon received a Master's in education from Walden University. She taught in the public school system for several years before resigning to be a full-time, stay-at-home mom.

Ronnie Dauber is a Canadian Christian author who enjoys writing both nonfiction and inspirational books, as well as short stories and a weekly blog. Ronnie is a cancer survivor who looks for the bright side of each new day. She lives in Ontario, Canada with her husband and their seven children and sixteen grandchildren.

NancyLee Davis had been writing since age twelve, had her own weekly newspaper special-interest column, while farming, raising her kids, showing dogs, and sports car racing. Now retired and raising orchids, she shares her adventures through her forever hobby, writing.

Julie de Belle received a Bachelor of Arts and Literature in 1984 and a degree in teaching in 1988. She has been dedicating all her time to writing and hosting poetry events since her retirement in 2014. She has had many of her poems and translations published in both French and English in various magazines.

Jennifer Quasha Deinard is a published nonfiction author and editor, public speaker, certified life coach, and has been a contributor to over twenty-five *Chicken Soup for the Soul* books. Learn more at www.jotcoach.com.

Kathy Dickson, received her Bachelor of Science, with honors, from Southeast Missouri University in 2001. She is a professional artist and retired Park Ranger. She loves the outdoors, coffee, and her family. A prior heatstroke may keep her home but she plans to write inspirational stories and art books for children.

Cassidy Doolittle grew up on a Midwest apple orchard and then became a psychiatric nurse and boy mom in Texas. She is a freelance writer and artist who is working on her first children's book and motherhood comic strip.

Joan Dubay is a retired kindergarten/first grade teacher, an observer of life, and a writer in search of a genre.

Sharon Rosenbaum Earls graduated from Tennessee Wesleyan College. Her three wonderful grandchildren, Andrew, Ella, and Ava, are her main focus in life, but her hobbies include reading, writing, sewing, and gardening.

J. E. Erickson resides in Alberta, Canada, where she enjoys music, the outdoors, and other artistic ventures.

Like most things in her life, **Sara Escandon** became a librarian by accident. But, it was a happy little accident that led her to a life full of stories — both real and unreal. She spends her time exploring various comedy venues, sharing stories, and caring for her plants, Spidey and Lemony Snicket.

Fred First is a life-long biology-watcher, naturalist, photographer, essayist, and speaker. His blog, "Fragments from Floyd," survives since 2002. His radio essays at WVTF were heard from 2003 to 2010. He has published two books and he has been an active teacher and community participant in Floyd County, VA since 1997.

Chelsea Walker Flagg is an award winning, bestselling author of both adult and children's books. She lives in Boulder, CO with her husband, three practically perfect daughters, and her cat, Gladys.

Lynne Daroff Foosaner is a political activist, freelance writer and grandmother… not necessarily in that order!

Carole Fowkes is an RN and though originally from Cleveland, OH has lived in Chicago and Tampa. She currently resides in Dallas, TX with her husband. She is the author of a humorous cozy mystery series, *The Terrified Detective*. E-mail her at cmsldfowkes@gmail.com.

Gail Gabrielle has seen her dream of becoming a published author come true thanks to the *Chicken Soup for the Soul* series. In her fourth contribution to the series, she continues to chronicle events from her fabulous children and family. Her interests center on autism, animal rights, completion of her book, and time with her kids.

Matt Geiger is a Midwest Book Award winner and a Next Generation Indie Book Awards and Best Book Award finalist. He is also the winner of numerous journalism awards. Matt's books include *Astonishing Tales!* and *The Geiger Counter: Raised by Wolves and Other Stories*.

James A. Gemmell's favourite hobby is long distance hiking. He tries to indulge himself each summer by walking across Spain or France. James's other favourite hobbies are playing the guitar, writing short stories, drawing and painting portraits.

Kathleen Gemmell pens for an array of publications. Kathleen is also an animal rights proponent, a storyteller, and a psychology buff.

Daniel Ginsberg, a former Brooklynite, has degrees in art (SVA) and science (LSU, BS & MS). He served in the Army as a Military

Policeman and Criminal Photographer and later worked as a New York City fashion photographer. Today, Daniel lives in Colorado where he writes, draws and paints.

Barry M. Grey is a nonfiction producer, writer, ghostwriter and book editor with diverse experience in television, print and on the Internet. He holds a Bachelor of Arts degree in English from UCLA and lives in Los Angeles with his wife Ann and their four dogs. Their daughter Lulu is away at college.

Stacey Gustafson is the bestselling author of *Are You Still Kidding Me?* as well as an inspirational speaker, blogger and comedian. She's been named Erma Bombeck Writers' Workshop Humor Writer of the Month and performs stand-up throughout the East Bay, CA. Read her blog, "Are You Kidding Me?" at StaceyGustafson.com.

Terry Hans is a previous contributor to the *Chicken Soup for the Soul* series. She is compiling a collection of humorous stories drawing on forty-five years as a Dental Hygienist. Terry has two very accomplished daughters and four athletic grandsons. Most days you will find Terry and her husband cheering at one of their grandson's sporting events.

Wendy Hobday Haugh's short stories, articles, and poems have appeared in dozens of national and regional publications. This is her thirteenth story to appear in the *Chicken Soup for the Soul* series. 2020 marks Wendy's forty-first year as a freelance writer. Happily, she reports that the thrill of writing never wanes.

Hailing from north Georgia, **Butch Holcombe** has been a writer for most of his life and now publishes *American Digger Magazine*, which he founded sixteen years ago. In addition, Butch records a weekly podcast, "Relic Roundup." He is also the author of *Never Mace a Skunk*, *Never Mace A Skunk II* and the e-novel *Becoming*.

Combining two of her passions — humor and championing for children — **Shayna R. Horowitz** has sprung her debut novel *Penina Pinkowitz and the Summer Situation* into the world of middle graders worldwide. Currently studying and practicing IFS, Shayna lives in Monsey, NY with her eight children and twenty grandchildren.

David Hull is a retired teacher who lives in Holley, NY. He enjoys gardening, reading, writing and has had several stories published in the *Chicken Soup for the Soul* series.

Justin Hunter lives in Missouri with his wife and four adopted boys. E-mail him at justinhntr@yahoo.com.

Wife, mother, karate instructor — these are just a few of the labels **Debby Johnson** wears with pride. She lives in Southern California with her husband and youngest son, and an assortment of pets. Having raised five children, she now fills her spare time with writing, painting and watching an occasional movie.

Sharon Landeen, mother, grandma, great-grandma and retired elementary teacher, believes that working with children helps keep her young. She stays busy volunteering at schools, being a reading mentor and helping with the 4-H program. She enjoys traveling, reading and following the University of Arizona's basketball team.

John J. Lesjack is a retired teacher, graduate of San Francisco State College's (1965) write program, member of Redwood Writers and lives in Santa Rosa, CA where he collects *Chicken Soup for the Soul* books. He has been published in several of them, among other national publications. E-mail him at jlesjack@gmail.com.

Barbara LoMonaco received her BS from the University of Southern California and has an elementary teaching credential. Barbara has worked for Chicken Soup for the Soul since February 1998. She wears many hats there, including Senior Editor.

Crescent LoMonaco is a frequent contributor to the *Chicken Soup for the Soul* series. She is an avid reader, writer and artist. She used her experience as a previous salon owner to write the "Ask a Stylist" column for the *Santa Barbara Independent*. She lives on the California coast with her husband of twenty-two years and their son.

Maureen Longnecker is a freelance writer, speaker, and the author of *The Other Side of the Tapestry: Choosing to Trust God When Life Hurts*. She writes nature articles and puzzles for children, and plans to write more books, Lord willing. She enjoys reading, writing, teaching, nature, photography, and time with her family.

Corrie Lopez is a teacher in a small town in Missouri where she lives with her parents, husband, and two children. Corrie's life is full of things to laugh about and people to love.

Kaye Lucas is a retired reading specialist and creative writing teacher. She holds an undergraduate degree from Erskine College and an advanced degree from The Citadel. Kaye is always happiest puttering in her garden, volunteering at church, surrounded by books, or lost in the characters of her latest writing project.

DeLila R. Lumbardy has completed her second novel in the *Sandhills Saga Series*. Both are available online or signed copies can be obtained from the author at delilalumbardy@gmail.com. She blogs monthly at www.delilalumbardy.com. Besides writing, she loves playing pickleball. She resides in South Dakota.

Carol L. MacKay's funny stories and poems for kids have been published in *Highlights*, *Cricket*, and *Babybug* magazines. Carol lives on Vancouver Island with her husband, James, and their cat, Victoria, who have both provided many laughs over the years. This is her third story published in the *Chicken Soup for the Soul* series.

Elaine Maly teaches the art of creative engagement for meaningful connections with elders through her work with TimeSlips. She writes about her life as a native Milwaukeean and is an active participant in her local storytelling community. She's the grandmother of three spunky grandsons who give her plenty of material.

Irene Maran, retired and living at the shore with her four cats and six turtles, enjoys writing about life, family and everyday topics humorously expressed in her two bi-weekly newspaper columns, *The News-Record of Maplewood/South Orange* and *The Coaster of Asbury Park*. She is also a storyteller and artist.

Debbi Mavity retired from the Federal Government and now resides in the beautiful state of West Virginia. She is an active member of Doddridge County Lions Club. Her first published story is in *Chicken Soup for the Soul: Life Lessons from the Dog*. Dogs and humor usually show up in her stories. Follow her on Twitter @MavsMutthouse.

Lisa McCaskill enjoys spending time with family and friends, and whenever there's a free moment, she writes stories of faith, hope, and love.

Robin K. Melvin is a mom, grandma, and wife of an Army veteran. She writes the faith column for a newspaper and is writing her first inspirational book. Robin writes to inspire others to live large and love well. She loves coffee and hiking. Connect with her at www. RobinMelvin.com, Robinkmelvin@gmail.com, or on Facebook.

Ann Morrow is a writer, humorist and frequent contributor to the *Chicken Soup for the Soul* series. She and her husband live in the Black Hills of South Dakota. Recently, she committed to living "gluten free" and no longer accepts gifts disguised as baked goods.

Mary Lee Moynan has a keen sense of humor and it's often reflected in her published articles on faith, family, and friends. E-mail her at moynan-marylee@hotmail.com.

Alice Muschany lives in Flint Hill, MO. She loves retirement. It's true — every day is Saturday. When she's not spending time with her grandchildren, she's busy hiking, taking pictures, reading and writing. E-mail her at aliceandroland@gmail.com.

Sandy Nadeau spent thirty years exploring the back country of Colorado. She loves writing stories connected to that time. She has published two inspirational fiction books: *Red Gold* and *Rescue Me*. She and her husband now live in Texas two miles from their grandchildren, discovering even more adventures. E-mail her at sandy@sandynadeau.com.

January Gordon Ornellas is a comedy writer, teacher, wife, and mom. She enjoys traveling, working out, and spending time with her family. She writes humorous stories on her blog at midlifebloomer.com and recently published one of her short stories, "Rookie's Triathlon Lessons" in the *Los Angeles Times*, June 2019.

Deb Palmer is the author of *In Spite of Us: A Love Story about Second Chances*. She has published an array of fiction and nonfiction articles in numerous print and online magazines and she writes an inspirational blog known for gut-wrenching truth and humor with a message.

Nancy Emmick Panko is a retired pediatric nurse with fifteen stories published in the *Chicken Soup for the Soul* series. She is the author of award-winning *Guiding Missal* and is working on her second novel. A member of the Cary Senior Writing Circle, Nancy enjoys being in, on, or near Lake Gaston with her children and grandchildren.

Marsha Porter has co-authored a movie guide and published numerous articles. She got her start in writing when the 500-word essay was the preferred punishment at her Catholic school.

Phyllis Reilly is seventy-seven years old. She returned to writing after a ten-year absence and has been writing her memoirs. She lives in Croton-on-Hudson, NY with her husband and cat, and runs a writing group. Her stories have been published in literary magazines. She says that in spite of this crazy world, "Life is Good."

Heather Rae Rodin is an award-winning writer and author of three books. Her last book, *Appointed,* was co-written with her daughter Becki. Heather also serves as Executive Director of the charity Hope Grows Haiti and much of her writing comes from those experiences. She is mother to six and grandma to thirteen. She and her husband Gord live in Ontario Canada.

Carol Senn Ruffin teaches music and drama at Maranatha Baptist University, is Music Director of her church, plays viola in a chamber group, and hosts *Carol's Kitchen*, a cable TV show. Her hobbies are song writing and pressed flower art. She and her husband John share their home with their cat, Lalie and their dog, Mocha.

Sue-Ellen Sanders is community development manager for a nonprofit promoting early childhood education, a community activist, local journalist and host of a radio talk show. A 1981 University of Florida grad, she is married with two young adult children and loves running, reading, rescue puppies and adventures.

Melanie A. Savidis is a teacher in the Rochester City School District. She and her husband, Mike, have three sons. She received her Bachelor of Arts from Allegheny College and her Masters of Education from the University of Rochester.

John M. Scanlan is a 1983 graduate of the United States Naval Academy, and retired from the United States Marine Corps as a Lieutenant Colonel aviator with time in the back seat of both the F-4S Phantom II and the F/A-18D Hornet. He is currently pursuing a second career as a writer.

Susan Schuerr is a former English/Drama teacher, and a current blogger at www.lifewithlarry.org. She has a Master's degree from

Concordia University. Sue and her husband, Larry, have three adult children and five grandchildren. She loves biking, skiing, volunteering and spending time with family and friends.

Joyce Newman Scott worked as a flight attendant while pursuing an acting career. She started college in her mid-fifties and studied screenwriting at the University of Miami and creative writing at Florida International University. She is thrilled to be a frequent contributor to the *Chicken Soup for the Soul* series.

Jennifer Sienes taught middle school for years but at the encouragement of her husband left that career to pursue her life-long dream of writing. She now has two women's contemporary novels published through Celebrate Lit — *Surrendered* and *Illusions* — with a third scheduled to release in 2021.

Doug Sletten grew up in the cold of the Dakotas. He is currently retired and living in Mesa, AZ. Doug received a Bachelor's degree from Concordia College in Moorhead, MN. in 1964. He has a son, Mitch, and a daughter, Sara. Doug enjoys reading, car trips, skiing, and writing. E-mail him at douglas4146@gmail.com.

Heather Norman Smith's other published works include *Grace & Lavender* and *Where I Was Planted*, both inspirational novels, and a thirty-day devotional titled *Timeout for Jesus*. She lives in the foothills of North Carolina with her husband, their four children, and several pets. Learn more at www.heathernormansmith.com.

Sheryn Smith is a serial cereal cooker, along with a variety of other foods. Her career centered around communications. Beginning in an advertising agency as a copywriter, she went on to freelance writing to accommodate her active role as a mom, moving into the classroom for fifteen years. The kitchen is her playground.

Diane Stark is a wife, mother, and freelance writer. She writes about the important things in life: her family and her faith. She is a frequent contributor to the *Chicken Soup for the Soul* series, as well as many magazines.

Christina Tolan lives in a Bavarian village on the outskirts of Munich. She writes comedy in memoir about her daily interactions with the Bavarians and raising two bilingual children and a trilingual dog. She is currently completing *CAR BY CAR*, reflections on owning thirty cars over sixteen years together with her husband.

Daniela Trivino has been writing short stories since she was young. She continues to post her stories on her blog at www.wordpress. com/storiesivenevertold. She has dabbled in teaching and has most recently joined the publishing industry.

Jennifer Clark Vihel writes from her cabin in the redwoods of Northern California. Born in Texas, she performed with the famed Kilgore Rangerettes before life choices took her away to many exciting new places. In addition to her nonfiction projects, as Jennifer Clark she writes novels about life, love, and second chances.

Nick Walker is a meteorologist, speaker, writer and voice over narrator with more than forty years experience in broadcasting, most recently appearing on *The Weather Channel*. As the Weather Dude he teaches weather to young people through educational songs. He has produced several recordings of original music.

Roz Warren writes for everyone from the *Funny Times* to *The New York Times* and has appeared on both the *Today Show* and *Morning Edition*. This is the eleventh *Chicken Soup for the Soul* book she's been included in. E-mail Roz at roswarren@gmail.com.

Rachel Weaver is the author of the novel *Point of Direction*, which *O, The Oprah Magazine* named a "Top Ten Book to Pick Up Now." *Point of Direction* was chosen by the American Booksellers Association as a Top Ten Debut for Spring 2014, and won the 2015 Willa Cather Award for Fiction.

Gwen Sheldon Willadsen is a retired professor. Her retirement hobbies include spending time with her grandkids, genealogy research, travel, and writing memoir and genealogy stories. Her stories are published in *The Sun*, *Boomer Café*, and *Raven's Perch* magazines as well as the *Chicken Soup for the Soul* series.

Curt Zeck would like to thank his wife, Sheri, for writing this story for him. Sheri's work has appeared in numerous *Chicken Soup for the Soul* books, *Guideposts* and *Angels on Earth*. Sheri writes about her faith, family and shares many other embarrassing stories at www. sherizeck.com.

Gary Zenker is an award-winning marketing strategist who has written marketing plans and content for nearly every media. By night, he writes flash fiction and runs the Main Line Writers Group, which he founded in 2010. He is also the creator of Writers Blox, a storytelling game and writer's tool. E-mail him at garyzenker@gmail.com.

Meet Amy Newmark

Amy Newmark is the bestselling author, editor-in-chief, and publisher of the *Chicken Soup for the Soul* book series. Since 2008, she has published 165 new books, most of them national bestsellers in the U.S. and Canada, more than doubling the number of Chicken Soup for the Soul titles in print today. She is also the author of *Simply Happy*, a crash course in Chicken Soup for the Soul advice and wisdom that is filled with easy-to-implement, practical tips for enjoying a better life.

Amy is credited with revitalizing the Chicken Soup for the Soul brand, which has been a publishing industry phenomenon since the first book came out in 1993. By compiling inspirational and aspirational true stories curated from ordinary people who have had extraordinary experiences, Amy has kept the twenty-seven-year-old Chicken Soup for the Soul brand fresh and relevant.

Amy graduated *magna cum laude* from Harvard University where she majored in Portuguese and minored in French. She then embarked on a three-decade career as a Wall Street analyst, a hedge fund manager, and a corporate executive in the technology field. She is a Chartered Financial Analyst.

Her return to literary pursuits was inevitable, as her honors thesis in college involved traveling throughout Brazil's impoverished northeast region, collecting stories from regular people. She is delighted to have come full circle in her writing career — from collecting stories "from the people" in Brazil as a twenty-year-old to, three decades later, collecting stories "from the people" for Chicken Soup for the Soul.

When Amy and her husband Bill, the CEO of Chicken Soup for the Soul, are not working, they are visiting their four grown children and their grandchildren.

Follow Amy on Twitter @amynewmark. Listen to her free podcast — "Chicken Soup for the Soul with Amy Newmark" — on Apple Podcasts, Google Play, the Podcasts app on iPhone, or by using your favorite podcast app on other devices.

Thank You

We owe huge thanks to all of our contributors and fans. We were overwhelmed by the thousands of submissions we received for this popular topic, and we had a team that spent months reading all of them. Laura Dean, Barbara LoMonaco, and Crescent LoMonaco read all of them, and then Associate Publisher D'ette Corona and Publisher and Editor-in-Chief Amy Newmark made the final selections and created the manuscript.

Susan Heim did the first round of editing, D'ette chose the perfect quotations to put at the beginning of each story, and Amy edited the stories and shaped the final manuscript.

As we finished our work, D'ette Corona continued to be Amy's right-hand woman in working with all our wonderful writers. Barbara LoMonaco and Kristiana Pastir, along with Elaine Kimbler, jumped in at the end to proof, proof, proof. And yes, there will always be typos anyway, so feel free to let us know about them at webmaster@chickensoupforthesoul.com, and we will correct them in future printings.

The whole publishing team deserves a hand, including our Senior Director of Marketing Maureen Peltier, our Vice President of Production Victor Cataldo, our Executive Assistant Mary Fisher, and our graphic designer Daniel Zaccari, who turned our manuscript into this entertaining book.

Sharing Happiness, Inspiration, and Hope

Real people sharing real stories, every day, all over the world. In 2007, *USA Today* named *Chicken Soup for the Soul* one of the five most memorable books in the last quarter-century. With over 100 million books sold to date in the U.S. and Canada alone, more than 250 titles in print, and translations into nearly fifty languages, "chicken soup for the soul®" is one of the world's best-known phrases.

Today, twenty-seven years after we first began sharing happiness, inspiration and hope through our books, we continue to delight our readers with new titles, but have also evolved beyond the bookshelves with super premium pet food, television shows, a podcast, video journalism from aplus.com, licensed products, and free movies and TV shows on our Popcornflix and Crackle apps. We are busy "changing the world one story at a time®." Thanks for reading!

Share with Us

We all have had Chicken Soup for the Soul moments in our lives. If you would like to share your story or poem with millions of people around the world, go to chickensoup.com and click on Submit Your Story. You may be able to help another reader and become a published author at the same time. Some of our past contributors have launched writing and speaking careers from the publication of their stories in our books!

We only accept story submissions via our website. They are no longer accepted via mail or fax. Visit our website, www.chickensoup.com, and click on Submit Your Story for our writing guidelines and a list of topics we are working on.

To contact us regarding other matters, please send us an e-mail through webmaster@chickensoupforthesoul.com, or fax or write us at:

Chicken Soup for the Soul
P.O. Box 700
Cos Cob, CT 06807-0700
Fax: 203-861-7194

One more note from your friends at Chicken Soup for the Soul: Occasionally, we receive an unsolicited book manuscript from one of our readers, and we would like to respectfully inform you that we do not accept unsolicited manuscripts, and we must discard the ones that appear.

Chicken Soup for the Soul

The Magic of Cats

101 Tales of Family, Friendship & Fun

Amy Newmark

Royalties from this book go to
AMERICAN·HUMANE
FIRST TO SERVE™

Paperback: 978-1-61159-066-1
eBook: 978-1-61159-301-3

More Family Fun

Chicken Soup for the Soul

The Magic of Dogs

101 Tales of Family, Friendship & Fun

Royalties from this book go to
AMERICAN·HUMANE
FIRST TO SERVE

Amy Newmark

Paperback: 978-1-61159-067-8
eBook: 978-1-61159-302-0

and Laughter

Chicken Soup for the Soul® : Be You

101 Stories of Affirmation, Determination and Female Empowerment

Amy Newmark

Paperback: 978-1-61159-065-4
eBook: 978-1-61159-300-6

Finding Yourself

Chicken Soup for the Soul

Listen to Your Dreams

101 Tales of Inner Guidance,
Divine Intervention
and Miraculous Insight

Amy Newmark

Paperback: 978-1-61159-068-5
eBook: 978-1-61159-303-7

and Your Future

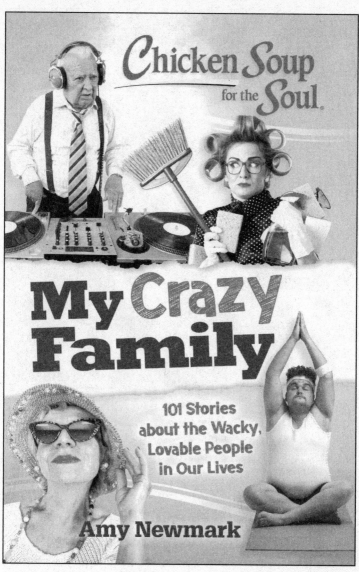

Chicken Soup for the Soul

My Crazy Family

101 Stories about the Wacky, Lovable People in Our Lives

Amy Newmark

Paperback: 978-1-61159-977-0
eBook: 978-1-61159-277-1

Hilarious

Chicken Soup for the Soul

for the Soul®

Family Matters

101
Unforgettable
Stories about
Our Nutty
but Lovable
Families

WARNING:
MAY
CONTAIN
NUTS

Jack Canfield,
Mark Victor Hansen,
Amy Newmark and Susan M. Heim
Foreword by Bruce Jenner

Paperback: 978-1-935096-55-9
eBook: 978-1-61159-136-1

and Unbelievable

Changing the world one story at a time®
www.chickensoup.com